New Ideas in the Four Knights

JOHN NUNN

An Owl Book
Henry Holt and Company
New York

Henry Holt and Company, Inc.
Publishers since 1866
115 West 18th Street
New York, New York 10011

Henry Holt ® is a registered
trademark of Henry Holt and Company, Inc.

First published in the United States in 1993 by
Henry Holt and Company, Inc.
Originally published in Great Britain in 1993 by
B. T. Batsford Ltd.

Library of Congress Catalog Card Number: 92-56749

ISBN 0-8050-2629-0 (An Owl Book: pbk.)

First American Edition—1993

Printed in the United Kingdom
All first editions are printed on acid-free paper.∞

10 9 8 7 6 5 4 3 2 1

Adviser: R. D. Keene, GM, OBE
Technical Editor: Andrew Kinsman

Contents

Summary of Variations

5 Introduction 5

The Four Knights Opening has a long history, stretching back about 400 years. Readers may wonder if, after all this time, there are any new ideas left to be discovered in the Four Knights. However, fashions in openings tend to run in cycles, and the Four Knights has been alternately in and out of favour for at least 150 years. Although it was recognised as one of the standard openings in the 19th century, it suddenly became very popular in the first decade of the 20th century. Most of the top players in the world adopted it with one side or the other and in this book you will find games by Lasker, Rubinstein, Capablanca, Nimzowitsch, Marshall, Tarrasch and other leading players of the pre-1914 period. After the First World War it suffered something of a decline and was less frequently employed by the top players. Immediately after the Second World War it once again came into fashion and was used by Petrosian and Botvinnik, amongst others. However, this revival was relatively short-lived and it more or less disappeared from tournament play, except for the occasional outing in pre-arranged draws.

Now, however, the wheel has turned and thanks mainly to Nigel Short the Four Knights is once again appearing in grandmaster events. Short revived the opening for his Candidates' match against Speelman in January 1991, scoring a win and two draws from three games. Although Short employed the Four Knights mainly as a surprise weapon, he has used it occasionally since, for example to defeat Anand at Linares 1992. Short's good results with the Four Knights encouraged other British players to follow his example, and both Chandler and I have used the opening with some success. Kamsky and Speelman himself are recent converts.

I would like to say a few words about the style of this book. Given that the title of this book includes the words *New Ideas*, readers may be surprised to find a certain number of old games in the book. The reason is that many ideas which seem modern were actually played and understood decades ago by players of earlier generations. Therefore I have included the predecessor games in cases where they are directly relevant to the lines played today. I have also included some older material in lines which are poorly analysed by contemporary opening books. However, the concept behind the *New Ideas* series is to concentrate on lines which are currently relevant, and in order to achieve this I have had to restrict coverage of certain variations. Readers who require a detailed knowledge of such lines will have to look in one of the standard opening reference works, such as *ECO*, but so far as possible this book is self-contained and should provide an adequate background for anyone wishing to adopt the Four Knights with either colour.

It is also worth pointing out which lines are covered in this book and which are not. The scope has been made as wide as possible within the limits set by the size of the book.

Thus it covers lines such as 1 e4 e5 2 ♘f3 ♘c6 3 ♘c3 g6 and 1 e4 e5 2 ♘f3 ♘f6 3 ♘c3 ♗b4, which are not really part of the Four Knights, but which White players need to know if they intend playing the Four Knights. I have also included some lines which arise after 1 e4 e5 2 ♘f3 ♘c6 3 ♘c3 ♘f6 4 d4, but which are not part of the Scotch. These lines are the Belgrade Gambit, 4...exd4 5 ♘d5, and the variation 4...♗b4. On the other hand I have excluded all lines which originate from 4 d4 exd4 5 ♘xd4, as these form part of the Scotch.

I have tried to give some comments to all the complete games in this book. These days computer databases make it very easy for authors to include complete games in a chess book, but I believe that readers learn little from totally unannotated games. The comments vary greatly in depth from game to game, and it is not possible to do some of the games justice in the limited confines of an opening book. However, I hope that readers will be able to appreciate at least the general outlines of each game.

Finally I would like to thank ChessBase for supplying some of the games included in the book, Rolf Schlösser for providing the fonts used in the typesetting and The Advanced Software Company for providing a Chess Machine which was used to help in the analysis of certain positions.

7 Unusual Black third moves 7

We have to distinguish between the two possible move-orders 1 e4 e5 2 ♘f3 ♘f6 3 ♘c3 and 1 e4 e5 2 ♘f3 ♘c6 3 ♘c3. In the former case there aren't many third move alternatives for Black except for 3...♗b4, which we cover in chapter 3. The only other serious idea is 1 e4 e5 2 ♘f3 ♘f6 3 ♘c3 d6 (3...♗c5 is good for White after 4 ♘xe5 ♗d4 5 ♘f3 ♗xc3 6 dxc3 ♘xe4 7 ♗d3 ♘c5 8 0-0 with a big lead in development for White), but after 4 d4 ♘bd7 play transposes into the Philidor Defence, which is not covered in this book.

Black has a wider choice after 1 e4 e5 2 ♘f3 ♘c6 3 ♘c3. We consider 3...g6 in chapter 2 and here we deal with 3...d6 (games 1-3) and 3...♗c5 (game 4). Other moves are playable but give White at least a slight advantage, for example 3...f5 4 d4, 3...♗b4 4 ♘d5 or 3...♘ge7 4 ♗c4.

After 1 e4 e5 2 ♘f3 ♘c6 3 ♘c3 d6, game 1 deals with the reply 4 ♗b5, a favourite of Campora's. However, the main line is 4 d4, which may be met either by 4...exd4 (game 2) or 4...♗g4 (game 3). Neither move equalises.

The dubious variation 3 ♘c3 ♗c5 is covered in game 4.

Game 1

Campora-Murey
Moscow 1989

1 e4 e5 2 ♘f3 ♘c6 3 ♘c3 d6 4 ♗b5 ♘ge7

⇨ 4...♗g4 (4...♘f6 will probably transpose to the Ruy Lopez) 5 h3 ♗xf3 6 ♕xf3 ♘f6 7 ♘d5 a6 8 ♘xf6+ ♕xf6 9 ♗xc6+ bxc6 10 ♕b3 ♗e7 11 ♕b7 ♔d7 12 ♕b3 g5 13 ♔e2 h5 14 ♕f3 ♕xf3+ 15 ♔xf3 g4+ 16 ♔e2 ♖ag8 17 ♔f1 d5 18 d3 ♗c5 19 ♗d2 g3 20 f3 h4 21 ♔e2 ♖h5 22 b4 ♗f2 23 ♗e3 ♗xe3 24 ♔xe3 f5 25 c4 d4+ ½-½, Campora-Romanishin, Biel 1987.

5 d4 a6 6 ♗c4 b5 7 ♗e2 ♘xd4 8 ♘xd4 exd4 9 ♕xd4 ♘c6 10 ♕e3 g6

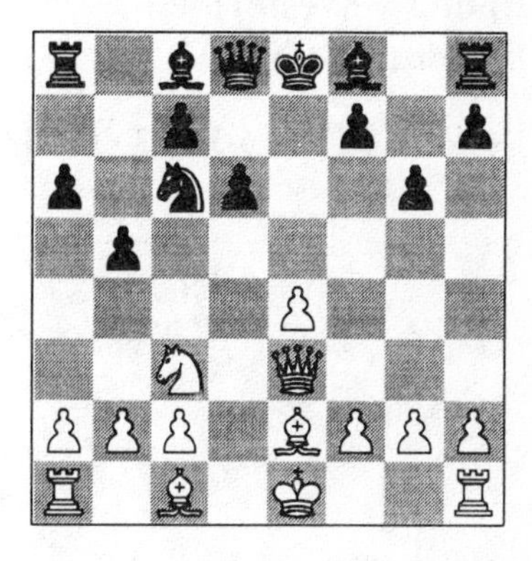

11 ♘xb5!? (at first sight crushing but Black manages to hold on) **11...axb5 12 ♗xb5 ♗d7 13 ♗xc6 ♗xc6 14 ♕c3 ♗xe4 15 0-0 ♖g8 16 ♖e1 f5 17 f3 d5 18 fxe4 dxe4 19 ♕c6+ ♔f7 20 ♗f4 ♗d6 21 ♖ad1 ♕e8 22 ♕d5+ ♕e6 23 ♗xd6 ♕xd5 24 ♖xd5 cxd6 25 ♖a1 ♖gc8 26 c3 ♔e6 27 ♖b5 ♖c5 28 ♖b4 ♖d5 29 a4 ♔e5 30 ♖b7 ♖d3 31 b4 ♖c8 32 ♖c1 f4 33 a5 ♖d2 34 a6 ♖a2 35 b5 e3 36 g3 g5 37 a7 f3 38 ♖e7+ ♔f5 39 ♖xe3 ♖xa7 40 ♖xf3+ ♔g4 41 ♔g2 ♖a2+ 42 ♖f2 ♖xf2+ 43 ♔xf2 ♔h3 44 ♔g1 ♖c5 45 ♖b1 ♖xc3 46 b6 ♖c8 47 b7 ♖b8 48 ♖b3 d5 ½-½**

The main line is undoubtedly 4 d4, whereby White preserves the option of playing ♗b5 to reach a favourable Ruy Lopez, or of developing the bishop elsewhere according to circumstances. Black has tried the two replies 4...exd4 and 4...♗g4, but White can retain an advantage in either case.

Game 2

Radulov-Westerinen
Hamburg 1981

1 e4 e5 2 ♘f3 ♘c6 3 ♘c3 d6 4 d4 exd4 5 ♘xd4 ♗d7

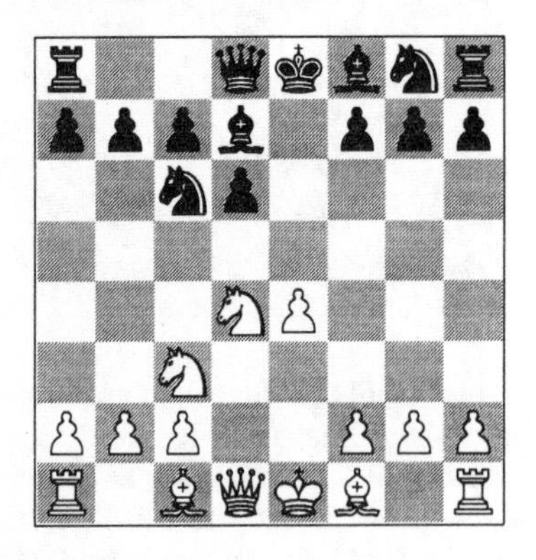

6 ♗e3

➪ 6 ♘xc6 ♗xc6 7 ♗d3 ♘f6 8 ♗f4 ♗e7 9 ♕d2 0-0 10 0-0-0 ♘d7 11 ♖he1 ♗f6 12 f3 ♘e5 13 ♕f2 b5 14 ♘e2 ♕c8 15 ♘d4 ♕a6 16 ♔b1 ♘c4 17 ♗xc4 bxc4 18 e5 dxe5 19 ♗xe5 ♗d7 20 ♗xf6 ♕xf6 21 ♕d2 ♖fb8 22 ♕c3 ♕b6 23 ♘e2 ♗f5 24 ♘f4 ♗g6 25 h4 h5 26 ♘d5 ♕c5 27 ♘e7+ ♔h7 28 ♘xg6 ♔xg6 29 g4 ♖d8 30 gxh5+ ♔h7 31 a3 ♕xh5 32 ♕xc4 ♕xf3 33 ♖xd8 ♖xd8 34 ♕xc7 ♖d2 35 ♕c4 ♖d1+ 36 ♖xd1 ♕xd1+ 37 ♔a2 ♕h5 38 ♕d3+ f5 39 c4 ♕xh4 40 ♕xf5+ ♔h6 41 ♕e6+ g6 42 c5 ♕h2 43 c6 ♔h5 44 ♕f7 ♕c2 45 c7 1-0, Mihevc-B.Hund, Manila Women's Ol. 1992.

6...♘f6 7 ♗e2 g6 8 ♕d2 ♗g7 (this type of position can also arise from the lines in chapter 2) **9 0-0-0 0-0 10 f3 a6 11 g4 b5 12 g5 ♘e8** (normally White would play h4 and h5 in this type of position, but here he makes use of the fact that 12...♘h5 13 ♘xc6 ♗xc6 14 ♘d5 followed by f4 is good for White to drive Black's knight to a bad square) **13 ♘xc6 ♗xc6 14 h4 ♗d7 15 h5 c6 16 ♗d3 ♕e7 17 ♕h2 ♗h8 18 ♕h4 ♘c7 19 ♗e2 ♘e6**

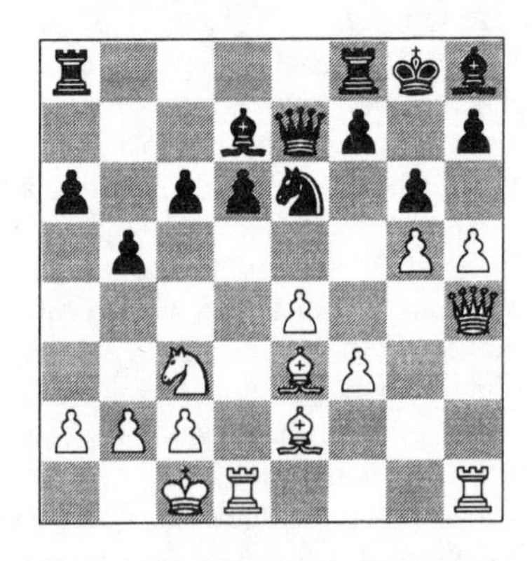

20 e5! (an obvious but attractive move to clear the knight's path towards f6) **20...♗xe5 21 ♘e4 ♘c7 22 ♖xd6 ♗f5 23 ♗c5 ♘e6 24 hxg6 ♗xg6 25 ♘f6+ ♗xf6 26 gxf6 ♕c7 27 ♗d3 ♘xc5 28 ♕h6 ♘e6 29 ♖d4!** (of course 29 ♖xe6 fxe6 30 ♗xg6 isn't bad, but this move is even stronger) **29...♕g3 30 ♗xg6 ♕g5+ 31 ♕xg5 ♘xg5 32 ♗xh7+ ♘xh7 33 ♖g4+ ♔h8 34 ♖g7 1-0**

Game 3

Nunn-Steinbacher
London (Lloyds Bank) 1992

1 e4 e5 2 Nf3 Nc6 3 Nc3 d6 4 d4 Bg4 5 Bb5 (without doubt the best reply) **5...exd4 6 Qxd4 a6**

Or 6...Bxf3 (6...Nge7 7 Qe3 a6 8 Be2 is also slightly better for White because the e7 knight is badly placed) 7 gxf3 Qd7 8 Qa4 and now:

⇨ 8...a6 9 Be3 Rb8 10 Be2 Nf6 11 0-0-0 Be7 12 Rhg1 0-0 13 f4 Qc8 14 Nd5 Re8 15 Nxf6+ Bxf6 16 e5! (leading to the forced win of material) 16...dxe5 17 Bg4 b5 18 Qe4 Qb7 19 Bd7 Na5 20 Qxb7 Nxb7 21 Bxe8 and White won in Czerniak-Van Scheltinga, Beverwijk 1966.

⇨ 8...Nge7 9 Be3 (A.Ivanov already assesses this position as clearly better for White and suggests no real improvements for Black in the remainder of the game) 9...a6 10 Nd5 Rc8 11 Be2 Nxd5 12 exd5 Ne7 13 Qb3 c6 14 dxc6 Nxc6 15 Rg1 g6 16 0-0-0 Bg7 17 f4 Qe7 18 f5 Qf6 19 h4 with a large plus for White, A.Ivanov-Beliavsky, USSR 1982.

7 Bxc6+ bxc6 8 Be3 c5 9 Qc4 Nf6 (Black had to try 9...Be6, but even then 10 Qe2 gives White a formidable lead in development)

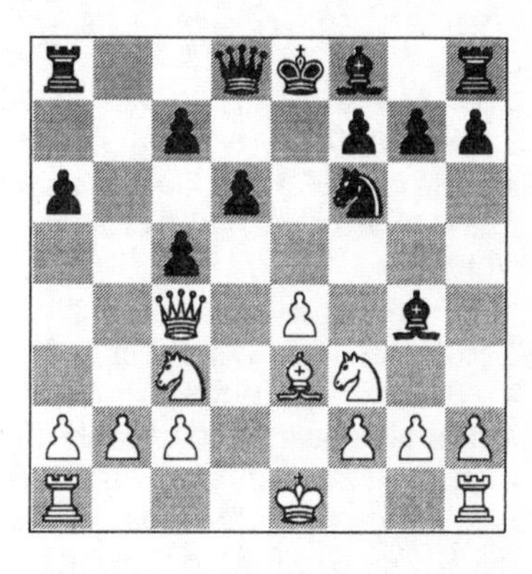

10 e5! (opening up the position while Black's king is still trapped in the centre) **10...Be6** (10...dxe5 11 Nxe5 Be6 12 Qa4+ is also very bad, while 10...Bxf3 11 exf6 Bc6 12 Nd5 is crushing because 12...gxf6 loses to 13 Qe4+ Kd7 14 Qf5+) **11 Qa4+ Nd7** (11...Bd7 12 Qa5 dxe5 13 0-0-0 threatens both Nxe5 and Bxc5) **12 0-0-0 Be7** (there is nothing better, but now White can win the d6 pawn) **13 Bf4 Qb8 14 Qc6 0-0 15 exd6 cxd6 16 Bxd6 Bxd6 17 Qxd6 Qb7 18 Ng5?** (the simple 18 Rhe1 should win without problems) **18...Rfb8 19 b3** (19 Nxe6? Qxb2+ 20 Kd2 Nb6! is unclear) **19...Nf8 20 Qxc5** (I had intended 20 Nd5 based on the line 20...Rd8 21 Ne7+ Kh8 22 Qxe6!, but 20...h6! is awkward for White)

20...♖c8 21 ♕e3 ♗f5 (this makes it easy; Black should have regained one pawn by 21...♕xg2, when White must still work hard for the win) **22 ♘ge4 ♖e8 23 ♖he1** (the tactical point is 23...♗xe4 24 ♘xe4 f5 25 ♘d6!, so White keeps his two extra pawns) **23...♖ac8 24 ♕f3 ♗xe4 25 ♘xe4 ♕c7 26 ♖e2 ♖e6 27 h3 ♘g6 28 ♔b1 ♘f4 29 ♖ed2 ♘d5 30 c4 ♖xe4 31 ♖xd5 ♖e7 32 ♕d3 g6 33 ♖d8+ ♖e8 34 ♖xc8 ♕xc8 35 ♕d7 ♕b8 36 c5 ♕e5 37 c6 ♕e4+ 38 ♔b2 ♕e5+ 39 ♕d4 ♕e7 40 ♖c1 ♖d8 41 ♕f4 1-0**

Now we move on to 1 e4 e5 2 ♘f3 ♘c6 3 ♘c3 ♗c5. White can reply 4 ♗b5, with a type of Spanish, but the critical continuation is undoubtedly 4 ♘xe5. Examination of published theory gives the impression that this line is very bad for Black, which is probably true, but White must be careful. The main line runs 4 ♘xe5 ♘xe5 5 d4 ♗d6 6 dxe5 ♗xe5 7 f4 ♗xc3+ 8 bxc3 ♘f6 9 e5, and now 9...♕e7 10 ♗e2 ♘e4 11 ♕d4 is analysis going back to the last century. A couple of recent games have featured 9...♘e4, but I doubt if this will lead to a reassessment of the variation since White can keep a clear advantage with accurate play.

Game 4

Martorelli-Bellia
Italian Ch. 1986

1 e4 e5 2 ♘f3 ♘c6 3 ♘c3 ♗c5 4 ♘xe5 ♘xe5 5 d4 ♗d6 6 dxe5 ♗xe5 7 f4 ♗xc3+ 8 bxc3 ♘f6 9 e5 ♘e4

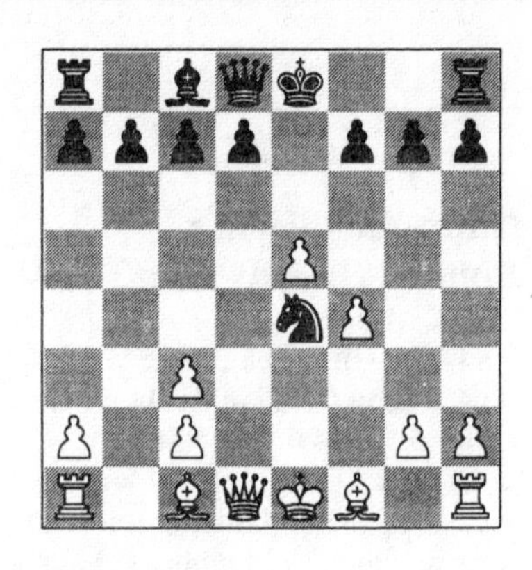

10 ♕d5!

⇨ 10 ♕f3 (this causes relatively few problems for Black) 10...d5 11 ♗d3 ♕h4+ 12 g3 ♕h3 13 c4 ♗g4 14 ♕f1 ♘c5 15 ♗e2 ♕xf1+ 16 ♗xf1 ♗f3 17 ♖g1 0-0-0 18 ♗a3 ♘e6 19 cxd5 ♗xd5 20 ♗d3 with an edge for White, V.Orlov-Mitkov, USSR-Yugoslavia Junior match 1991.

10...♕h4+ (10...♘xc3 11 ♕c4 wins a piece) **11 g3 ♘xg3 12 hxg3 ♕xg3+ 13 ♔d1 d6 14 ♕d3** (14 ♗d2! ♗g4+ 15 ♔c1 ♗f3 16 ♕d3 would have been a distinctly more convincing refutation) **14...♗g4+ 15 ♗e2 ♕g2 16 ♖h4 ♕f1+ 17 ♔d2 ♕xf4+ 18 ♔e1 ♗xe2 19 ♗xf4 ♗xd3 20 cxd3 dxe5 21 ♗xe5** (Black has three pawns for the piece, but they are all on the second rank) **21...0-0-0?** (21...f6 was better, with real drawing chances) **22 ♔d2 f6 23 ♗d4 ♖d7 24 ♖ah1** (now White has a clear advantage) **24...h6 25 ♖4h3 ♔d8 26 ♖g1 a6 27 ♖hg3 c5 28 ♗xc5 ♖h7 29 ♔e3 ♔e8 30 c4 ♔f7 31 a4 g5 32 ♖f1 ♔g6 33 ♖gf3 ♖hf7 34 ♖f5 h5 35 d4 h4 36 d5 h3 37 ♗d4 ♖de7+ 38 ♔d3 g4 39 ♗xf6 h2 40 ♖g5+ ♔h6 41 ♖xg4 1-0**

If Black wants to avoid the main lines of the Four Knights, then this is his most common choice. However, it is objectively weaker than the main lines and offers White good attacking chances. White has a choice of three possible replies to Black's system. The first is to pay no attention to Black's plan and simply develop by ♗c4, d3 and 0-0. Although this cannot be completely wrong, it poses relatively few problems for Black. Some examples are given in game 5. The second is the sharp continuation 4 d4 exd4 5 ♘d5, which we examine is games 6 and 7. Although Black must defend accurately he has excellent equalising chances. Finally there is the simple 4 d4 exd4 5 ♘xd4, which currently appears most dangerous for Black. This line often leads to castling on opposite flanks, with White launching a kingside attack much as in the Yugoslav Attack against the Dragon. However, in the Dragon Black has the half-open c-file to aid his attack, but in this line Black finds it much harder to create serious threats. This variation is covered in games 8 and 9.

Game 5

Degraeve-Volzhin
Oakham 1992

1 e4 e5 2 ♘f3 ♘c6 3 ♘c3 g6 4 ♗c4

⇨ 4 h4!? (a remarkable idea, but I wonder what White intended after 4...♘f6?) 4...h5 5 d4 exd4 6 ♘d5 ♗g7 7 ♗g5 ♘ce7 8 e5 (without the interpolation of h4 and ...h5 Black may equalise now by playing ...h6; lacking this Black has no route to equality) 8...d6 9 ♘f6+ ♔f8 (Black had to try 9...♗xf6 10 exf6 ♘d5 11 ♕xd4 ♘dxf6, although it is clear that White has excellent compensation for the pawn) 10 ♕xd4 ♗g4 11 0-0-0 ♘f5 12 ♕c3 ♗xf6 13 exf6 ♘gh6 14 ♖e1 ♗xf3 15 gxf3 ♔g8 16 ♖e7! ♔h7 17 ♗h3 ♖f8 18 ♖he1 d5 19 ♗xh6 d4 20 ♕xc7 ♕xc7 21 ♖xc7 ♔xh6 22 ♗xf5 gxf5 23 ♖xb7 ♖ad8 24 ♖ee7 ♔g6 25 ♖xa7 ♔xf6 26 ♖ed7 ♔e5 27 ♖xd8 ♖xd8 28 ♖xf7 ♖a8 29 a3 ♔f4 30 ♔d2 ♖a5 31 ♖h7 ♔xf3 32 ♖xh5 ♔e4 33 ♖h8 f4 34 h5 ♔f3 35 h6 ♖h5 36 h7 ♖h2 37 ♔d3 ♖h4 38 a4 1-0, Hector-Iskov, Malmo Open 1986.

4...♗g7

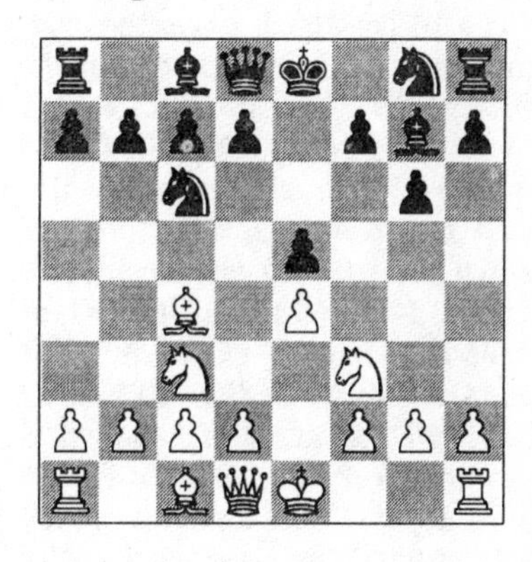

5 a3

⇨ 5 d3 ♘f6 6 0-0 0-0 7 ♗g5 h6 8 ♗e3 d6 9 a3 ♔h7 10 b4 ♘h5 11 b5 ♘a5 12 ♗a2 ♗e6 13 ♘d5 c6 14 bxc6 bxc6 15 ♘b4 ♘f4 16 c4 c5 17 ♘d5 g5 18 ♗xf4 exf4 19 d4 ♘c6 20 dxc5 dxc5 21 e5 ♘xe5 22 ♘xe5 ♗xe5 23 ♕c2+ ♔g7 24 ♖ad1 ♗d4

(Black is clearly better at this stage, but a combination of his slightly exposed king and especially his clock led to a reversal of fortune) 25 ♗b1 ♖h8 26 ♖fe1 ♕d6 27 ♘c3 ♗g4 28 ♖d2 ♖ae8 29 ♖xe8 ♖xe8 30 h3 ♗h5 31 ♕h7+ ♔f8 32 ♘b5 ♕f6 33 ♗e4 g4 34 hxg4 ♗xg4 35 ♘xd4 cxd4 36 c5 ♗d7 37 ♖d1 ♗a4 38 ♖c1 f3 39 ♗xf3 ♖e5 40 c6 ♕f4 41 ♕b1 ♖b5 42 ♕a1 ♖b8 43 ♖c4 ♗b3 44 ♖xd4 ♕f6 45 c7 ♖e8 46 ♕c3 ♗e6 47 ♕c5+ ♔g7 48 ♗g4 ♗c8 49 ♗xc8 ♖xc8 50 ♖g4+ ♔h7 51 g3 ♕a1+ 52 ♔h2 ♕f6 53 ♖f4 ♕e6 54 ♕xa7 ♕d5 55 ♕b6 h5 56 a4 ♕d7 57 ♕c5 ♔g6 58 ♕e5 f5 59 ♖d4 ♕f7 60 ♖d6+ ♔h7 61 ♖f6 1-0, Calvo-Averbakh, Palma de Mallorca 1972.

5...d6 6 d3 ♘f6 7 ♗e3 0-0 8 ♕d2 (White has at most a very small advantage, but Black plays too optimistically and runs into trouble) **8...♗g4?! 9 ♘g5 ♘d4 10 h3 ♗d7 11 f4 c6 12 0-0 b5 13 ♗a2 a5 14 ♖ae1** (now White has a clear plus, with a lead in development and pressure down the f-file to the sensitive f7 square) **14...♗e8 15 ♘d1 h6 16 fxe5 dxe5 17 c3 hxg5 18 cxd4 ♘h7 19 d5 cxd5 20 ♗xd5 ♖c8 21 ♖f2 a4 22 ♖ef1 ♕e7 23 ♗a2** (the knight is heading for d5) **23...♔h8 24 ♘c3 f6 25 ♘d5 ♕b7 26 d4 exd4 27 ♗xd4 ♗f7 28 h4!** (White is able to launch a direct attack) **28...gxh4 29 ♖xf6! ♘xf6 30 ♖xf6 ♔h7 31 ♖f4 ♗xd4+ 32 ♕xd4 ♖c1+ 33 ♔h2 ♕b8 34 ♘f6+ ♔h6 35 e5 g5 36 ♗xf7 ♖xf7 37 ♖xh4+ 1-0**

In the lines after 4 d4 exd4 5 ♘d5 ♗g7 6 ♗g5 ♘ce7, we consider two possibilities. In game 6 we cover the lines in which White meets ...c6 by ♘xe7, answering ...h6 by ♗h4. In game 7 we examine the idea of responding to ...c6 with ♘c3, when the bishop retreats to e3 after ...h6. Recent games have not featured the retreat to f4, probably because this leads only to equality.

Game 6

J.Szmetan-Frey
Bogota 1977

1 e4 e5 2 ♘f3 ♘c6 3 ♘c3 g6 4 d4 exd4 5 ♘d5 ♗g7 6 ♗g5 ♘ce7 (not 6...♘ge7? 7 ♘xd4! ♗xd4 8 ♕xd4 ♘xd4 9 ♘f6+ ♔f8 10 ♗h6 mate) **7 ♘xd4** (one of the games below continued with the move-order 7 ♕d2 h6 8 ♗h4 c6 9 ♘xe7 ♘xe7 10 ♘xd4 d5, but this is less flexible) **7...c6 8 ♘xe7 ♘xe7 9 ♕d2 h6**

⇨ 9...d5 10 0-0-0 dxe4 (it is more risky to play this without ...h6 and ...g5 interpolated)

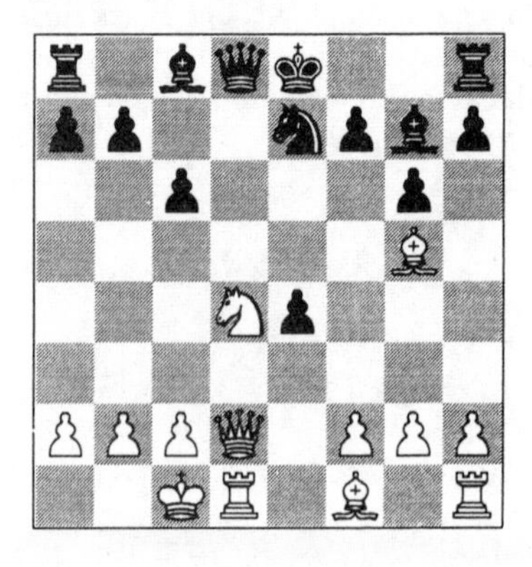

11 ♘b5!? (an incredible but probably unsound idea; 11 ♕e3 is objec-

tively better, with a promising position for White) 11...♕xd2+ 12 ♖xd2 ♗e5 (Black cannot take the knight) 13 ♗c4 (calm development, and the knight is still invulnerable) 13...h6! (after 13...♗f5 14 ♘d6+ ♗xd6 15 ♖xd6 White has enough for the pawn) 14 ♗f6 ♗xf6 15 ♘c7+ ♔f8 16 ♖d8+ ♔g7 17 ♖xh8 ♔xh8 18 ♘xa8 ♔g7 19 a4 ♗e5 20 a5 ♔f8 (or the simple 20...♘d5 followed by ...♗e6 when Black has fantastic compensation for the exchange; she is not winning the knight, but the knight cannot safely emerge) 21 h3 ♘f5 22 ♖d1 ♔e7 23 ♖e1 ♘d6 24 ♗d3 f5 25 c3 ♗e6 26 ♗e2 ♔d7 27 a6 b6?? (a miserable blunder; after 27...b5! Black is still clearly better, since it is hard to see a long-term defence to the threat of ...♔c8-b8) 28 ♘xb6+ ♔c7 29 ♘a4 ♘c4 30 ♔c2 ♘a5 31 ♘c5 ♗d5 32 b4 ♘c4 33 ♖d1 ♘a3+ 1-0, Micic-Dabrowska, Novi Sad Women's Ol. 1990.

10 ♗h4 d5 11 0-0-0 g5 (11...dxe4 12 ♕e3 ♕a5 fails to 13 ♗xe7! ♔xe7 14 ♘b5 ♕b6 15 ♕a3+, as in Fichtl-Udovcic, Berlin 1961) **12 ♗g3 dxe4 13 ♕e3**

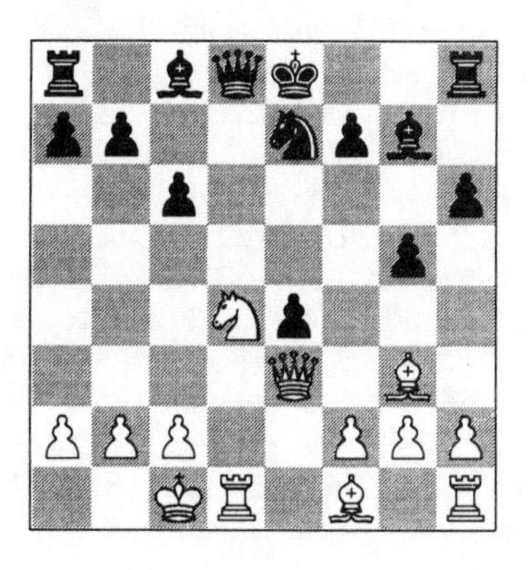

13...♕d5?

⇨ 13...♕b6! (this is a better move, although the position is very double-edged) 14 ♗d6 ♗e6 15 ♗xe7 ♔xe7 16 ♕a3+ c5 17 ♘xe6 fxe6 18 ♗c4 (Black's king position appears insecure, but White has to fight his way past two e-pawns to reach the king and meanwhile the g7 bishop is very strong) 18...♖ad8 19 ♖de1 ♕c6 20 ♕b3 a6 21 f3 b5 22 ♗xe6 c4 23 ♕a3+ (23 ♗xc4 bxc4 24 ♕a3+ followed by ♖xe4 was a better chance, although still very good for Black) 23...♔xe6 24 ♖xe4+ ♔f5 25 h4 ♖he8 26 hxg5 hxg5 27 ♕e3 ♖xe4 28 fxe4+ ♔f6 29 ♖h5 ♔e7 30 e5 ♕xg2 31 ♕c5+ ♔e8 32 b3 ♕d5 0-1, Morgulov-Shereshevsky, USSR 1975.

14 ♘b5! (the start of a spectacular attack) **14...♗xb2+ 15 ♔xb2 ♕xd1 16 ♘c7+ ♔d8 17 ♗d3! ♕xh1 18 ♕d4+ ♘d5 19 ♕xh8+ ♔e7 20 ♕e8+ ♔f6 21 ♕e5+ ♔g6 22 ♗xe4+ f5 23 ♕e8+ 1-0**

Game 7

Nei-Helle
Finland 1968

1 e4 e5 2 ♘f3 ♘c6 3 ♘c3 g6 4 d4 exd4 5 ♘d5 ♗g7 6 ♗g5 ♘ce7 7 ♘xd4 c6 8 ♘c3 h6 9 ♗e3 (the bishop cannot retreat to h4 in this line because 9 ♗h4 d5! 10 exd5 ♕b6 11 ♘b3 ♕b4 exploits the tactical weakness of the h4 bishop) **9...d5?!** This is too risky; 9...♘f6 is a more sensible line and appears to be satisfactory for Black, as in the following examples:

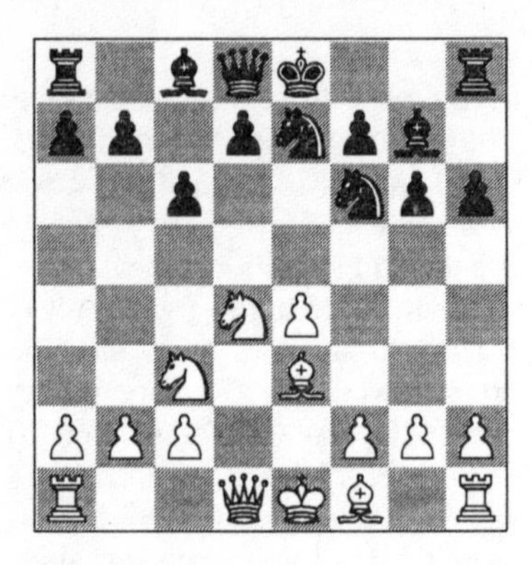

⇨ 10 ♕e2?! 0-0 11 0-0-0 b5 (Black already has a good position) 12 f3 b4 13 ♘a4 ♕a5 14 b3 d5 15 e5 ♘d7 16 ♔b1 c5 17 ♘b5 d4 18 e6 ♘b6 19 exf7+ ♖xf7 20 ♗c1 ♘xa4 21 bxa4 ♗b7 22 ♘d6 ♘d5? (time-trouble starts to affect the play; 22...♗d5! 23 ♘xf7 ♕xa4 24 ♗b2 ♕xa2+ 25 ♔c1 c4 would have given Black a crushing attack) 23 ♗b2 d3?? 24 ♕xd3 ♖d8 25 ♕xg6 ♖xd6 26 ♕xd6 ♗d4 27 ♗c4 1-0, Utasi-Westerinen, Havana 1986.

⇨ 10 ♗c4 0-0 11 ♕f3? (a tactical blunder) 11...d5! 12 exd5 c5 (Black is winning) 13 ♘db5 (after other knight moves ...♗g4 wins material because White's queen is trapped) 13...a6 14 d6 ♘f5 15 ♘c7 ♘xd6! 16 0-0-0 ♕xc7 17 ♗f4 ♗g4 18 ♕d3 b5 19 ♗d5 ♖ad8 20 f3 b4 21 ♕xg6 ♔h8 22 ♕d3 bxc3 23 fxg4 ♕b6 24 b3 ♕b4 0-1, Gufeld-T.Petrosian, Moscow 1969.

⇨ 10 ♗c4 0-0 11 e5 (certainly better than Gufeld's 11 ♕f3?, but even here Black has no problems) 11...♘e8 12 ♕d2 d5 13 exd6 ♘xd6 14 ♗b3 ♘ef5 15 ♘xf5 ♘xf5 16 0-0-0 ♕xd2+ 17 ♗xd2 ♘d4 18 ♗e3 ♘xb3+ 19 axb3 ♗f5 20 ♗d4 ♖fd8 21 ♗xg7 ♔xg7 22 ♖xd8 ♖xd8 23 ♖e1 ♖d4 24 g3 h5 25 ♖e7 ♗d7 26 ♖e4 ♖d6 27 ♖e1 ♗g4 28 ♘e4 ♖d5 29 ♘d2 g5 (Black has a slight advantage and Keres suggested 29...♖f5 as a better winning chance) 30 f3 ♗e6 31 ♘c4 ♔f6 32 ♘e3 ♖d8 33 ♖d1 ♖h8 34 ♔d2 h4 35 g4 ♖d8+ (the game peters out to a draw) 36 ♔e2 ♖xd1 37 ♘xd1 ♔e5 38 ♔e3 f5 39 ♘f2 f4+ 40 ♔e2 a5 41 ♘h3 ½-½, Tarve-Keres, Parnu 1971.

10 exd5 ♘xd5 11 ♘xd5 ♕xd5 (attentive readers will have no trouble guessing White's next move)

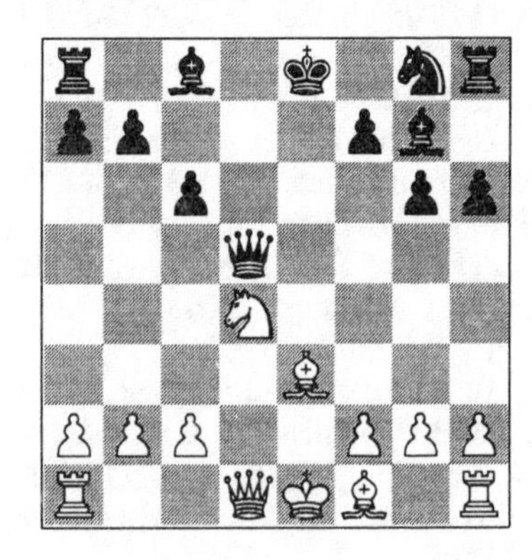

12 ♘b5! (once again this move causes severe problems for Black) **12...♗e5** (after 12...♕xd1+ 13 ♖xd1 cxb5 14 ♗xb5+ ♔e7 15 ♗c5+ ♔e6 16 ♗c4+ ♔f5 17 ♖d5+ ♔e6 18 ♔d2! White has a colossal attack for the sacrificed piece) **13 ♕xd5 cxd5 14 0-0-0 ♘e7 15 ♗xa7 ♗e6 16 a3 0-0 17 ♗c5 ♖fe8 18 ♗d6 ♗xd6 19 ♘xd6 ♖eb8 20 ♗d3 ♖a5 21 ♘b5 ♗d7 22 ♘d4 b5 23 ♖he1 ♔f8 24 c3 ♘c8 25 ♖e3 ♖a7 26 ♖de1 ♘d6 27 ♖e5 1-0**

The next topic is the line 4 d4 exd4 5 ♘xd4. Black can meet this in two ways, according to whether he develops his knight on e7 or f6. The former keeps open the bishop's diagonal, but gives White a free hand with h4-h5. We consider this in game 8. If Black plays ...♘f6, there are two lines for White; the first involves exchanging knights on c6 and playing e5. This is the theoretical recommendation and it appears to guarantee a slight plus for White. The alternative is to continue with the attacking plan of ♕d2, 0-0-0 and a kingside pawn advance. This is more double-edged and it is not clear if White can gain an advantage. We examine this line in game 9. In both lines White must take care not to allow Black to break open the position with a favourable ...d5.

Game 8

Nunn-Beliavsky
Belgrade 1991

1 e4 e5 2 ♘f3 ♘c6 3 ♘c3 g6 4 d4 exd4 5 ♘xd4 ♗g7 6 ♗e3 ♘ge7 7 ♕d2 d5?!

This move is not justified. The alternative is 7...0-0 (see following diagram):

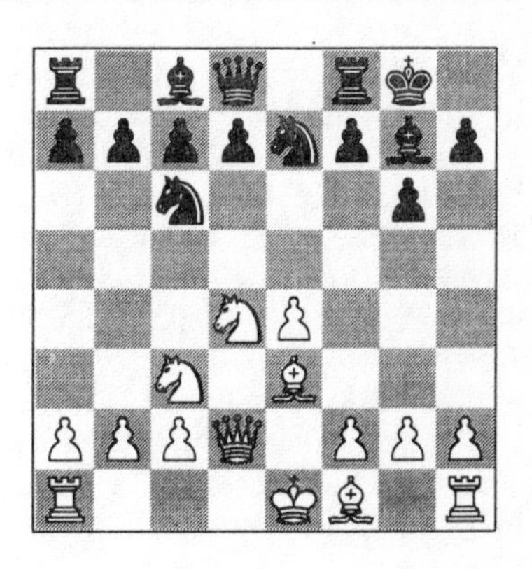

⇨ 8 h4?! (White should play 0-0-0 before starting his attack) 8...d5 9 ♘xd5? (9 ♘xc6 bxc6 10 0-0-0 is better, with equality) 9...♘xd5 10 exd5 ♕xd5 11 c4 ♕e4 12 ♘xc6 ♕xc6 13 0-0-0 ♗f5 14 a3 ♗f6 15 ♗d3 ♖ad8 16 ♕c2 ♖xd3 17 ♖xd3 ♕xg2 18 ♖hd1 ♗xd3 19 ♖xd3 ♕h1+ 20 ♖d1 ♕xh4 21 ♗xa7 ♖d8 22 ♖xd8+ ♗xd8 23 ♗e3 ♗g5 24 ♕e2 ♗xe3+ 25 fxe3 ♕e4 26 b4 h5 27 c5 h4 28 ♕d2 h3 29 ♕d8+ ♔g7 30 ♕xc7 ♕h1+ 31 ♔b2 ♕g2+ 32 ♔c3 h2 33 ♕e5+ ♔h7 34 ♕f6 ♔g8 35 ♕d8+ ♔g7 36 ♕d4+ f6 0-1, Joksimovic-V.Sokolov, Belgrade 1966.

⇨ 8 0-0-0 d6 9 h4 (when the knight is on e7 White need not play the preliminary f3, but 9 ♗e2 is another idea, waiting to see Black's reply before deciding on an attacking plan) 9...h5 10 f3 ♘xd4 11 ♗xd4 ♗xd4 12 ♕xd4 ♘c6 13 ♕d2 ♗e6 14 ♗e2 ♕f6 15 f4 ♖ae8 16 f5 gxf5 17 ♗xh5 (White is clearly better) 17...f4 18 ♖df1 ♕e5 19 ♗e2 ♘d4 20 ♗d3 c5 21 ♕xf4 (21 ♖xf4 c4 22 ♗f1 would have been very good for White, keeping the queens on for the attack) 21...c4 22 ♕xe5 (22 ♗e2 was better; the move played cements the knight on d4 and improves Black's pawn structure) 22...dxe5 23 ♗e2 b5 (Spassky's experience enables him to escape from a dangerous situation) 24 ♗h5 ♔g7 25 ♘e2 ♖h8 26 ♗f3 b4 27 ♘xd4 exd4 28 ♖d1 ♖d8 29 c3 dxc3 30 bxc3 a5 31 ♖xd8

♖xd8 32 ♖d1 ♖b8 33 ♔b2 ♖h8 34 h5 ♖b8 35 ♖d6 bxc3+ 36 ♔xc3 ♖b4 37 ♗d1 ♖b1 38 ♔c2 ♖b5 39 ♖c6 ♖e5 40 ♗f3 ♖b5 41 ♖a6 c3 42 ♔xc3 ♗xa2 43 ♗e2 ♖g5 44 g4 ♗e6 45 ♔d4 ♔h7 46 e5 ♗xg4 47 ♗d3+ ♗f5 48 ♖xa5 ♗xd3 49 ♔xd3 ♖xh5 50 ♔e4 ♔g7 51 ♖a1 ½-½, Sterten-brink-Spassky, Bundesliga 1986/7.

8 ♘xc6 bxc6 9 0-0-0 ♗e6 10 ♗d4 0-0 11 ♗xg7 ♔xg7 12 ♕d4+ f6 (Black should have tried 12...♔g8)

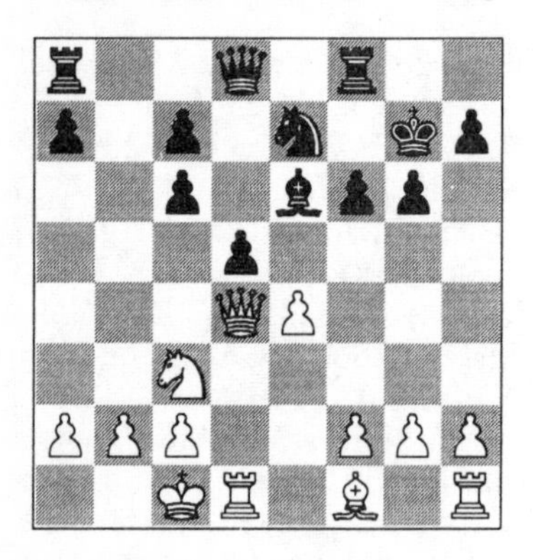

13 ♕c5! (this move decides the game; the threat is ♗c4 and Black cannot hold on to all his pawns) **13...♕d7 14 ♗c4 ♖ad8** (or 14...♖fd8 15 ♖he1 and there are too many loose pieces sitting on the e-file) **15 ♕xa7 ♕d6 16 ♗b3 ♗f7 17 exd5 cxd5 18 ♘b5 ♕f4+ 19 ♔b1 ♖d7 20 ♕c5 ♘f5 21 g3 ♕f3 22 ♘xc7 ♖fd8 23 ♖he1 ♖e7 24 c3 ♖dd7 25 ♘b5 ♖xe1 26 ♖xe1 d4 27 ♗xf7 ♕xf2 28 ♖c1 ♔xf7 29 g4 ♘e3 30 cxd4 ♘xg4 31 ♘d6+ ♔g7 32 ♕c8 ♖xd6 33 ♕c7+ ♔h6 34 ♕xd6 ♘e3 35 a4 g5 36 ♕f8+ ♔g6 37 ♕g8+ ♔h6 38 ♕e6 ♕f4 39 ♖c3 ♘f1 40 ♖h3+ 1-0**

Game 9

Makarychev-Tukmakov
Palma de Mallorca 1989

1 e4 e5 2 ♘f3 ♘c6 3 ♘c3 g6 4 d4 exd4 5 ♘xd4 ♗g7 6 ♗e3 ♘f6 7 ♕d2

The theoretical recommendation 7 ♘xc6 bxc6 8 e5 hasn't been seen much recently, which is surprising because it virtually guarantees White a safe (if small) advantage. When it has appeared the outcome has been successful, for example:

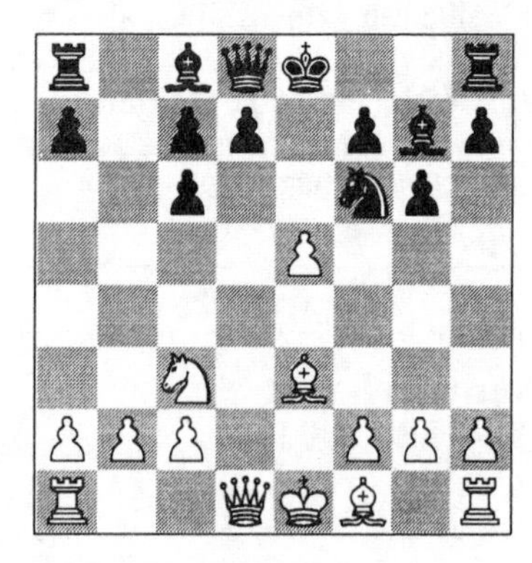

⇨ 8...♘d5 (this pawn sacrifice is a new idea, but it is not convincing) 9 ♘xd5 cxd5 10 ♕xd5 ♖b8 11 ♗xa7 ♖xb2 12 ♗d4 ♖b8 13 ♗c4 0-0 14 0-0 ♗b7 15 ♕a5 ♕g5 16 f3 d6 17 ♖f2 (to meet 17...dxe5 by 18 f4) 17...c5 18 f4 ♕h4 19 ♗c3 dxe5 20 ♕c7 (threat 21 ♗xf7+) 20...♕d8 21 ♕xd8 ♖bxd8 22 fxe5 ♗d5 23 ♗xd5 ♖xd5 24 ♖e2 ♖e8 25 a4 (Black finally regains the pawn, but the a-pawn is too strong) 25...♗xe5 26

♖xe5 ♖dxe5 27 ♗xe5 ♖xe5 28 a5 ♖e7 29 ♔f2 ♔f8 30 ♔f3 ♔e8 31 a6 ♖a7 32 ♔e4 ♔d7 33 ♔d5 c4 34 ♔xc4 ♔c6 35 ♔d4 f5 36 h4 ♔b6 37 ♔d5 ♔c7 38 c4 ♔b8 39 ♖b1+ ♔a8 40 c5 ♖d7+ 41 ♔c6 ♖d2 42 ♔b6 ♖d8 43 a7 1-0, Campora-E.Geller, Berne 1988.

⇨ 8...♘g8 9 f4!? (an interesting new idea; after 9 ♗d4 ♕e7 10 ♕e2 f6 11 exf6 ♘xf6 12 0-0-0 White has a small advantage) 9...f6 10 ♕d2 fxe5 11 fxe5 ♗xe5 12 0-0-0 (for the pawn White has a large lead in development) 12...d6 13 ♖e1 ♘f6 14 ♗g5 ♕e7 (14...0-0? 15 ♖xe5 wins) 15 ♗c4 ♗e6 16 ♘e4! ♘xe4 17 ♖xe4 ♕d7 18 ♗f6 ♖f8 19 ♗xe5 dxe5 20 ♕xd7+ (keeping the queens on by 20 ♕e2 was probably even better) 20...♔xd7 21 ♖d1+ ♗d5 22 ♗xd5 cxd5 23 ♖xd5+ ♔c6 24 ♖dxe5 and with a clear extra pawn the position should be a win. White eventually netted the full point in Shabanov-Vorotnikov, USSR 1977.

⇨ 7 ♗e2 with the idea of castling kingside was played in the well-known game Spassky-Larsen, Malmo match 1968. It was the only game Larsen won in this Candidates' match and it proved that without the attacking chances afforded by castling on opposite wings White has no advantage: 7...0-0 8 0-0 ♖e8 9 ♘xc6 bxc6 10 ♗f3 ♗b7 11 ♕d2 d6 12 ♗h6 ♗xh6 13 ♕xh6 ♖e5 14 ♖ae1 c5 15 ♖e3 ♕e7 16 ♖fe1 ♖e8 17 h4 ♕e6 18 ♕f4 ♔g7 19 b3 h6 20 ♕g3 ♕d7 21 ♕f4 ♖8e7 22 ♘d5 ♗xd5 23 exd5 g5 24 hxg5 hxg5 25 ♕g3 ♕f5 26 c4 ♖xe3 27 fxe3 ♖e5 28 ♗d1 ♕d3 29 ♗f3 ♕c3 30 ♔h2 a5 31 ♔h1 ♔f8 32 ♖f1 ♕xe3 33 ♕h3 ♔g7 34 g3 ♕d4 35 g4 a4 36 ♗d1 ♖e3 37 ♕g2 ♖d3 38 ♗e2 ♖d2 0-1.

7...0-0

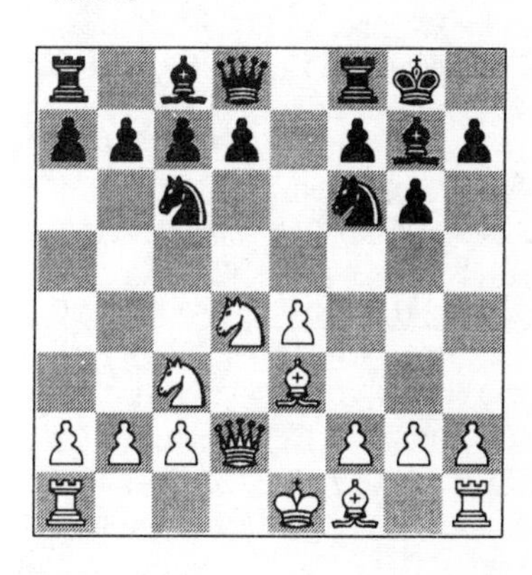

8 0-0-0

This is the best plan. It is possible to play 8 f3, but since White can often manage without this move it might cause a loss of time. In Radulov-Planinc, Wijk aan Zee 1974 Black tried to refute 8 f3 by 8...d5, but after 9 ♘xc6 bxc6 10 0-0-0 ♗e6 11 ♗h6 ♖b8 12 ♗xg7 ♔xg7 13 ♕e3 ♕e7 14 exd5 cxd5 15 ♘xd5 ♘xd5 16 ♖xd5 ♕f6 17 ♖e5 ♖fd8 18 ♗e2 White had a definite advantage.

8...♘xd4

Other ideas:

⇨ 8...♘g4 9 ♗g5! (9 ♘xc6 bxc6 10 ♗d4 ♗xd4 11 ♕xd4 ♕f6 12 f3 ♘e5 13 ♕d2 d6 14 f4 ♘d7 15 g3 ♘b6 16 h4 h5 17 f5 ♘d7 18 ♗e2 ♘e5 19 ♖dg1 ♖b8 20 ♕h6 ♗d7 21 g4 hxg4 22 ♗xg4 ♕h8 ½-½, Svidler-Lev, Gausdal 1991) 9...f6 (9...♗f6!? 10 ♗xf6 ♕xf6 11 f3 ♕xd4 12 ♕xd4 ♘xd4 13 ♖xd4 ♘f6 14 e5 ♘e8 15 ♘e4 followed by ♗c4 is better for White) 10 ♗f4 ♘xd4 11 ♕xd4 f5 12

♕c4+ ♔h8 13 ♗xc7 ♕f6 14 ♕e2 with advantage to White according to Makarychev.

⇨ 8...♖e8 (this may be Black's best move) 9 ♘xc6 (9 f3 d5 10 ♗b5 ♗d7 11 exd5 ♘e5 12 f4 ♘eg4 13 ♗g1 ♗xb5 14 ♘dxb5 a6 15 ♘d4 ♘xd5 16 ♘xd5 ♕xd5 17 ♘b3 ♕xd2+ 18 ♘xd2 ♖e2 19 g3 ♖ae8 20 ♘f3 ♘f2 21 ♗xf2 ♖xf2 22 ♖hf1 ♖xf1 23 ♖xf1 ♖e2 24 ♖e1 ♖f2 25 ♖e8+ ♗f8 26 ♘e5 ♔g7 27 ♖b8 b5 28 ♖d8 ♗d6 29 ♖d7 ♗xe5 30 fxe5 ♖xh2 31 e6 ♖f2 32 ♖xc7 h5 33 ♖a7 g5 34 exf7 ♖xf7 35 ♖xa6 ♖f3 36 a4 bxa4 37 c4 ♖xg3 38 ♔d2 h4 39 ♔e2 h3 40 ♔f2 h2 41 ♖a7+ ♔g6 42 ♖a6+ ♔h5 0-1, Denny-Castro, St.Martin Open 1991, but after 12 ♗e2! it is far from clear how Black can justify his pawn sacrifice; therefore 9 f3 is probably the critical move) 9...bxc6 10 ♗g5 and now:

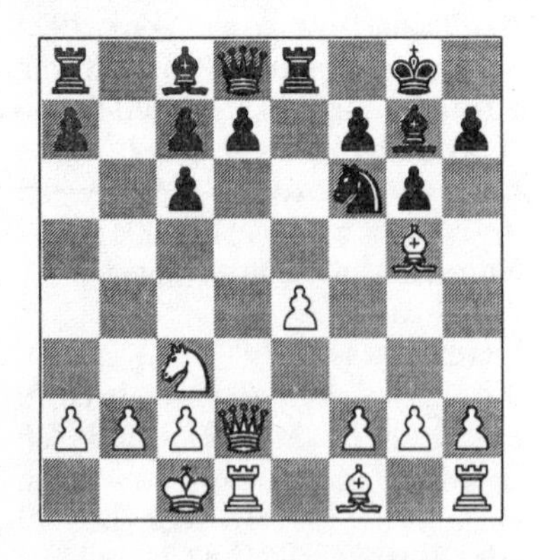

1) 10...♕e7 11 ♗c4 ♕e5 12 ♖de1 d6 13 f4 ♕a5 14 e5 dxe5 15 ♖xe5 ♖xe5 16 fxe5 ♕xe5 17 ♕d8+ ♘e8 18 ♖f1 ♗b7 19 ♗xf7+ ♔h8 20 ♕e7 (White has just an edge) 20...♘d6 21 ♗b3 ♖e8 22 ♕xe5 ♗xe5 23 ♘a4 c5 24 ♘xc5 ♗xg2 25 ♖f2 ♗c6 26 ♘d3 ♗d4 27 ♗f6+ ♗xf6 28 ♖xf6 ♔g7 29 ♖f4 g5 30 ♖f2 h5 31 ♘c5 ♖e1+ 32 ♔d2 ♖e5 33 ♘e6+ ♖xe6 34 ♗xe6 ♘e4+ 35 ♔e3 ♘xf2 36 ♔xf2 with an eventual draw, Abdennabi-Van der Sterren, Lucerne World Team Ch. 1989.

2) 10...♖b8 11 ♖e1 d6 12 ♗c4 ♗e6 13 ♗b3 ♕c8 14 ♔b1 c5 15 e5 dxe5 16 ♗xf6 ♗xf6 17 ♘e4 ♗e7 18 ♕c3 c4 19 ♗xc4 ♗xc4 20 ♕xc4 ♕b7 21 b3 with equality, although White later won a long rook and pawn ending in the game Abdennabi-J.Nikolac, Bahrain 1990.

9 ♗xd4 d6 10 f3 ♗e6 11 g4! (Yurtaev's innovation poses more problems for Black than the previously played 11 ♔b1) **11...c5 12 ♗e3 ♕a5 13 ♗h6! ♗xh6!? 14 ♕xh6 b5!?** (14...♗xa2 15 h4 ♗e6 16 h5 gives White a very strong attack) **15 ♗xb5 ♖ab8 16 a4! a6 17 ♖xd6!** (a spectacular temporary piece sacrifice) **17...axb5 18 e5 ♘xg4!** (Black is forced to return the material because 18...♘e8 19 ♘e4 threatens both 20 ♘f6+ and 20 ♘g5) **19 fxg4 ♕b4! 20 a5!** (White must keep the b-file closed) **20...♕xg4 21 ♖e1** (threat ♘e4) **21...♕f5!? 22 ♕h4 b4?!** (after 22...h5!? the situation would be less clear) **23 ♘e4 h5 24 ♖d2!** (threat ♖f2) **24...♔g7! 25 ♕f6+ ♔h6 26 ♘xc5 ♖b5 27 ♘xe6 fxe6 28 ♕xf5 ♖xf5?!** (28...exf5 was a better chance because the passed f-pawn offers counterplay) **29 a6 ♖fxe5 30 ♖xe5 ♖xe5 31 ♖d6! ♔g5 32 c4! ♔h4 33 ♔c2 ♔h3 34 ♔b3 ♔xh2 35 ♔xb4 ♖e1 36 a7 ♖a1 37 ♖d2+ 1-0**

This system can only arise via the Petroff move-order, but since many players adopt the Four Knights against both 2...♘c6 and 2...♘f6 we will examine it in detail. The critical reply is 4 ♘xe5, but first we will consider some other options. The line 4 a3 ♗xc3 5 dxc3 is a poor choice because it is a direct transposition into the variation 1 e4 e5 2 ♘f3 ♘c6 3 ♗b5 a6 4 ♗a4 ♘f6 5 ♗xc6 dxc6 (with colours reversed), and therefore loses a tempo. The main alternative to 4 ♘xe5 is 4 ♗c4, but here we run into problems with transpositions. Perhaps the most common answer to 4 ♗c4 is 4...♘c6, but 5 d3 leads to a line from C28 in *ECO* which is normally considered part of the Vienna Opening. We will consider it briefly in game 10.

The main line runs 4 ♘xe5 0-0 5 ♗e2 ♖e8 6 ♘d3 ♗xc3 7 dxc3, when White gains the two bishops but the symmetrical pawn structure makes it hard for White to achieve anything. White probably has a slight advantage, but no more. However, Black's winning chances are even more remote, and normally Black can only win if White overpresses. This line is rather depressing for Black, but would probably appeal to Petroff players. We look at it in game 11.

Game 10

Larsen-Davies
London (WFW) 1989

1 e4 e5 2 ♘f3 ♘f6 3 ♘c3 ♗b4 4 ♗c4 ♘c6 5 d3 d6 (5...0-0 is a major alternative; readers should refer to standard theoretical works for coverage) **6 0-0 ♗xc3 7 bxc3 ♗g4** (theory gives 7...♘a5 8 ♗b3 ♘xb3 9 axb3 0-0 10 c4 b6 as equal, but in my view White's preponderance of pawns in the centre must give him a slight advantage) **8 h3 ♗h5**

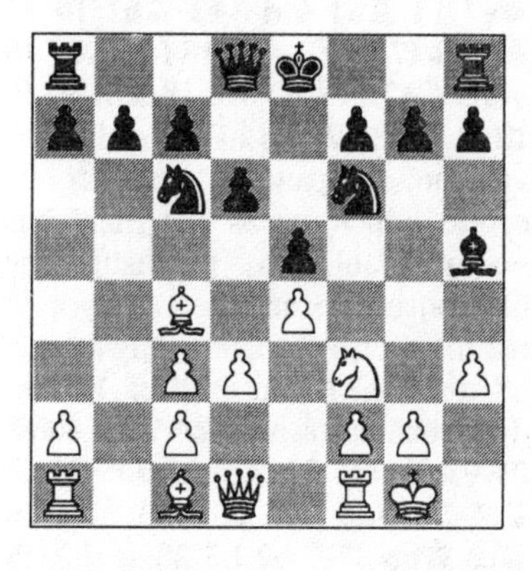

9 ♗b3

⇨ 9 ♖e1 ♕d7 (the idea is to prevent g4, and to make White worry about ...0-0-0 followed by ...♖dg8 and ...g5-g4) 10 ♗b5?! (the exchange of this bishop gives Black a comfortable game) 10...a6 11 ♗xc6 ♕xc6 12 c4 b5 (Black is already slightly better) 13 g4 ♗g6 14 cxb5 axb5 15 a3 ♘d7 (of course the g6 bishop is out of play, but it can return by ...f6 and ...♗f7, while White must worry both about the weak a-pawn and about the damage he has done to his own kingside) 16 ♖b1 ♘c5 17 ♖b4 0-0 18 c4 ♖fb8 19 ♘h4 bxc4 20 ♖xc4 d5 (opening lines exposes White's kingside weaknesses) 21 ♖c3 ♕d6 22 ♕f3 d4 23 ♖c4 ♖b3 24 ♘xg6 hxg6 25 ♖d1 ♖c3! (decisive) 26 ♖xc3 dxc3 27 d4 exd4 28 e5 ♕d8

29 ♖xd4 ♕xd4 30 ♕xa8+ ♔h7 31 ♗e3 ♕xe3 32 fxe3 c2 0-1, Seppeur-Nunn, Bundesliga 1984/5.

9...♘d7?! (the ...♕d7 plan is also appropriate here; Black must generate some active play or else White's two bishops and central pawns will prove the dominant factor) **10 ♗e3 ♕e7 11 ♖b1 ♘d8 12 ♔h2 f6 13 ♕d2 ♗f7 14 ♘h4 g6 15 f4 ♗xb3 16 axb3 ♘f7 17 ♘f3 0-0 18 ♖f2 a6 19 ♖bf1 ♔h8** (White has a lasting advantage; his pawns are nearer the centre, which means that Black has no favourable way to change the pawn structure, and there is a potential long-term problem along the a1-h8 diagonal because Black has no dark-squared bishop) **20 ♔h1 ♖ae8 21 ♘h2 exf4 22 ♗xf4 ♘fe5 23 c4 ♖f7 24 ♕a5 ♖c8 25 ♘f3 ♘c6 26 ♕c3 ♔g8 27 ♘h2 h5 28 ♗c1 ♕f8 29 ♘f3 ♕g7 30 b4 ♘ce5 31 ♘d4** (White starts to make use of his advantages; the move c5 will undermine the e5 knight)

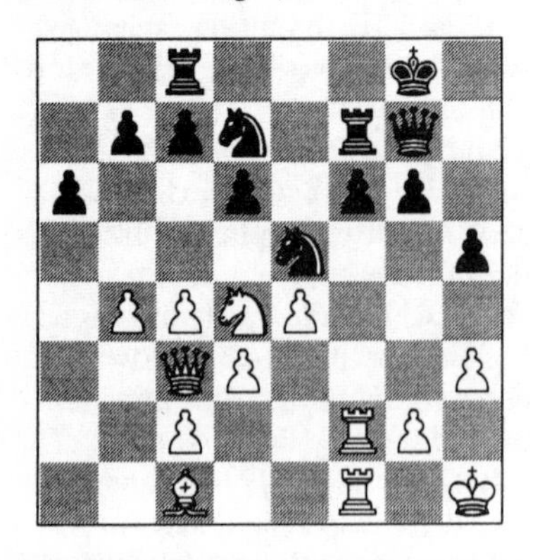

31...♖e8 32 c5 dxc5 33 bxc5 c6 34 ♘b3 g5 (the f5 square is the last straw) **35 ♘d4 ♕f8 36 ♘f5 ♘xc5 37 ♗a3 ♘ed7 38 ♕a1 b5 39 d4 ♖xe4 40 ♗xc5 1-0**

Game 11

Bastian-Röder
Bundesliga 1985

1 e4 e5 2 ♘f3 ♘f6 3 ♘c3 ♗b4 4 ♘xe5 0-0

This looks better than 4...♕e7 5 ♘d3 ♗xc3 6 dxc3 ♘xe4 7 ♗e2 0-0 8 0-0 d5 9 ♘f4 c6 10 c4 dxc4 11 ♗xc4 and now:

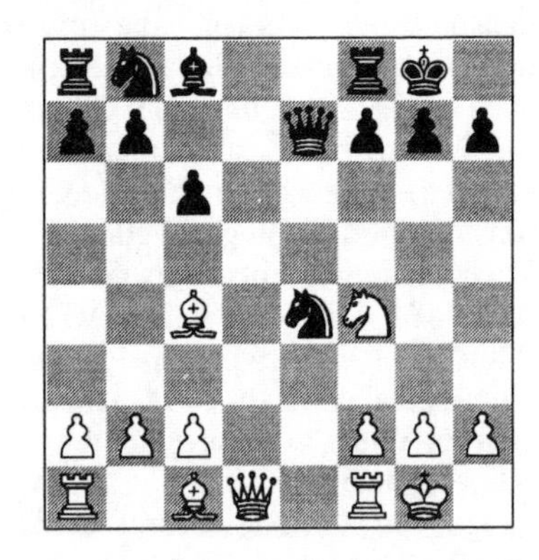

➯ 11...♘d6?! (a weak move) 12 ♖e1 ♕c7 13 ♗b3 ♗f5 14 ♘h5 ♕d7 15 ♕d4 ♘e8 16 ♕c3 ♗g6 17 ♗h6! (White finishes neatly) 17...♗xh5 (17...gxh6 18 ♖xe8 ♗xh5 19 ♖xf8+ ♔xf8 20 ♕h8+ ♔e7 21 ♖e1+ ♔d6 22 ♕e5 mate) 18 ♖xe8 ♕g4 19 ♖xf8+ ♔xf8 20 h3! ♕g6 21 ♕b4+ ♔g8 22 ♕xb7 gxh6 23 ♕xa8 ♕d6 24 ♕xa7 ♘d7 25 ♕e3 ♗g6 26 a4 ♘c5 27 a5 1-0, Istratescu-Wijesundara, Manila Ol. 1992.

➯ 11...♗f5 (Alekhine found a better move 80 years earlier, but it does not equalise) 12 ♕e2 (this threatens f3; 12 ♕h5 was another idea) 12...♖e8 13 ♖e1 ♕d7 14 ♗e3 b5 15 ♖ad1 (in his book of best games, Alekhine gives the immediate 15 ♗b3 as better for White) 15...♕c7 16 ♗d3 (the tournament book recommends 16 ♗b3) 16...♘d7 17 f3 (if White wanted to play g4, he should have done so immediately) 17...♘d6 18 g4? (now this is just a mistake) 18...♗xd3 19 ♕xd3 ♘e5! (White is suddenly much worse) 20 ♕f1 ♘dc4 21 ♗c1 ♕a5 22 ♖e2 ♕xa2 23 ♖de1 f6 24 ♘d3 ♖f8 25 b3 ♘d6 26 ♘xe5 fxe5 27 ♕g2 ♖ae8 28 f4 e4 29 f5 ♕a1 30 ♕g3 (30 ♗f4 gives drawing chances) 30...♘f7 31 c3 b4 32 ♗b2 ♕a5 33 ♖xe4 ♖xe4 34 ♖xe4 ♕d5 35 ♖e2 ♕d1+ 36 ♕e1 ♕xb3 37 cxb4 ♘g5 38 ♕c3 ♘h3+ 39 ♔f1 ♕d1+ 40 ♕e1 ♕d5 41 ♖e4 ♘g5 (41...h5! wins more quickly) 42 ♕c3 ♖f6 43 ♖d4 ♕h1+ 44 ♔e2 ♕xh2+ 45 ♔d1 h5 46 ♖d7 ♘f7 47 g5 ♕g1+ 48 ♕e1 ♖d6+ 49 ♖xd6 ♕xe1+ 50 ♔xe1 ♘xd6 51 f6 gxf6 52 ♗xf6 ♔f7 53 ♗d4 a6 54 ♔e2 ♔g6 55 ♔d3 ♔xg5 56 ♗e5 ♘f5 57 ♔c4 h4 58 ♗h2 ♔g4 59 ♔c5 ♔h3 60 ♗c7 ♔g2 61 ♔xc6 h3 62 ♔b6 ♘g3 63 ♔xa6 h2 64 b5 h1♕ 65 b6 ♘e4 66 b7 ♘c5+ 0-1, Alapin-Alekhine, Carlsbad 1911.

5 ♗e2 ♖e8

Black can also play 5...d6, which gives him the possibility of delaying or avoiding ...♖e8. However, the result is a transposition into positions which are not fundamentally different from those in the main line. After 5...d6 6 ♘d3 ♗xc3 7 dxc3 ♘xe4 8 0-0 Black has tried:

➩ 8...♗f5 9 ♗e3 ♘d7 10 ♖e1 ♖e8 11 c4 ♘dc5 12 ♗f1 ♘xd3?! (this is dubious for tactical reasons) 13 cxd3 ♘f6 14 ♕f3 ♗c8 (14...♕c8 15 ♗g5 is very awkward) 15 ♗g5 ♖xe1 16 ♖xe1 ♔f8 17 ♕e4! (the threat of ♗xf6 wins a pawn) 17...♗e6 18 ♗xf6 ♕xf6 19 ♕xb7 ♕d8 20 g3 ♖b8 21 ♕xa7 ♖xb2 22 d4 ♖b4 23 a3 ♖b2 24 d5 ♗d7 25 ♕d4 ♕f6 26 ♕xf6 gxf6 27 ♔g2 c5 28 ♖e2 ♖b1 29 ♖a2 ♗a4 30 ♗d3 ♖c1 31 ♖b2 ♖c3 32 ♗xh7 ♖xc4 33 ♔f3 ♖d4 34 ♗e4 f5 35 ♗xf5 ♖xd5 36 ♔f4 c4 37 ♖b4 ♗b3 38 h4 ♖d2 39 ♔g5 ♔g7 40 ♖b7 ♖xf2 41 h5 ♗a4 42 h6+ ♔f8 43 ♖b8+ ♔e7 44 h7 ♖xf5+ 45 ♔xf5 ♗c2+ 46 ♔f4 ♗xh7 47 ♖c8 ♗d3 48 ♖c7+ ♔e6 49 ♔e3 d5 50 ♔d4 f5 51 a4 ♔d6 52 ♖c5 ♗c2 53 a5 ♗a4 54 ♖xd5+ ♔e6 55 ♖e5+ ♔f6 56 ♖c5 1-0, Rührig-Grünberg, Bundesliga 1984.

➩ 8...♘c6 9 ♘f4 ♘f6 10 c4 ♗f5 11 b3 ♘b4?! 12 a3 ♘c6 13 ♗b2 (Black has wasted time and White stands well) 13...♖e8 14 f3 ♘e5 15 ♕d2 ♘g6 16 ♘d3?! (16 ♘d5 gives White some advantage) 16...d5 17 c5? (and this is just wrong) 17...♕e7 18 ♖f2 ♗xd3 19 ♗xd3 ♕xc5 20 ♗xf6 gxf6 21 f4 ♖e7 22 ♖af1 ♕e3 23 ♗xg6 ½-½, Svidler-Delanoy, Groningen Open 1990.

6 ♘d3 ♗xc3 7 dxc3 ♘xe4 8 ♘f4

The purpose of this move is to prevent ...d5. If White plays 8 0-0, then Black can transpose to the lines below or try to take advantage of White's omission, as in the following example:

➩ 8 0-0 d5 9 ♘f4 c6 10 ♗e3 ♘d7 (10...♘d6 is the theoretical recommendation, in order to prevent c4) 11 c4 dxc4 12 ♗xc4 ♘e5 13 ♕xd8 ♖xd8 14 ♗e2 ♗f5 (a typical position from this variation; can White make use of his two bishops?) 15 g4 ♗d7 16 f3 ♘f6 17 ♖ad1 ♘g6 18 ♘xg6 hxg6 19 c4 ♗e6 20 b3 b6 21 ♔f2 c5 22 h4 ♔f8 23 ♖h1 (the start of a plan which leads nowhere; gradual preparation for a3 and b4 might have been better, but it is obviously hard work to make progress) 23...♖xd1 24 ♗xd1 ♖e8 25 h5 gxh5 26 gxh5 ♗f5 27 ♗g5 ♘g8 28 ♗e2 f6 29 ♗f4 ♔f7 30 ♖d1 ♘e7 31 ♗d3 ♖d8 32 ♗c2 ♖xd1 33 ♗xd1 ♘c6 (Black has completely equalised) 34 ♔e3 ♔e6 35 ♗g3 ♘e5 36 ♗e1 ♘c6 37 ♗c3 ♗h7 38 a3 a5 39 f4 ♗b1 40 ♗f3 ♔d6 41 ♗e4 ♗xe4 42 ♔xe4 ♘e7 43 f5 ♘g8 44 ♗d2 ♘h6 45 ♗f4+ ♔c6 0-1 (presumably this was a loss on time as the position is completely drawn), Si.Popov-Oniscuk, USSR-Yugoslavia Junior match 1991.

8...d6 9 0-0 ♘c6

⇨ Or 9...♘d7 (this doesn't make much difference, because the knight normally goes to e5 in any case) 10 ♗e3 ♘e5 11 ♖e1 ♗d7 12 f3 ♘f6 13 ♗f1 ♗c6 14 c4 a6 15 a4 d5 16 cxd5 ♘xd5 17 ♘xd5 ♗xd5 18 b3 (once again the typical structure arises) 18...h5 19 ♗f2 ♖e6 20 ♗g3 ♕d6 21 ♕d4 ♖ae8 22 c4 ♗c6 23 ♕xd6 cxd6 (on this occasion White has made concrete progress; Black has to defend his weak d-pawn as well as fight against the two bishops) 24 ♖ed1?! h4 25 ♗xh4 ♗xf3 26 ♖d2 ♗h5 27 h3 f5 28 ♖f2 ♖f8 29 ♗g5 ♖g6 30 ♗f4 ♘f3+ 31 ♔h1 ♘g5 32 ♗xg5 ♖xg5 33 ♗d3 (White is still slightly better) 33...♖f6 34 ♔h2 a5 35 ♖af1 ♗g6 36 ♖f4 ♔f7 37 ♗e2 ♖e6? (Black doesn't notice the threat to his rook on g5) 38 ♗f3 ♖e3 39 h4 ♖xf3 40 ♖1xf3 ♖h5 41 ♖d3 ♔e7 42 ♖d5 ♗e8 43 ♖dxf5 b6 44 ♖xh5 ♗xh5 45 ♖f5 ♗e8 46 ♔g3 ♗d7 47 ♖g5 ♔f6 48 ♔f4 ♗c6 49 g4 d5 50 cxd5 ♗d7 51 h5 ♗e8 52 ♖f5+ 1-0, Heidrich-Rührig, Bundesliga 1986.

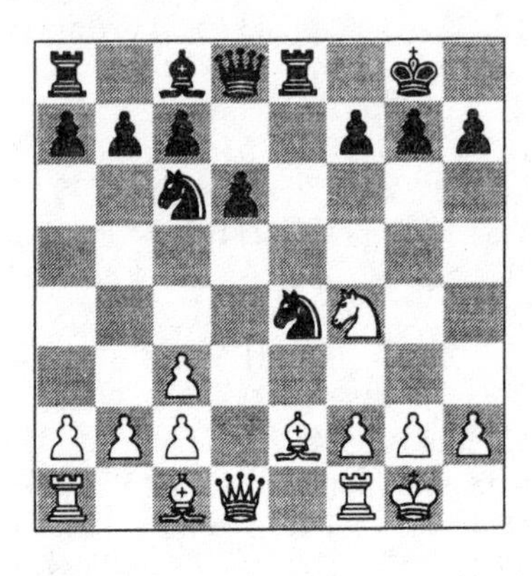

10 ♖e1

⇨ 10 c4 a5 11 ♘d5 ♘c5 12 b3 ♘e5 13 ♗b2 c6 14 ♘e3 ♕e7 15 ♕d2 (White can also consider 15 ♖e1 followed by ♗f1) 15...f5 16 ♘d1 ♘e4 17 ♕e3 ♕f7 18 f3 ♘f6 19 ♕d2 d5 20 cxd5 ♕xd5 21 ♕xd5+ ♘xd5 22 ♖e1 (Black's active pieces almost compensate for the two bishops, but the move ...f5 has weakened the kingside) 22...♘f7 23 ♘c3 ♘e3 24 ♗d3 f4 25 ♗c1 ♗f5 26 ♖xe3 ♖xe3 27 ♗xe3 ♗xd3 28 cxd3 fxe3 29 ♔f1 (the e3 pawn is in trouble as White can cut off the e-file by ♘e4) 29...b5 30 ♔e2 a4 31 b4 ♘d6 32 ♔xe3 and White won with his extra pawn, Marciano-Miralles, Montpellier 1991.

10...♗f5 11 ♗e3 h6 12 a4 ♕d7 13 a5 ♘e5 14 c4 ♕c6 15 ♕d4 ♘g5 16 ♘d5 ♘e6 17 ♕c3 ♗e4 18 ♖ad1 (as usual White is slightly better) **18...b6 19 f3 ♗xd5 20 ♖xd5 ♘g6 21 ♕d2 ♖ad8 22 b3 ♘ef8 23 axb6 axb6 24 ♗d3 ♘e7 25 ♖h5 d5 26 cxd5 ♘xd5 27 ♗e4**

27...♘xe3 (Black attempts to escape from an awkward situation tactically) **28 ♗xc6** (28 ♕xd8 was probably stronger; after 28...♕c3 29 ♕h4 or 28...♖xd8 29 ♗xc6 White is clearly better) **28...♖xd2 29 ♗xe8 ♘xg2 30 ♖e7 ♘g6 31 ♖d7** (Black has counterplay after 31 ♗xf7+ ♔f8 32 ♖xc7 ♘6f4, for example 33 ♖f5 ♖d1+ 34 ♔f2 ♖d2+ 35 ♔g3 ♘e2+!) **31...♖xc2 32 ♗xf7+ ♔h7 33 ♗xg6+ ♔xg6 34 ♖hd5** (34 ♖e5 ♘h4 35 ♖e3 may be better, but now White's winning chances are poor) **34...♘e1 35 ♔f1 ♘xf3 36 h3 ♖b2 37 ♖d3 ♘e5 38 ♖g3+ ♔f6 39 ♖xc7 g5 40 ♖b7 ♔f5 41 ♖xb6 h5 42 ♖b5 ♔f4 43 ♖c3 g4 44 hxg4 hxg4 45 ♖xe5 ♔xe5 46 b4 ♔f4 47 b5 g3 48 ♖c8 ♖xb5 49 ♖f8+ ♔g4 50 ♔g1 ♖b1+ 51 ♔g2 ♖b2+ 52 ♔g1 ♖c2 53 ♖g8+ ½-½**

As explained in the introduction, the variation 1 e4 e5 2 ♘f3 ♘c6 3 ♘c3 ♘f6 4 d4 exd4 5 ♘xd4 is part of the Scotch Opening and is therefore not analysed in this book. However, we do consider alternatives on Black's 4th move and White's 5th move. The main 5th move alternative is 5 ♘d5, the so-called Belgrade Gambit. This aggressive continuation involves the sacrifice of a second pawn, which Black may either accept or decline. Unlike most of the chapters in this book, a large percentage of the analysis is pure tactics, and readers who are considering adopting this line with either colour should be aware that even a small slip can be fatal.

We first consider the three main methods of declining the offer. The first is by 5...♘b4, which is analysed in game 12. This is a relatively safe continuation. After 6 ♗c4 White can only hope for a very slight advantage, so the critical lines are those after 6 ♘xd4, but even these pose few problems for Black. The second way to decline the gambit is by 5...♘xd5 6 exd5 ♘b4 (or 6...♗b4+), as in game 13. My view is that this is much more risky for Black. After 6...♗b4+ White has good chances for a small positional advantage, while 6...♘b4 allows White to develop a dangerous initiative. Finally we come to 5...♗e7 (game 14), which is perhaps the safest continuation of all. Black has adopted this line in most recent games with the Belgrade Gambit, and the practical results suggest that he has little to fear.

Black may also accept the second pawn by 5...♘xe4. The older reply to this is 6 ♕e2 (game 15), but although the play is complicated the evidence suggests that the only question is whether or not White can draw. More recent games have centred on the direct 6 ♗c4 (game 16). In this case White abandons any attempt to regain his material and concentrates on rapid development. Admittedly this line has not been completely explored, but it is hard to believe that White's attack is really correct.

The Belgrade Gambit does not have a very good theoretical reputation and recent games have done nothing to change this assessment. If Black doesn't know what he is doing then he can easily get into trouble, particularly in some of the sharpest lines, but the line with 5...♗e7 spoils White's fun at little risk. The alternative 5...♘xe4 is also adequate, although in this case Black must be prepared to enter some complications.

Game 12

Prie-Psakhis
Paris 1990

1 e4 e5 2 ♘f3 ♘c6 3 ♘c3 ♘f6 4 d4 exd4 5 ♘d5 ♘b4 (5...d6 is an inferior continuation because after 6 ♘xd4 the line 6...♘xe4? 7 ♘b5 is too risky for Black, for example 7...♗e6 8 ♘dxc7+! ♔d7 9 ♘xa8 and Black has inadequate compensation for the sacrificed material)

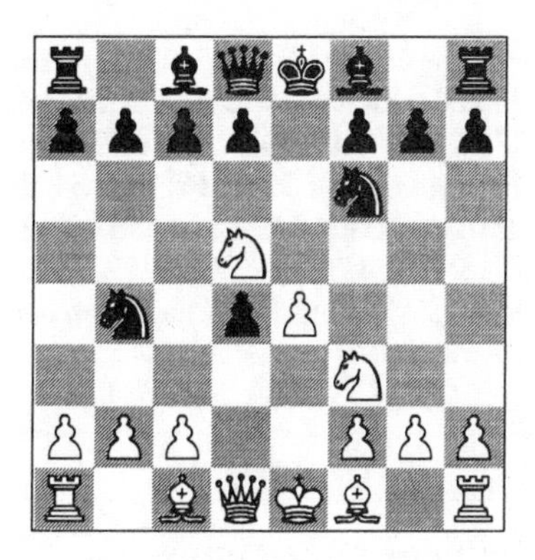

6 ♘xd4

Or 6 ♗c4 ♘bxd5 7 exd5 ♗b4+ and now:

➯ 8 ♔f1 (a typical Hector idea) 8...0-0 9 ♕xd4 h6 10 h4 d6 11 ♗g5 ♗c5 12 ♗xf6 (12 ♕d3 is roughly equal) 12...♕xf6 13 ♕xf6 gxf6 (in this ending White must be careful because the two bishops can become dangerous) 14 ♗d3 ♖e8 15 ♘d2 ♖e5 16 c4? (after 15 ♘e4 the result should be a draw) 16...♗f5 17 ♗xf5 ♖xf5 18 f3 b5! (suddenly White is in trouble) 19 b3 bxc4 20 bxc4 ♖b8 21 ♔e2 ♖e5+ 22 ♔d1 ♖b2 23 ♖b1 ♖xa2 24 ♖b8+ ♔g7 25 ♖h3 f5 26 f4 ♖a1+ 27 ♔c2 ♖e2 28 ♖g3+ ♔f6 29 ♔d3 ♖f2 30 ♘b3 ♖a3 31 ♔c3 a5 32 ♖f3 ♖xf3+ 33 gxf3 a4 0-1, Hector-Karolyi, Copenhagen 1985.

➯ 8 ♗d2 (this is more sensible) 8...♕e7+ 9 ♕e2 ♕xe2+ 10 ♔xe2 ♗c5 11 b4 ♗b6 12 a4 a5 13 bxa5 ♗xa5 14 ♘xd4 (White has a slight edge) 14...♗xd2 15 ♔xd2 ♘e4+ 16 ♔e3 ♘d6 17 ♗b3 b6 18 ♘b5 ♘xb5 19 axb5 ♗b7 20 ♖xa8+ ♗xa8 21 ♖a1 ♔e7 22 ♔d4 ♗b7 23 ♖a7 ♖b8 24 c4 d6 25 ♗c2 ♔d8 26 g4 h6 27 h4 ♖a8! (forcing the draw) 28 ♖xa8+ ♗xa8 29 h5 ♗b7 30 ♗f5 ♗c8 31 ♔e4 ♗b7 32 ♔f4 ♔e7 33 g5 ♔f8 34 ♔g4 ♔e7 35 ♔h4 ♔f8 36 ♗g4 ♔e7 37 f4 ♔f8 38 ♗h3 ♔e7 39 ♗g4 ♔f8 40 f5 f6 ½-½, Fahrner-Wells, Graz 1991.

6...♘xe4

Psakhis gives 6...♘bxd5 7 exd5 ♗c5 as equal, but 8 ♕e2+ may be slightly better for White.

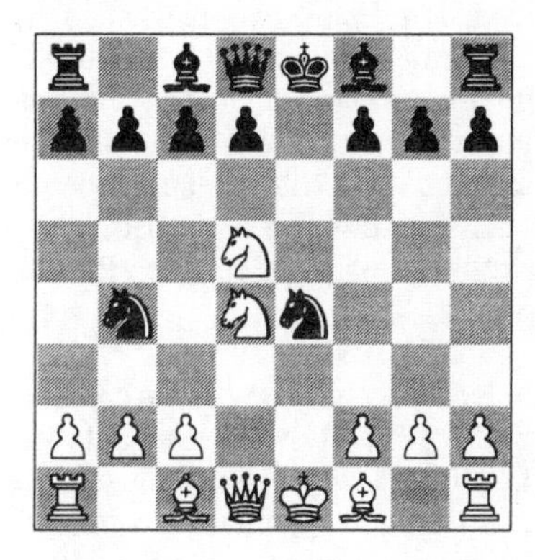

7 ♘f5!

➯ 7 ♗c4 ♘xd5 8 ♗xd5 ♗b4+ 9 c3 ♘xc3 (magnificently greedy play by Black, but in this example White could find no refutation) 10 bxc3 ♗xc3+ 11 ♔f1 ♗xa1 12 ♗a3 d6 13 ♕xa1 0-0 (Black has ♖+3♙ v ♗+♘, but White has a big lead in development) 14 h4 c6 15 ♗b3 a5? (this must be too slow; 15...c5 followed by ...♗e6 looks strong) 16 h5 h6 17 ♕c3 a4 18 ♗c2 c5 19 ♕d3 f5 (suddenly Black's position is full of holes) 20 ♘b5 ♕f6 21 ♖h3 b6 22 ♖e3 ♗a6 23 ♗xa4 ♔h8 24 ♔g1 ♗b7 25 ♗b3 d5 26 ♕d2 d4 27 ♖e6 ♕g5 28 ♕xg5 hxg5 29 ♖xb6 ♗a6 30 ♘c7 (what is wrong with 30 ♗xc5?) 30...c4 31 ♗d1 ♖fb8! 32

♖xb8+ ♖xb8 33 ♘xa6 ♖b1 34 ♔f1 ♖xd1+ 35 ♔e2 ♖a1 36 ♘b4 ♔h7 37 ♔d2 ♖f1 38 ♔e2 ♖b1 0-1, Federau-Behrmann, Bundesliga 1986.

7...c6! 8 ♘xb4 ♕a5!?

A new move. 8...♗xb4+ 9 c3 ♕f6 10 ♘xg7+ (10 ♕f3 ♘xc3 11 a3 was played in Tal-Averbakh, USSR Team Ch. 1954, and now 11...♕e5+ 12 ♔d2 ♘e4+ 13 ♔c2 ♗f8 would have left Black two pawns up for very little) 10...♕xg7 11 cxb4 0-0 12 g3!? is given as unclear by Psakhis, but it is interesting to note that Tal mentions 10...♔d8! as the refutation. Therefore this line is probably even stronger than the move Psakhis played.

9 ♕f3! ♗xb4+ 10 ♔d1?

Psakhis gives 10 c3! ♘xc3 11 a3 ♘d5+ 12 ♔d1 as unclear, but after 12...0-0 it is up to White to justify his sacrifice, for example 13 ♗h6 ♖e8 14 ♗xg7 d6 gives Black the advantage.

10...♕e5! 11 ♘xg7+ ♔d8 12 ♘f5

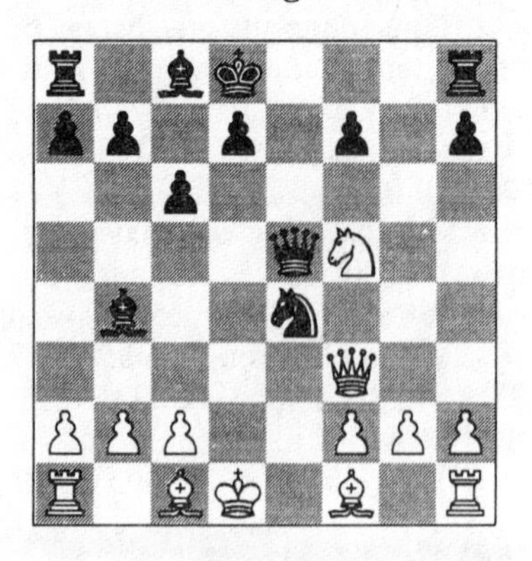

12...d5 (White has restored material equality but Black has a strong initiative) **13 ♘h6!? ♕d4+ 14 ♗d3 ♘xf2+ 15 ♔e2 ♖e8+ 16 ♗e3 ♘xd3 17 c3! ♘f4+ 18 ♔f2 ♘d3+ 19 ♔e2 ♕c4! 20 ♘xf7+ ♔c7 21 ♔d2 ♗c5! 22 ♕g3+ ♔b6 23 ♘d6! ♗xe3+ 24 ♕xe3+ ♖xe3 25 ♘xc4+ dxc4 26 ♔xe3 ♗g4! ♖e8 27 b3** (27 ♔d4 ♖d8+! 28 ♔xc4 ♗e6 is a nice mate) **27...♔c5 0-1**

Game 13

Bellon Lopez-Jamieson
Wijk aan Zee II 1977

1 e4 e5 2 ♘f3 ♘c6 3 ♘c3 ♘f6 4 d4 exd4 5 ♘d5 ♘xd5 6 exd5 ♘b4

The alternative is 6...♗b4+ 7 ♗d2 ♕e7+ 8 ♕e2 (8 ♗e2 ♗xd2+ 9 ♕xd2 ♘e5 10 ♘xd4 d6 11 0-0-0 ♗d7 12 f4 ♘g6 13 g3 was slightly better for White in Borg-Nawa, Dubai Ol. 1986, but 8...d3!? is interesting) 8...♗xd2+ 9 ♔xd2 ♕xe2+ 10 ♗xe2 and now:

⇨ 10...♘e7 11 d6 ♘c6 12 ♖ad1 cxd6 13 ♔c1 d5 (13...b6 may be better, for example 14 ♖he1 ♔d8 15 ♗c4 ♗b7 16 ♗xf7 ♘e5 17 ♘xe5

dxe5 18 ♖xe5 ♖f8 19 ♗d5 ½-½, Svidler-Cherepkov, Leningrad 1990) 14 ♘xd4 ♘xd4 15 ♖xd4 d6 16 ♖xd5 ♔e7 17 ♗f3 (White has a small but permanent endgame advantage) 17...♖b8 18 ♖hd1 ♖d8 19 ♗e4 g6 20 f4 f5 21 ♗f3 ♗e6 22 ♖5d3 b6 23 ♖a3 ♖d7 24 ♖e3 ♔f6 25 ♗c6 ♖dd8 26 ♖de1 ♗f7 27 ♖e7 ♖bc8 28 ♗a4 a6 29 ♗b3 d5 30 ♖a7 ♖a8 31 ♖b7 ♖ab8 32 ♖ee7 ♖xb7 33 ♖xb7 ♖d6 34 ♔d2 h6 35 ♔d3 g5 36 g3 gxf4 37 gxf4 ♗h5 38 ♖h7 ♔g6 39 ♖a7 ♗f3 40 ♔d4 ♖e6 41 ♗xd5 ♗xd5 42 ♔xd5 ♖e2 43 ♖xa6 ♖xc2 44 ♖xb6+ ♔h5 45 h3 ♖e2 46 a4 ♖e4 47 a5 ♖xf4 48 b4 ♖f3 49 a6 ♖xh3 50 ♖b5 1-0, Svidler-Badzharani, Leningrad 1990.

⇨ 10...♘b4 11 d6 c5 12 ♖he1 0-0 13 ♗c4 a6 14 a4 ♖b8 15 a5 b5 16 axb6 ♖xb6 17 ♘g5 ♖xd6 18 ♘xf7 ♖e6 19 ♗xe6 dxe6 20 ♘d6 ♗d7 21 f3 ♖b8 (White should win this ending) 22 ♖e5 ♖b6 23 ♘c4 ♖b5 24 ♘d6 (24 c3 is very strong) 24...♖b6 25 ♘c4 ½-½, Volpinori-Schepel, Manila Ol. 1992.

The conclusion is that 6...♗b4+ gives White a slight advantage.

7 ♘xd4 ♘xd5 8 ♘f5

⇨ 8 ♕f3 (this appears inadequate) 8...♘f6 9 ♗g5 ♕e7+ 10 ♗e2 ♕e5 11 ♗xf6 ♕xf6 12 ♕e4+ ♗e7 13 ♘b5 ♔d8 14 0-0-0 c6 15 ♘c3 d6 16 ♔b1 ♗f5 17 ♕a4 ♔c7 (Black has consolidated his extra pawn) 18 g4 ♗e6 19 f4 g6 20 h3 ♖hd8 21 ♗d3 ♕h4 22 f5 gxf5 23 ♗xf5 ♗f6 24 ♖d3 ♗e5 25 ♕e4 ♖e8 26 ♗xe6 ♖xe6 27 ♕c4 ♗xc3 28 ♕xc3 ♖ae8 29 a3 ♕f6 30 ♖f3 ♕xc3 31 bxc3 f6 32 ♖hf1 ♖e1+ 33 ♖xe1 ♖xe1+ 34 ♔b2 ♖e6 35 ♖f5 ♔d7 36 c4 ♔e8 37 ♖h5 ♖e7 38 ♖h6 ♖f7 39 ♔c3 ♔f8 40 ♖h5 ♔g7 41 ♖f5 ♖e7 42 ♖f3 ♔g6 43 ♔d2 ♖e5 44 ♖d3 d5 and Black won in Reefschläger-Riedel, Bundesliga 1988.

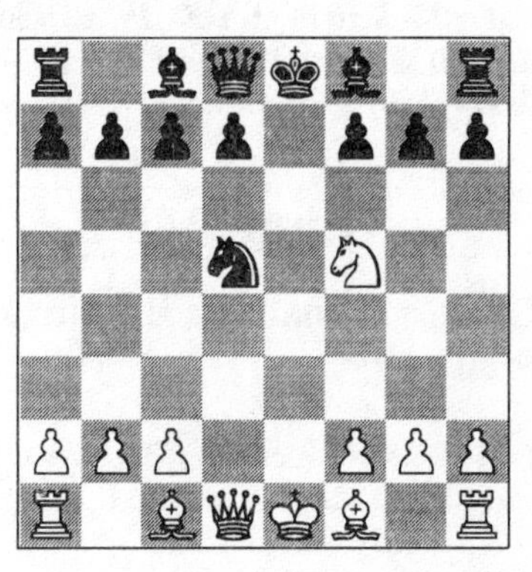

8...♘e7 9 ♗g5 f6 10 ♗xf6 gxf6 11 ♕h5+ ♘g6 12 0-0-0 (Tal once suggested 12 ♗c4) **12...d6 13 ♘h4** (13 ♗d3 looks more dangerous to me) **13...♗g7 14 ♗c4** (threat 15 ♖he1+ ♔f8 16 ♕xg6!) **14...♕d7 15 ♖he1+ ♔d8 16 ♘xg6 hxg6 17 ♕xg6 ♗h6+ 18 ♔b1 ♕g7 19 ♕e4** (it is hard to believe that White has enough for the piece)

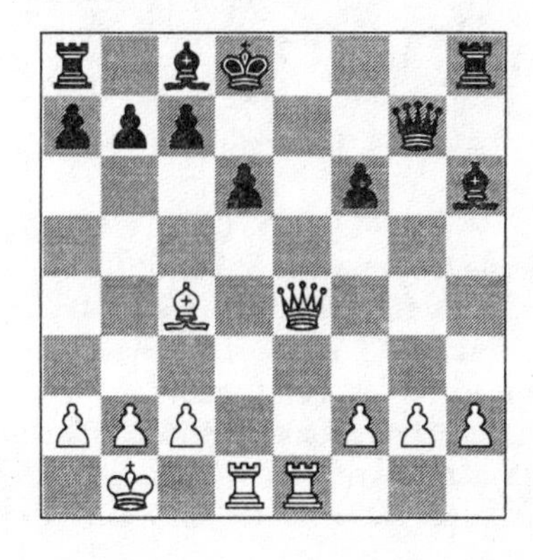

19...♖b8 20 ♖d3 f5 21 ♕d5 ♕f6 (21...♗d7 appears good for Black) **22 ♕a5 b5 23 ♖e6!** (this move surprisingly leads to a forced draw) **23...♕xb2+ 24 ♔xb2 bxc4+ 25 ♔c3 ♗g7+ 26 ♔d2 ♗xe6 27 ♖xd6+ ♗d7 28 ♖xd7+ ♔xd7 29 ♕xf5+ ♔e7 30 ♕c5+ ♔d7 31 ♕f5+ ♔e7 32 ♕e4+ ♔d8 33 ♕d5+ ♔e7 ½-½**

Game 14

Hector-Fernandez Garcia
Spain 1990

1 e4 e5 2 ♘f3 ♘c6 3 ♘c3 ♘f6 4 d4 exd4 5 ♘d5 ♗e7 (the safest way to decline the gambit) **6 ♗f4**

Or 6 ♗c4 0-0 (for 6...♘xe4 see game 16) and now:

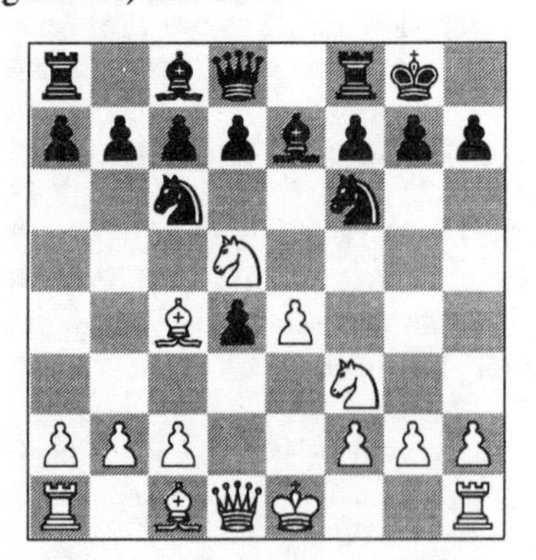

➪ 7 ♘xd4 ♘xd5 (7...♘xe4 still leads to game 16) 8 ♗xd5 ♘xd4 9 ♕xd4 ♗f6 10 ♕d3 c6 11 ♗b3 d5 12 0-0 dxe4 13 ♕xe4 ♖e8 (Black has equalised very comfortably and soon starts playing for a win) 14 ♕f3 ♗e6 15 ♗xe6 ♖xe6 16 ♗e3 ♕a5 17 c3 ♕b5 18 ♖ab1 a5 19 ♖fd1 ♖e7 20 ♗d4 (giving Black a permanent advantage) 20...♗xd4 21 cxd4 ♖d8 22 ♖d2 ♕g5 23 ♕c3 ♕d5 24 b3 ♖e4 25 h3 ♖e6 26 ♕c4 ♕f5 27 ♖bd1 ♖de8 28 ♕c1 h6 29 d5 ♖e2 30 ♖xe2 ♖xe2 31 ♕c5 ♖xa2 32 ♖c1 ♖d2 33 d6 ♕xc5 34 ♖xc5 ♖xd6 35 ♖xa5 ♖d1+ 36 ♔h2 ♖b1 37 ♖a8+ ♔h7 38 ♖a3 ♖b2 39 ♔g3 ♔g6 40 h4 ♔f5 41 f3 ♔e5 42 h5 ♔f5 43 ♖a5+ ♔f6 44 ♖a3 ♔g5 45 ♖a5+ f5 46 f4+ ♔xh5 47 ♖xf5+ ♔g6 0-1, Morris-Wedberg, New York Open 1991.

➪ 7 0-0 d6 (very passive; 7...♘xe4 is much better, as in game 16) 8 ♘xd4 ♘xd4 9 ♕xd4 ♘xd5 10 ♗xd5 ♗f6 11 ♕d3 a5 12 a4 ♕e7 13 c3 c6 14 ♗b3 (White has a perceptible advantage and Black goes downhill very quickly) 14...♗e6 15 ♗c2 g6 16 f4 ♗g7 17 f5 ♗c8 18 ♗e3 c5 19 ♖ad1 ♖a6 20 ♗f4 ♖d8 21 ♕g3 gxf5 22 exf5 f6 23 ♖fe1 ♕f8 24 ♗b3+ ♔h8 25 ♗e6 ♗xe6 26 fxe6 ♕e7 27 ♗xd6 1-0, Trajkovic-Stieg, corr. 1967.

6...d6

Sanz has suggested 6...0-0!? 7 ♗xc7 (7 ♘xc7 ♘h5 and 7 ♘xd4 ♘xd5 8 exd5 ♘xd4 9 ♕xd4 ♗f6 are good for Black) 7...♕e8 and now:

1) 8 ♘xf6+ ♗xf6 9 ♕e2 ♕e7! 10 e5 ♕b4+ 11 ♘d2 ♘xe5 12 ♗xe5 (12 0-0-0 d3! 13 ♕e4 ♘c4 14 ♘xc4 ♗xb2+ 15 ♔b1 ♗a3+ wins) 12...♖e8 is good for Black.

2) 8 ♗e2 d6 9 ♘xf6+ gxf6 10 ♕d2 b6 11 ♘xd4 ♘xd4 12 ♕xd4 ♕d7 13 ♕c4 ♗b7 and White cannot save the trapped bishop.

However, in *Informator* Minev proposed the improvement 10 ♘xd4!? in line 2 and this does seem to be good for White.

7 ♘xd4 0-0 8 ♘b5 ♘xd5 9 exd5

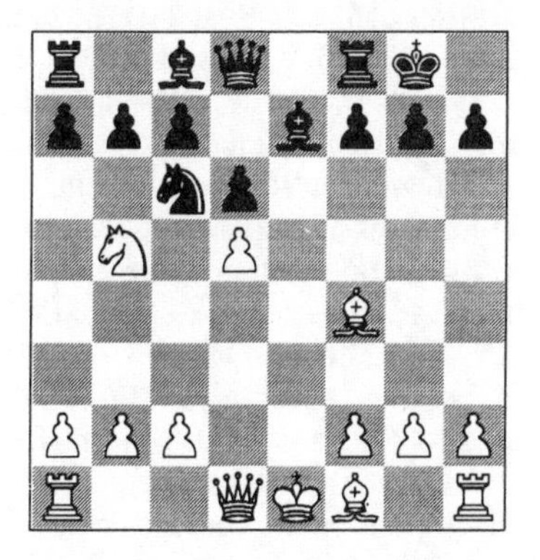

This is the key position for the assessment of 5...♗e7. There are three possible lines. The first, 9...♘b4, is very risky although Black survived in the first game below. The safest line is 9...♘e5, which enables Black to equalise with no risk. The final possibility is 9...♗g5, which we take as the main line. Play becomes very sharp and the assessment of the move depends on the main line game Hector-Fernandez Garcia. The notes by Fernandez Garcia in *Informator* suggest that Black's sacrificial idea is sound, but his analysis is heavily biased in Black's favour and he repeatedly overlooks defences for White. Therefore I view 9...♗g5 with some scepticism.

⇨ 9...♘b4 10 c3 a6!? (a remarkable move, because Black's knight has no way back from b4, so he has to resort to tactics) 11 ♘a3 ♖e8 12 ♗e2 ♗h4 (to meet 13 cxb4 by 13...♗g4) 13 ♘c4 ♗g4 14 ♘e3 ♗xe2 15 ♔xe2 ♕d7 16 g3 ♗f6 17 h4 (17 cxb4 g5 is unclear) 17...♕b5+ 18 ♔f3 ♖xe3+ 19 ♗xe3 ♘xd5 (the knight finally escapes; Black has just enough for the exchange) 20 ♕d2 ♕c6 21 ♔g4 ♕d7+ 22 ♔f3 ♕c6 23 ♔g4 ♕d7+ 24 ♔f3 ♕c6 ½-½, Skrobek-Pinkas, Polish Ch. 1987.

⇨ 9...♘e5 10 ♕d2 c6 (10...g5 11 ♗g3 f5 is too weakening and White won after 12 f3 f4 13 ♗f2 c5 14 dxc6 bxc6 15 ♘d4 c5 16 ♘b3 ♗e6 17 0-0-0 ♕b6 18 h4 a5 19 ♕c3 ♕b4 20 ♕e1 ♗xb3 21 cxb3 ♕xe1 22 ♖xe1 h6 23 ♗c4+ ♔g7 24 hxg5 hxg5 25 ♗xc5 ♖ac8 26 ♖xe5 dxe5 27 ♗xe7 ♖h8 28 ♖xh8 ♖xh8 29 ♗xg5 ♖h2 30 ♗d5 1-0 in Kapic-Aronin, corr. 1967) 11 ♘c3 and now:

⇨ 11...♗f5 12 ♗e2 ♗f6 13 0-0 c5 14 ♖fe1 a6 15 a4 ♖e8 (Black's pieces are all active and he has no problems) 16 ♗f1 ♕b6 17 ♘d1 ♘g6 18 ♖xe8+ (giving up the e-file is a serious concession; 18 ♘e3 was better, with the tactical point 18...♘xf4 19 ♘c4) 18...♖xe8 19 a5 ♕d8 20 ♗g3 h5 21 ♘e3 ♗g5 (with an excellent position for Black) 22 ♕c3 ♗xe3 23 fxe3 h4 24 ♗f2 ♖e4 25 ♖a3 ♕g5 26 ♔h1 h3 27 ♗g3 ♘h4 28 ♕d2 ♖g4 29 ♔g1 ♗e4 30 ♗xh4 ♕xh4 31 ♖a4 hxg2 32 ♗xg2 ♕g5 0-1, Bellon Lopez-I.Ivanov, Benidorm 1982.

⇨ 11...♘g6 12 ♗e3 c5 13 ♗e2 f5 (Van der Wiel's approach is much more aggressive, but risks blocking in the c8 bishop) 14 f4 ♗f6 15 ♘d1 ♕e8 16 0-0 b5 17 ♗f2 a6 18 ♗f3 ♖a7 19 g3 ♖e7 20 c3 ♘h8 21 ♘e3 g5 22 ♖ae1 gxf4 23 gxf4 ♘g6 24 ♘g2 ♖ff7 25 ♖xe7 ♖xe7 26 ♖e1 ♖xe1+ 27 ♗xe1 ♗g7 28 ♗f2 ♕e7 29 b4?! (the position should be a draw, but White weakens his queenside) 29...cxb4 30 cxb4 ♕f6 31 ♘e1

♕c3 32 ♕xc3 ♗xc3 33 ♘d3 ♗b7 34 ♗b6 ♗d2 35 ♗c7 ♘xf4 36 ♘xf4 ♗xf4 37 h3 ♔f7 38 ♔f2 ♔f6 39 ♔e2 ♔e5 0-1, Prie-Van der Wiel, match France-Netherlands, Cannes 1990.

9...♗g5 10 ♗xg5 ♕xg5 11 ♕d2

After 11 ♘xc7 Black can play the simple 11...♕e7+ 12 ♗e2 ♕xc7 13 dxc6 bxc6 or the complicated 11...♗g4 12 ♗e2 ♗xe2 13 ♕xe2 ♖ac8 (13...♘d4 14 ♕e4 ♖ac8 is also fine for Black) 14 dxc6 ♕xg2 15 0-0-0 ♖xc7, with a roughly level position in both cases.

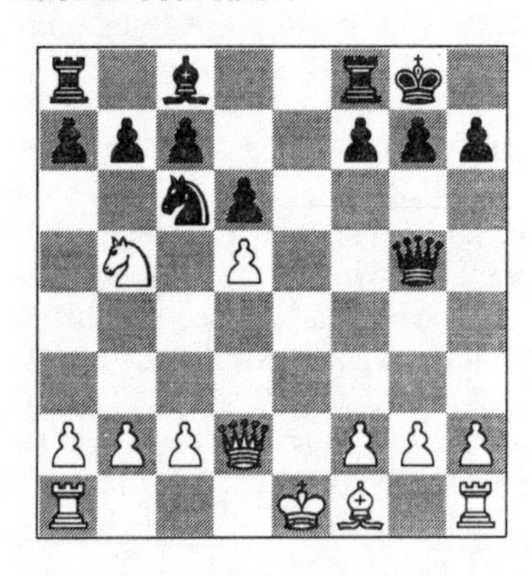

11...♕e5+!

➪ Not 11...♖e8+? (11...♕e7+ 12 ♗e2 ♘e5 13 0-0-0 is good for White) 12 ♔d1! (now White wins material) 12...♗g4+ 13 f3 ♖e3 (Black is already reduced to desperation) 14 dxc6 ♖ae8 15 cxb7 ♖xf3 16 ♗e2 ♕xd2+ 17 ♔xd2 ♖f2 18 ♖ae1 ♖fxe2+ 19 ♖xe2 ♖xe2+ 20 ♔c3 ♖e8 21 ♖e1 ♖b8 22 ♖e7 1-0, Bellon Lopez-Pomar, Las Palmas 1975.

12 ♗e2 a6

Not 12...♕xb2 13 0-0 ♘e7 (13...♘e5?? 14 ♖fb1 wins) 14 ♘xc7 ♖b8 15 ♘b5 with a clear plus.

13 ♘xc7 ♘d4 14 ♘xa8 ♗g4 15 c3

After 15 0-0 ♘xe2+ 16 ♔h1 ♖xa8 17 ♖ae1 ♖e8 18 f3 ♗d7 or 15 f3 ♗xf3 16 0-0 ♘xe2+ 17 ♔h1 ♗xg2+! 18 ♔xg2 ♕e4+ Black has the advantage. We are following the annotations of Fernandez Garcia, but he makes no mention of the interesting variation 15 ♘b6!? ♗xe2 (15...♘xe2 16 ♘c4 ♕e7 17 ♘e3) 16 f4 ♕e4 17 ♔f2, when 17...♘xc2 fails to 18 ♖ae1 ♘d4 19 ♘a4 followed by ♘c3. I cannot see how Black gains enough compensation in this line.

15...♘xe2 16 ♕e3 ♕f6

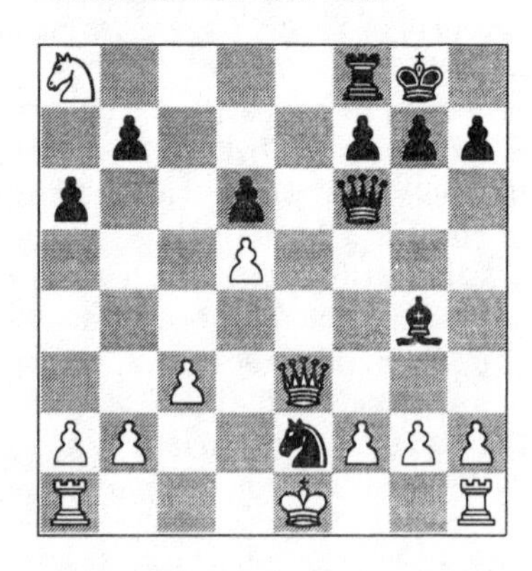

17 ♘b6?

Now White really is crushed. The alternatives were:

1) After 17 ♔d2 ♕d8! Fernandez Garcia gives the lines 18 ♖ae1 ♖e8 19 ♕b6 ♕g5+ 20 ♔c2 ♕f5+ and 18 f3 ♖e8 19 ♕b6 (19 ♕xe8+ ♕xe8 20 fxg4 ♘f4 wins) 19...♕g5+ 20 ♔c2 ♗f5+, both winning for Black. However, 18 ♘c7! is much stronger; after 18...♕xc7 19 f3 Black ends up material down for little compensation.

2) Against the obvious 17 f3 Fernandez Garcia only comments that 17...Bd7 intending ...Re8 wins for Black. However, it seems to me that after 17...Bd7 18 Nb6 Bb5 (18...Re8 19 Nxd7 Qh4+ 20 g3 wins) 19 Kd1 Re8 20 Qd2 it is very hard for Black to justify his play, for example 20...Qd8 21 a4.

3) 17 Kf1 Qd8! 18 h3 (18 f3 Re8 19 Qb6 Qxa8 20 fxg4 Qc8 threatening 21...Qc4 and 21...Qxg4 is given as good for Black by Fernandez Garcia, but even this is unclear after 21 Qb4) 18...Bh5 19 g4 Re8 20 Qb6 Qxa8 21 gxh5 Qc8 is also unclear.

17...Qd8! 18 Nc4

After 18 f3 Re8 19 Qxe2 Rxe2+ 20 Kxe2 Qxb6 21 fxg4 Qxb2+ Black wins at least two more pawns with a clear advantage.

18...Re8 19 h3 Rxe3

Missing the even stronger 19...Nf4!, but this doesn't affect the result of the game.

20 Nxe3 Qb6! 21 hxg4 Qxb2 22 Rd1 Nxc3 23 Rd2 Qb5! 24 Nd1 Ne4 25 Re2 Qb4+ 26 Kf1 h6 27 Rh3 Qd4 28 Re1 Qxd5 29 Kg1 b5 30 Rhe3 Nf6 31 Nc3 Qc4 d5 32 Ne4 Nxe4 33 Rxe4 Qxa2 34 f4 a5 35 f5 b4 36 Kh2 Qd2 37 R1e2 Qg5 38 Rb2 d5 39 Re8+ Kh7 40 Ra8 Qh4+ 0-1

Game 15

Mishuchkov-Malinin
corr. 1990

1 e4 e5 2 Nf3 Nf6 3 Nc3 Nc6 4 d4 exd4 5 Nd5 Nxe4 6 Qe2

This is the old way of meeting 5...Nxe4. Current theory suggests that Black has a very comfortable game and the only question is whether White can equalise.

6...f5 7 Ng5

⇨ 7 Bf4 (Black gains the advantage after 7 g4 Ne7 8 gxf5 Nxd5 9 Qxe4+ Qe7) 7...d6 8 0-0-0 Ne5? (8...Be6! is good for Black) 9 Rxd4 c6 10 Nxe5 dxe5 11 Rxe4 Bd6 (11...fxe4 12 Qh5+ is crushing) 12 Rxe5+ Kf7 13 Nc7! Qxc7 14 Qh5+ (14...g6 15 Bc4+ wins) 1-0, Bellon Lopez-Wagman, Cirella di Diamante 1977.

7...d3 8 cxd3 (8 Qxd3 Nb4 is excellent for Black) **8...Nd4**

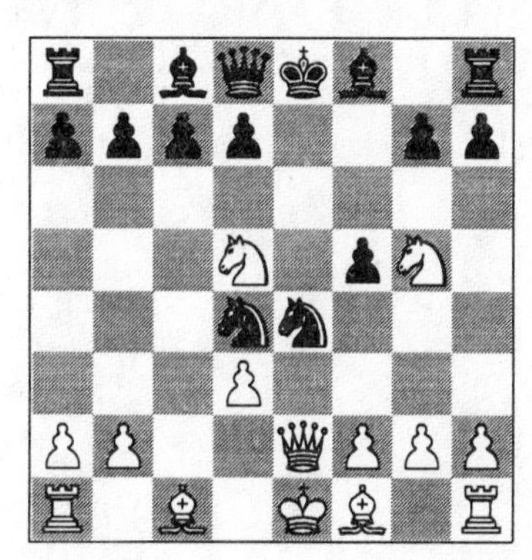

9 Qh5+

ECO gives the line 9 Nxe4 Nxe2 10 Bg5 Be7 11 Bxe7 Qxe7 12 Nxe7 fxe4 13 Nxc8 exd3 14 Bxe2 dxe2 15 Nd6+ as equal. There are two things wrong with this line; the first is that the improvement 13 Nd5! is good for White. The second is that the amazing 10...Nf4!! 11 Bxf4 (what else?) 11...Bb4+ 12 Kd1 0-0 is winning for Black.

9...g6 10 ♕h4 c6 11 dxe4 cxd5 12 exd5

⇨ 12 exf5 (this attempt to improve on the usual 12 exd5 is not successful) 12...♘xf5 13 ♕a4 (13 ♕g4 ♗c5 14 ♗d3 ♕e7+ 15 ♔d1 0-0 was good for Black in McCormick-Evans, corr. 1965) 13...♗g7 (the simple 13...♕e7+ followed by ...♗g7 is good for Black) 14 ♗e2 0-0? (14...♕e7 is still good, preventing castling) 15 0-0 h6 16 ♘h3 ♔h7 17 ♘f4 d4 18 ♗d3 d6 19 ♗d2 ♗d7 20 ♕b3 ♗e5 21 ♕xb7 ♘e7 22 ♘e2 ♗c6 23 ♕a6 ♕d7 24 ♘g3 ♖ab8 25 b3 ♘d5 26 ♖ac1 ♖b6 27 ♕a5 ♘f4 28 ♗xf4 ♖xf4 29 ♖fe1 ♖b8 30 ♕d2 ♖bf8 31 ♕c2 ♗d5 32 ♗xg6+ ♔h8 33 f3 ♖g8 34 ♗e4 ♗xe4 35 ♖xe4 ♖f7 36 ♕d2 ♖g6 37 f4 ♗f6 38 ♖ce1 ♗h4 39 f5 ♖gg7 40 ♖xh4 1-0, Pelling-Vickery, Great Britain 1984.

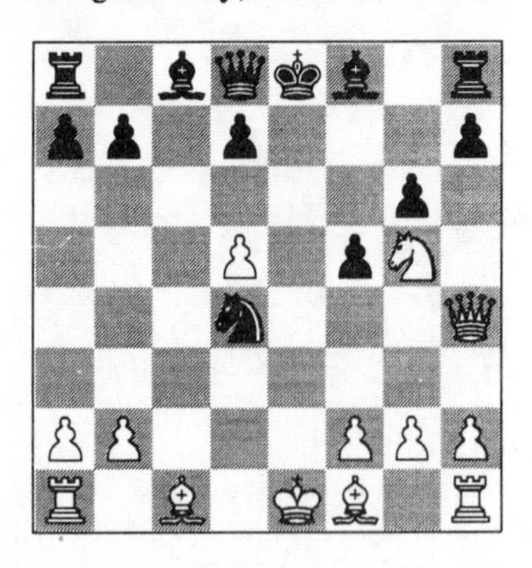

12...♗g7

This safe continuation guarantees at least a small advantage for Black. The very complicated alternative line runs 12...♕a5+ (12...♘c2+ is too dangerous) 13 ♔d1 (13 ♗d2 ♕a4! is fine for Black) 13...♕xd5 14 ♗c4 ♕xc4 15 ♖e1+ ♗e7 16 ♖xe7+ ♔xe7 17 ♘e4+ ♔e6 18 ♕f6+ ♔d5 19 ♘c3+ ♔c5.

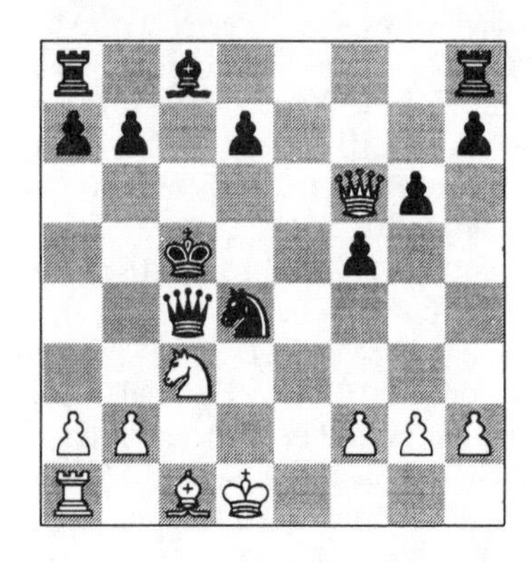

According to theory this critical position is a draw by perpetual check. In my view a draw is the best White can hope for. White has tried two ideas:

⇨ 20 ♗e3 (the more risky alternative) 20...♕d3+ (20...♖e8! looks better, since 21 ♖c1 ♕d3+ 22 ♔e1 ♖xe3+ 23 fxe3 ♕xe3+ 24 ♘e2+ ♔d5 appears good for Black, while 21 b4+ is met by 21...♕xb4, as below) 21 ♔e1 ♖e8 22 b4+ ♔c4 23 ♖c1 ♖e6 (23...b6!? is interesting) 24 ♘e2+? (24 ♘d5+! is a draw after 24...♔xd5 25 ♖c5+ ♔d6 26 ♕f8+ ♖e7 27 ♕f6+ ♖e6, while 24...♘c2+ 25 ♖xc2+ ♕xc2 26 ♕d4+ ♔b5 27 ♘c3+ ♕xc3+ 28 ♕xc3 b6 is unclear) 24...♔xb4 25 ♕f8+ d6 26 ♘xd4 ♕xd4 27 ♖b1+ ♔a4 28 ♖b3 ♕a1+ 29 ♔e2 ♕xa2+ 30 ♔f3 ♕xb3 0-1, Mardarowik-Veres, Hungary 1969.

⇨ 20 b4+ ♔xb4 21 ♕d6+ (21 ♖b1+ is also possible, when 21...♔xc3 22 ♖b3+ ♕xb3+ 23 axb3 ♖e8 looks rather risky, while 21...♔a5 22 ♗d2 ♕f1+ 23 ♗e1 ♕d3+ 24 ♗d2 is a draw, Lubensky-Schepanetz, Polish Ch. 1955) 21...♔xc3? (21...♔a5 22 ♕a3+ ♔b6 23 ♕d6+ is probably a draw because 23...♘c6 is very dangerous after 24 ♘d5+ ♔a6 25 ♘c7+ ♔a5 26 ♗d2+ ♔a4 27 ♖b1) 22 ♕a3+ ♘b3 23 ♕b2+ ♔d3?! (23...♔b4 24 ♗d2+ followed by axb3 is again very dangerous for Black) 24 axb3 (now White is winning) 24...♕d5 25 ♖a4 (missing mate in two by 25 ♕c2+) 1-0, Slastenin-Selivanovsky, Moscow Ch. Prelims 1960.

However, the big question is what happens after 20 b4+ ♕xb4!?; the best reply is probably 21 ♕e5+ (21 ♗e3 ♖e8 22 ♖c1 ♖xe3! 23 fxe3 ♘c6 appears good for Black) and then there are two lines:

1) 21...♔c6 22 ♕d5+ ♔c7 23 ♗f4+ (23 ♕e5+ is no draw because of 23...d6! 24 ♘d5+ ♔b8 25 ♕xh8 ♕a4+ 26 ♔e1 ♕c4! with decisive threats) 23...d6 24 ♖b1! (24 ♖c1 was given as good for White by Clarke, but after 24...♖d8! White has nothing better than 25 ♘b5+ ♔b8 26 ♘xd4 a5, intending ...♖a6, and White has insufficient compensation for the exchange and two pawns) 24...♗e6 25 ♖xb4 ♗xd5 26 ♘xd5+ ♔c6 27 ♖xd4 ♖he8 and White's well-placed pieces compensate for his small material deficit.

2) 21...♔c4 (risky, but perhaps the only way to play for a win) 22 ♗d2 (Clarke gave 22 ♕d5+ ♔xc3 23 ♗d2+, but he overlooked 22...♔d3!, which is very dangerous for White) 22...d6! 23 ♕xh8 (23 ♕d5+ ♔d3 doesn't seem to help) 23...♕b2 (23...f4!?) 24 ♖c1 ♔d3 is completely unclear, for example 25 25 ♘b1 (or 25 ♗e3 ♘c2, and again it is hard to say what is happening) 25...f4 26 f3 ♗d7! 27 ♕xa8 ♘e2! (threats 28...♘xc1 and 28...♗a4+ 29 ♔e1 ♕d4) 28 ♕xa7 (28 ♕d8 ♗a4+ 29 ♔e1 ♕d4 30 ♗e3 ♕xe3 31 ♕xd6+ ♘d4+ mates) 28...♘xc1 29 ♕a5 ♘b3 30 ♕d5+ ♘d4 31 ♕e4+ ♔c4 looks good for Black, if only because of his extra pawn.

13 ♕g3

13 ♔d1 h6 14 ♘f3 ♘xf3 15 ♕xd8+ ♔xd8 16 gxf3 is slightly better for Black after 16...d6 or 16...♗d4!?.

13...0-0 14 d6

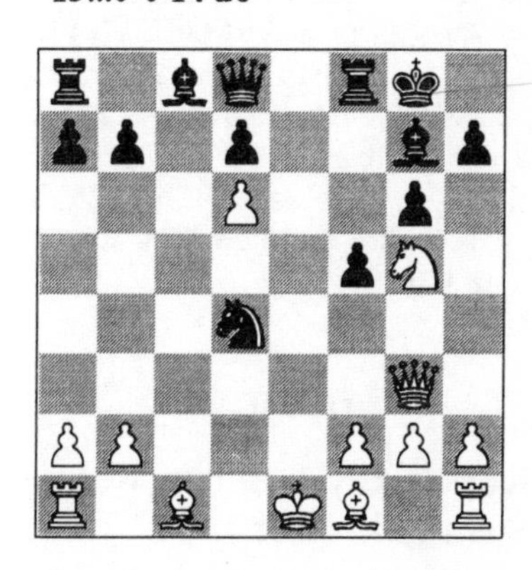

14 ♗d3? is bad after 14...♕a5+ 15 ♔f1 b6 16 ♕h3 h6 17 ♘f3 ♕xd5 with a distinct advantage for Black as in Nikonov-Yudovich, USSR 1949.

14...♕a5+!?

➪ 14...b5!? (this move is also promising) 15 ♗d3 ♕a5+ 16 ♗d2 (16 ♔f1 is less clear) 16...♖e8+ 17 ♔d1 ♕a4+ 18 b3 ♕a3 19 ♗c3 ♕c5 20

♖c1 ♗b7 21 ♕h4? (21 ♗b2 was a better chance, but Black must have the advantage with White's king stuck on d1) 21...h6 22 ♗xd4 ♕xd6 23 ♘f3 ♗xf3+ 24 gxf3 ♗xd4 25 ♕xh6 ♗e3 0-1, Szklarczyk-Brauer, corr. 1984.

15 ♗d2

Or 15 ♔d1!? ♕d5 (not 15...♕a4+? 16 b3 ♘xb3 17 axb3 ♕xa1 18 ♗c4+ ♔h8 19 ♘xh7! ♗h6 20 ♔c2 and White wins) 16 ♗d3 b5 with a position resembling the previous note. Again I would assess this as at least slightly better for Black.

15...♖e8+ 16 ♔d1 ♕a4+ 17 b3 ♘xb3! 18 ♗c4+! ♕xc4 19 axb3 ♕g4+! (not only is Black a pawn up but the g5 knight is horribly placed) **20 ♕xg4 fxg4 21 ♖a4 h6 22 ♖e4** (22 ♘e4 b5 23 ♖b4 a5 wins for Black) **22...♖f8 23 h4 hxg5 24 h5 a5! 25 ♗xg5** (25 hxg6 ♖a6 26 ♖e7 ♖xd6 27 ♖h7 ♖xg6! wins) **25...b5! 26 h6 ♗c3 27 ♖e3 ♗d4 28 ♖e4 ♗a1 29 ♔e2 ♗b7 0-1**

Game 16

Kenworthy-Van der Sterren
Ramsgate 1981

1 e4 e5 2 ♘c3 ♘f6 3 ♘f3 ♘c6 4 d4 exd4 5 ♘d5 ♘xe4 6 ♗c4

This is the modern method of meeting 5...♘xe4, pioneered by the correspondence player Trajkovic. Black should meet White's aggression by straightforward development, when he should encounter few problems despite the tactical nature of the position.

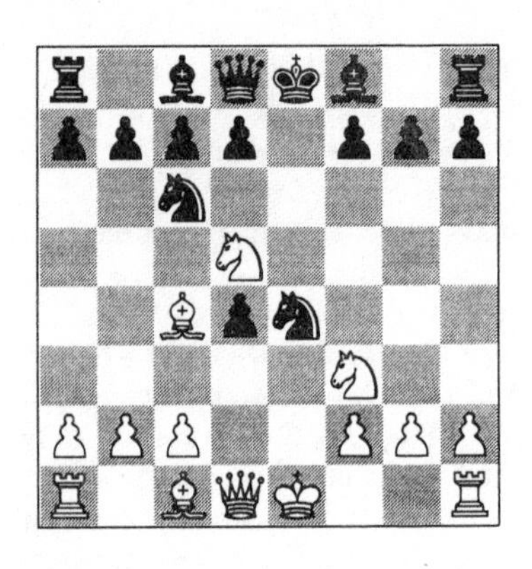

6...♗e7

The most natural move. Alternatives are more risky:

➩ 6...♘c5 (this is good for White) 7 ♗g5 f6 8 ♘h4 d6 (8...h5 looks horrible and was duly punished after 9 ♘g6 ♖h7 10 ♕f3 d6 11 ♗xf6 ♗g4 12 ♗xd8 ♗xf3 13 ♘xc7+ ♔xd8 14 ♘xa8 ♗e4 15 ♘xf8 ♖h8 16 f3 ♗f5 17 g4 hxg4 18 fxg4 ♗e4 19 0-0 d5 20 ♗d3 ♘e5 21 ♗xe4 dxe4 22 b4 1-0, Trajkovic-Henriksen, corr. 1967) 9 ♗xf6 ♘e7 (9...gxf6 10 ♕h5+ ♔d7 11 ♕f5+ ♘e6 12 ♘xf6+ ♔e7 13 ♘d5+ ♔e8 14 ♕h5+ ♔d7 15 ♕f7+ ♘e7 16 ♘f6+ ♔c6 17 ♗xe6 is very good for White) 10 ♕h5+ ♔d7

11 ♗xd4 (11 ♘f5! gxf6 12 ♘xf6+ ♔c6 13 ♘xd4+ ♔b6 14 b4 is also very awkward for Black) 11...♘xd5 12 ♗xd5 c6 13 0-0-0 ♔c7 14 ♗f3 (it is hard to understand why White didn't play 14 ♗xc6! winning a pawn) 14...♘e6 15 ♘g6 ♘xd4 16 ♖xd4 ♕f6 17 ♖h4 hxg6 18 ♕xh8 d5 (Black has fair compensation for the sacrificed exchange) 19 ♖d1 ♗d7 20 ♖hd4 ♖e8 21 ♕h7 ♗c5 22 ♖4d2 ♗a3 23 ♖d4 c5 24 ♕h4 cxd4 25 ♕xf6 ♗xb2+ 26 ♔xb2 gxf6 27 ♖xd4 ♗c6 28 h4 f5 29 ♗xd5 ½-½, Hunter-Steiner, corr.1972.

➪ 6...♘e7 7 ♘e5 (7 ♕xd4 is a weak move and after 7...c6 8 ♘xe7 ♕xe7 9 0-0 d5 10 ♗d3 ♘c5 11 ♗d2 ♘xd3 12 cxd3 ♗e6 Black had consolidated his extra pawn and went on to win in Csuri-Dobsa, corr. 1987) 7...♘xd5 8 ♗xd5 ♘d6 9 ♕h5 g6 10 ♕f3 f6 11 ♘g4 ♘f5 12 0-0 ♗g7 13 ♖e1+ ♔f8 14 ♗f4 (White has sufficient compensation) 14...d6 15 ♗c4 c6 16 ♕a3 b5 17 ♗e6 c5 18 ♗d5 ♖b8 19 ♕xa7 ♗d7 20 ♖e6 ♗xe6 21 ♗xe6 ♘e7 22 ♘h6 ♕b6 23 ♕a3 d5 24 ♖e1 1-0, Trajkovic-Svensson, corr. 1971.

7 ♘xd4

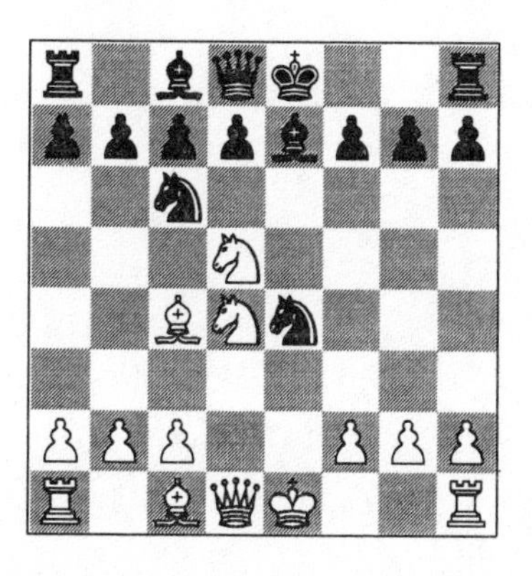

➪ This is probably better than the alternative 7 0-0 0-0, reaching a position which can also arise from game 14. In *Informator 4* Trajkovic gave the variation 8 ♖e1 ♘f6 9 ♘g5 ♘xd5 10 ♘xf7 as unclear, but in Burton-Nunn, Oxford 1971 the continuation was 10...♖xf7 11 ♗xd5 ♕f8 (Black is simply material up for no compensation) 12 ♕e2 ♔h8 13 ♗xf7 ♕xf7 14 ♗d2 d6 15 b4 ♗f5 16 b5 ♘e5 17 f4 ♘g6 18 ♖ac1 d5 19 ♕h5 ♗a3 20 ♖a1 ♗xc2 21 ♖e2 ♗c5 22 ♔h1 ♕f5 23 ♕xf5 ♗xf5 24 ♖ae1 ♗e4 25 f5 d3 0-1. There are better moves than 9 ♘g5, but nothing that appears adequate for White.

7...0-0

7...♘xd4 8 ♕xd4 ♘f6 9 0-0 0-0 10 ♘xe7+ ♕xe7 11 ♗g5 gives White enough for the pawn.

8 ♘b5

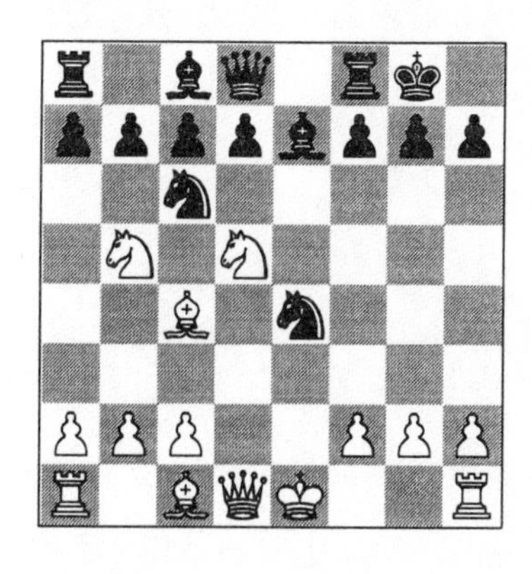

8...♗b4+

The alternatives are:

1) 8...♘e5 9 ♘bxc7 ♗c5 10 0-0 ♕h4 11 ♕e2 ♘xf2!? is unclear.

2) 8...♗c5! (probably best) 9 0-0 ♘xf2 (9...♕h4 10 ♗e3 ♘xf2 11 ♖xf2 ♕xc4 12 ♘bxc7! is very good

for White) 10 ♕h5 (10 ♖xf2 ♗xf2+ 11 ♔xf2 ♕h4+ wins) 10...♘e5! (10...g6 11 ♘f6+ wins) 11 ♘bxc7 d6! 12 ♖xf2 (not 12 ♘xa8 ♗g4 13 ♗g5 ♗xh5 14 ♗xd8 ♘e4+ 15 ♔h1 ♘xc4 with a clear advantage for Black) 12...♗g4 13 ♕g5 ♕xg5 14 ♗xg5 ♘xc4 15 ♘xa8 ♖xa8 leaves Black with an admittedly not very useful extra pawn.

9 c3 ♘xf2

9...♗a5 10 b4 ♗b6 11 0-0 gives White good compensation for the pawn, while 9...♗c5! is the same as line 2 above, except that White's pawn is on c3 instead of c2; it is hard to say who benefits from this change.

10 ♕h5! ♘xh1

Black could still play 10...♗c5 11 0-0 as above.

11 cxb4 ♘xb4??

A terrible blunder; after 11...♖e8+! 12 ♔f1 ♖e5 the position is absolutely unclear.

12 ♗g5!

Not 12 ♘xb4? ♕e7+.

12...♖e8+

12...♕e8+ 13 ♘e7+ ♔h8 14 ♘xc7 ♕d8 15 ♗xf7 wins.

13 ♔f1 ♖e5 14 ♖e1! 1-0

Because the lines 14...♕e8 15 ♖xe5 ♕xe5 16 ♘e7+ ♔h8 17 ♕xf7 and 14...♖xe1+ 15 ♔xe1 ♕e8+ 16 ♘e7+ ♔h8 17 ♗xf7 are easily winning for White.

This line is sometimes used by Black players aiming to avoid the Scotch or by those frightened of the Belgrade Gambit. Instead of taking on d4 Black simply develops a piece and prepares to castle. It is not surprising that such an obvious move should prove an effective weapon, and White players have not had an easy time proving any real advantage against 4...♗b4.

There are two main variations for White. The first is 5 d5 ♘e7, when the critical line continues 6 ♘xe5. We examine 6 ♘xe5 and some alternative ideas in game 17. The second plan is the obvious 5 ♘xe5, when Black may either play 5...♕e7 (game 18) or the very sharp 5...♘xe4 (game 19). The first is somewhat better for White, but 5...♘xe4 also fails to equalise completely, even though in the main line White has only a slight endgame advantage. Black players would be well advised to examine the sidelines, as some of these appear more promising than the main theoretical paths.

Game 17

Valenti-Arlandi
Lugano Open 1989

1 e4 e5 2 ♘f3 ♘f6 3 ♘c3 ♘c6 4 d4 ♗b4 5 d5 ♘e7

ECO mentions the variation 5...♘xe4 6 dxc6 ♘xc3 7 bxc3 ♗xc3+ 8 ♗d2 ♗xa1 9 ♕xa1 d6 10 ♗b5 0-0, assessing the final position as unclear. I prefer 10 cxb7 ♗xb7 11 ♗b5+ c6 12 ♗a4, which blocks in Black's bishop, and then White is probably slightly better. It is curious that I haven't been able to find any practical examples of this line.

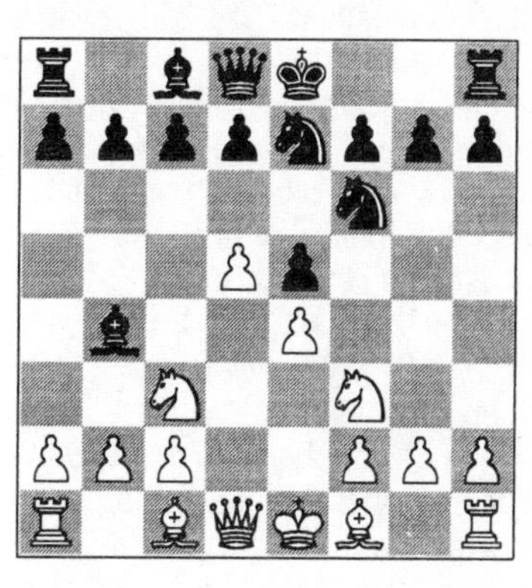

6 ♘xe5

⇨ 6 ♗d3 (this is a harmless attempt to avoid the main lines) 6...d6 7 0-0 (7 ♗d2 has been played before; in this game White allows his pawns to be doubled) 7...♗xc3 8 bxc3 0-0 9 ♗g5 ♘g6 10 h3 h6 11 ♗e3 ♘xe4 (this combination is playable, but the simple 11...♘d7 followed by ...♘c5 is fine for Black) 12 ♗xe4 f5 13 ♗d3 e4 14 ♘h2 exd3 15 ♕xd3 ♘e5 16 ♕d4 ♕e7?! (it must be wrong to put the queen opposite a white rook; 16...c5 is better) 17 ♖ae1 b6 18 f4 ♘d7 19 ♗f2 ♕f7 20 ♗h4 ♘f6 21 ♗xf6 ♕xf6 22 ♕d3 a5 23 ♘f3 (White has a very small advantage; in the rest of the game it isn't clear who is playing for the win, but White eventually triumphs) 23...♗a6 24 c4 ♖ae8 25 ♘d4 ♖e4 26 ♖xe4 fxe4 27 ♕xe4 ♗xc4 28 ♖f3 ♗xa2 29 ♖g3 ♖f7 30 ♘e6 c6 31 c4 cxd5 32 ♕xd5 ♔h8 33 ♕a8+ ♔h7 34 ♕e4+ ♔h8 35 ♕a8+ ♔h7 36 ♕d5 ♔h8 37

♕a8+ ♔h7 38 ♕e4+ g6 39 ♖e3 ♕f5 40 ♕d4 ♕f6 41 ♕d5 ♕f5 42 ♕c6 b5 43 ♘d8 ♕xf4 44 ♕e8 ♕f2+ 45 ♔h2 ♕f4+ 46 ♖g3 ♗xc4 47 ♘xf7 ♕xf7 48 ♕d8 a4 49 ♖f3 ♕g7 50 ♕xd6 h5 51 ♖e3 g5 52 ♖e7 ♗f7 53 ♕d7 ♔g6 54 ♕d3+ ♔h6 55 ♕f3 ♔g6 56 ♕d3+ ♔h6 57 ♕xb5 ♕f6 58 ♕c5 ♗g6 59 ♖e3 ♕f4+ 60 ♔g1 h4 61 ♕c3 ♕f8 62 ♖f3 ♕d8 63 ♕c5 ♕d1+ 64 ♔h2 ♕a1 65 ♕d6 ♕g7 66 ♖e3 ♔h5 67 ♖e5 ♕f7 68 ♖a5 ♕c4 69 ♕e5 1-0, Petrovic-Blauert, Graz Open 1987.

➩ 6 ♕d3 (another innocuous move; if White doesn't take the e5 pawn, then he cannot hope for an advantage) 6...0-0 7 ♗d2 d6 8 0-0-0 (an aggressive plan, but it rebounds because Black obtains a lead in development) 8...♘g4 9 ♕e2 f5 10 exf5 ♗xf5 11 h3 ♘f6 12 ♕b5 ♗xc3 (the initiative is more important than the two bishops) 13 ♗xc3 ♘e4 14 ♗e1 c6! (this amounts to a pawn sacrifice, but it is justified because it opens lines against White's king) 15 dxc6 bxc6 16 ♕b3+ ♘d5 17 ♗c4 ♖b8 18 ♗xd5+ ♔h8 19 ♕c4 cxd5 20 ♕xd5 ♕b6 21 ♕b3 ♕c7 22 ♕a4 22...♘xf2! 23 ♗c3 (23 ♗xf2 fails to 23...♖b4, so White loses material) 23...♘xh1 24 ♖xh1 ♖fc8 25 ♖e1 ♕c4 26 ♕a3 ♖b6 27 ♕xa7 ♖xb2 28 ♖e3 ♖xc2+ 29 ♔d1 ♖xc3 0-1, Mann-Mayer, German Junior Ch. 1988.

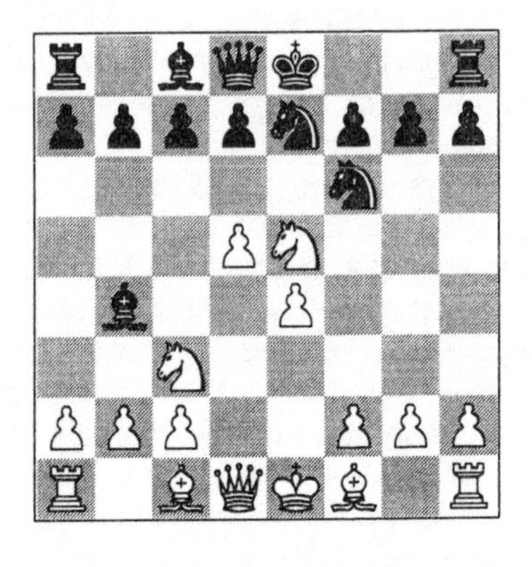

6...0-0

Or 6...d6 7 ♘f3 (the critical move is 7 ♗b5+ - see below) 7...♘xe4 8 ♕d4 ♗xc3+ (8...♘xc3 9 bxc3 ♗a5 is a safe alternative for Black because 10 ♕xg7 ♖g8 11 ♕d4 ♘xd5 is bad for White, but this line hasn't been seen recently) 9 bxc3 ♘f6 and now:

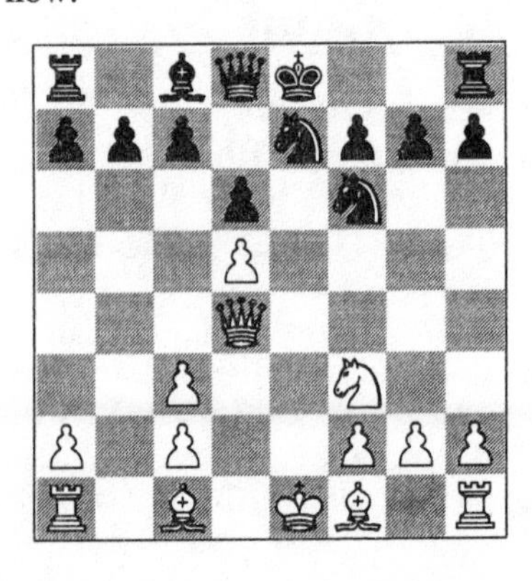

➪ 10 ♗g5 (this pawn sacrifice is not really correct) 10...♘exd5 11 0-0-0 ♗e6 12 ♗c4 c5 13 ♗xf6 cxd4 14 ♗xd8 ♖xd8 15 ♗xd5 ♗xd5 16 ♘xd4 0-0 17 f3 ♗xa2 (Black has kept his extra pawn, but in the following moves he becomes tangled up and never succeeds in exploiting his material advantage) 18 ♔d2 a6 19 ♖a1 ♗d5 20 ♖hb1 ♖d7 21 ♖b6 g6 22 ♖a5 ♗e6 23 ♖a4 ♖c8 24 ♖ab4 ♗d5 25 ♘b3 ♗xb3 26 cxb3 ♖cc7 27 h4 ♔f8 28 h5 ♔e7 29 hxg6 hxg6 30 ♔d3 ♔d8 31 ♖d4 ♖c6 32 ♖xc6 bxc6 33 ♖a4 ♖a7 34 ♖c4 ♔d7 35 ♖f4 ♔e6 36 ♖e4+ ♔d7 37 ♖f4 f5 38 ♖h4 ♔e6 39 ♖h8 ♖b7 40 b4 c5 41 bxc5 dxc5 42 ♖c8 ♖d7+ 43 ♔c4 ♖d2 44 ♖c6+ ♔f7 45 g4 fxg4 46 fxg4 ♖g2 47 ♖xa6 ♖xg4+ 48 ♔xc5 ½-½, Reefschläger-Neunhöffer, Bundesliga 1990.

➪ 10 c4 (this is a better chance) 10...0-0 11 ♗e2 ♘f5 12 ♕d1 ♘e4 13 ♗b2 ♘c5 (White has the two bishops, but the doubled c-pawns mean that the c5 knight is also well placed) 14 ♖b1 ♘h4 15 ♘xh4 ♕xh4 16 0-0 ♗f5 17 ♕d2 ♖fe8 18 ♖be1 h6 19 ♗d3 ♕h5 20 ♖e3 ♖xe3 21 fxe3 ♗e4 22 ♗d4 ♕g6 23 ♖f3 ♕h5 24 ♖f4 ♗g6 (the position is roughly equal, but White goes downhill as the time control approaches) 25 h4 ♗xd3 26 cxd3 b6 27 e4 f6 28 ♗f2 ♖e8 29 ♖f3 ♘d7 30 ♕f4 ♘e5 31 ♖g3 ♕d1+ 32 ♔h2 h5 33 ♗g1 ♘g4+ 34 ♔h1 ♕e1 35 ♖f3 g6 36 g3 ♕e2 37 ♗f2 ♕f1+ 38 ♗g1 ♕h3+ 0-1, Santo Roman-Hector, Manila Ol. 1992.

Based on the above analysis, 6...d6 may appear a good choice, but the critical reply is definitely 7 ♗b5+, as in the following example.

➪ 6...d6 7 ♗b5+ ♔f8 (7...c6 8 dxc6 0-0 9 ♘d7 is good for White) 8 ♘d3 ♗xc3+ 9 bxc3 ♘xe4 10 ♕f3

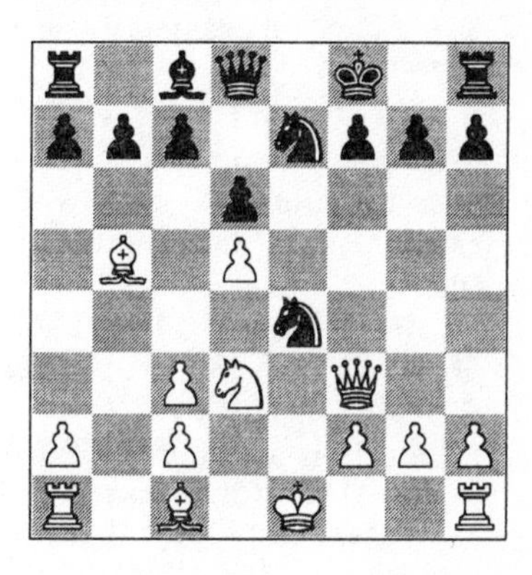

10...♘f6 (10...♘xc3 11 ♗c4 gives White good compensation for the pawn) 11 ♗c4 (not 11 c4 ♗g4 12 ♕f4 c6! and the b5 bishop is in trouble, Hort-Trifunovic, Sarajevo 1964) 11...h6 12 0-0 ♗g4 13 ♕g3 ♕d7 14 f3 ♗f5 15 ♗b2 ♗g6 16 ♗b3 a5 17 a4 ♘fxd5 (Black finally decides to take the pawn, but now the bishops cut loose and Black's bad king position proves fatal) 18 ♖fe1 h5 19 c4 ♘b4 20 ♘f4 ♖h6 21 ♕g5 ♘bc6 22 ♘d5 ♘xd5 23 cxd5 ♕d8 24 ♕d2 ♘b8 25 ♗c4 ♗f5 26 ♕f4 ♗d7 27 ♖e2 ♘a6 28 ♖ae1 ♘b4 29 ♖e7 f6 30 ♕g3 g5 31 h4 ♕xe7 32 ♖xe7 ♔xe7 33 hxg5 ♖g6 34 ♗xf6+ ♔f7 35 ♕h4 1-0, Peric-Rothgen, corr. 1967.

7 ♕d4

This is worth a try because the usual line 7 ♗d3 ♘exd5 8 exd5 ♖e8 9 0-0 ♖xe5 10 d6 ♗xd6 11 ♘b5 ♗f8 12 ♗f4 ♖c5 13 ♗e3 ♖e5 is a draw.

7...♗xc3+ 8 bxc3 ♖e8 9 ♗e3

ECO gives 9 ♗g5 ♘f5 10 exf5 d6, but 11 f4 dxe5 12 fxe5 may be better for White after 12...♕xd5 13 0-0-0; however, there are other replies to 9 ♗g5, for example 9...d6 or 9...c5!?.

9...♘g6 10 ♘xg6 ♖xe4 11 ♕d3 hxg6 12 ♗e2

Once again the two bishops are balanced against the doubled c-pawns.

12...d6 13 0-0 ♖e5 14 ♗d4 ♗f5 15 ♕c4 ♖e7 16 ♗d3 ♘g4 17 ♖fe1 ♘e5 18 ♕b5 b6

18...♘xd3 is also fine for Black after 19 cxd3 ♕e8! 20 ♕xe8+ ♖axe8 21 ♖xe7 ♖xe7 or 19 ♖xe7 ♕xe7 20 cxd3 ♖e8.

19 f4?

A horrible move weakening the kingside; 19 ♗xf5 is still level.

19...a6 20 ♕b4 ♘xd3 21 cxd3 ♕e8 22 c4 ♖e2 23 ♕c3 ♗xd3 24 ♗xg7 ♕e3+ 25 ♔h1 ♖e8 26 ♖xe2 ♗xe2 27 ♕f6?

27 ♖e1 was a much better chance.

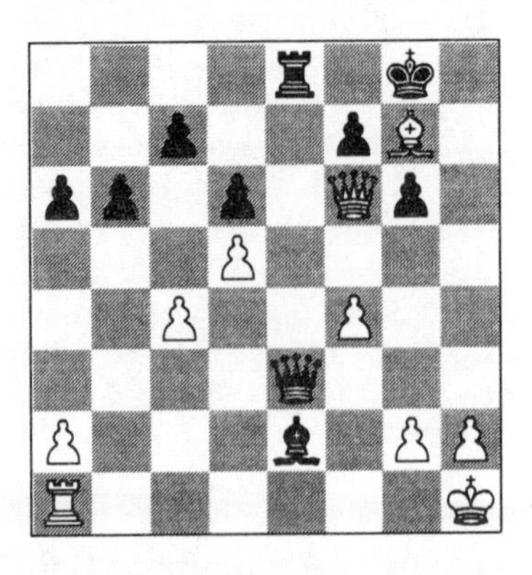

27...♗f3! 28 ♖g1

28 ♕c3 ♕f2! is no better, while 28 ♕d4 ♕e2! 29 ♖g1 ♕xg2+! 30 ♖xg2 ♖e1+ leads to a winning king and pawn ending.

28...♕f2 0-1

because 29 ♕g5 ♔xg7 30 gxf3 ♕xf3+ 31 ♕g2 ♕xf4 is hopeless.

Game 18

Miagmasuren-Bisguier
Tallinn 1971

1 e4 e5 2 ♘f3 ♘c6 3 ♘c3 ♘f6 4 d4 ♗b4 5 ♘xe5 ♕e7

➪ 5...0-0 6 ♕d3 ♖e8 7 ♗d2 d5!? (an interesting new idea, which deserves further tests; 7...♘xe5 8 dxe5 ♖xe5 9 0-0-0 is slightly better for White) 8 ♘xc6 bxc6 9 e5 c5 10 0-0-0 (the calm 10 ♗e2 cxd4 11 ♕xd4 c5 12 ♕f4 may be slightly better for White) 10...♘g4 11 ♗e3 c6! 12 ♘b1 (this unnatural move gives Black the advantage, but 12 ♗e2 cxd4 13 ♕xd4 ♘xe3 14 ♕xe3 f6 is also fine for him) 12...♘xe3 13 ♕xe3 cxd4 14 ♕xd4 ♕b6 15 ♕xb6 axb6 16 a3 ♗c5 17 ♖d2 ♖xe5 (Black has regained his pawn with a clear advantage due to his two bishops and more active pieces) 18 ♗d3 b5 19 ♔d1 ♗g4+ 20 f3 ♗d7 21 ♖e1 ♖xe1+ 22 ♔xe1 ♔f8 23 ♖e2 ♗d6 24 h3 g6 25 c3 c5 26 ♘d2 ♗g3+ 27 ♔d1 ♗c6 28 ♘f1 ♗f4 29 ♘d2 ♖d8 30 ♘b1 ♖d6 31 ♘d2 f5 32 ♖e1 ♔f7 33 ♔c2 ♔f6 34 ♗f1 ♗g3 35 ♖d1 ♗d7 36 ♘b3 ♗f2 37 ♘a5 ♔f7 38 b4?! (38 c4!? ♖a6 39 b4 is unclear) 38...c4 39 a4 f4 40 ♖a1? (40 axb5 ♔e6 is just slightly better for Black) 40...bxa4 41 ♗xc4 dxc4 42 ♘xc4 ♔e6??

(42...♖d5 wins) 43 ♘xd6 ♔xd6 44 ♖d1+ ♔c6 45 c4 ♗e6 46 ♔d3 ♗h4 47 ♖a1 ♗f5+ 48 ♔d2 ♗e6 49 ♔d3 ½-½, Polovodin-Berkovich, Liepaya 1979. It is strange that this successful new idea was never repeated.

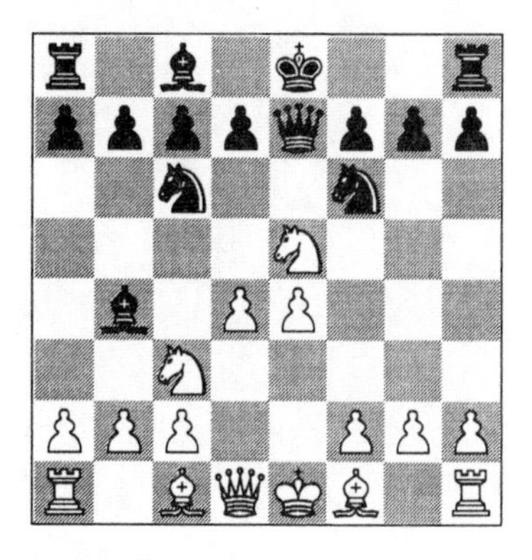

6 ♕d3

Or 6 ♘xc6 (this recent idea is quite promising) 6...♕xe4+ 7 ♗e2 ♕xc6 8 0-0 ♗xc3 9 bxc3 and now:

➪ 9...♕xc3 (it is reasonable to take the pawn because White's bishops will become strong in any case) 10 ♖b1 0-0 11 d5 (preventing ...d5 and opening the long diagonal for the black-square bishop) 11...♕a5 12 ♖b5 ♕a4 13 ♗b2 d6 14 ♗xf6 gxf6 15 ♕d2 ♗f5 16 ♖b3 (the position is hard to assess, but White's attacking chances are dangerous; in the game Black quickly went under) 16...c5 17 ♕h6 ♗g6 18 h4 c4 19 ♖g3 ♕xc2 20 ♗d1 ♕e4 21 h5 ♖ae8 22 hxg6 fxg6 23 ♖h3 ♕e7 (the piece is worth more than the pawns) 24 ♗a4 ♖d8 25 ♖e3 ♕g7 26 ♕xg7+ ♔xg7 27 ♖c1 ♖c8 28 ♖ec3 ♖f7 29 ♖xc4 ♖xc4 30 ♖xc4 ♖e7 31 ♔f1 f5 32 f4 ♔f6 33 ♔f2 g5 34 fxg5+ ♔xg5 35 ♖c8 ♖e4 36 ♗b3 a5 37 ♖g8+ ♔f4 38 g3+ ♔e5 39 ♖e8+ ♔d4 40 ♖b8 ♖e7 41 ♖a8 b6 42 ♖b8 ♔c5 43 ♖c8+ ♔b4 44 ♖c6 b5 45 ♖xd6 a4 46 ♗d1 ♖b7 47 ♖c6 ♔a3 48 d6 ♔xa2 49 ♗c2 a3 50 ♗xf5 ♖f7 51 g4 1-0, Reefschläger-Hertneck, Bundesliga 1988.

➪ 9...d5?! (weakening the a3-f8 diagonal is dubious) 10 ♖b1 0-0 (other moves are also not very attractive) 11 ♗a3 ♘e4 12 ♗xf8 ♘xc3 13 ♕d3 ♗f5? (Black had to play 13...♘xb1, when 14 ♗b4 a5 15 ♗e1 may appear strong, but after 15...♕b6 there is no clear way to round up the trapped knight; therefore White may not have anything better than 14 ♗xg7 ♔xg7 15 ♖xb1, when he can claim a slight advantage because of Black's broken kingside) 14 ♕xf5 ♘xe2+ 15 ♔h1 ♖xf8 (now Black is simply material down, although it is a hard technical task to win this position) 16 ♕d3 ♘c3 17 ♖b3 ♘e4 18 f3 ♘d6 19 ♖e1 a5 20 ♖e2 b5 21 ♖b1 ♘c4 22 ♖be1 a4 23 ♖e7 b4 24 ♕f5 ♘d6 25 ♕d7 ♕xc2 26 ♕xc7 ♕g6 27 ♖d7 ♘e8 28 ♕c5 ♘f6 29 ♕xf8+ 1-0, Sapfirov-Reviakin, Gorki 1974.

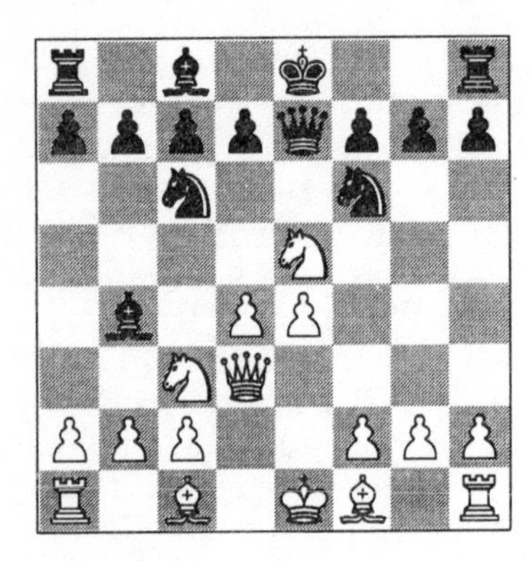

6...♘xe5

➪ 6...♘xd4 (this curious move has only been played once; it can lead to a position identical to the main line, except that Black's bishop is on c5 instead of b4) 7 ♕xd4 ♗c5 8 ♕d3 (8 ♘d5!? ♗xd4 9 ♘xe7 is interesting, since after 9...♔xe7 10 ♘f3 White has the advantage; however, 9...♗xe5 10 ♘xc8 ♘xe4!? may be an improvement since 11 f3 ♘f6 12 f4 ♗d4 13 c3 ♗c5 14 b4 ♗f8 15 ♘xa7 ♖xa7 is only very slightly better for White) 8...♕xe5 9 f4 (the bishop on c5 makes castling queenside harder, but the immediate f4 becomes possible) 9...♕d4 10 ♕xd4 (10 e5!? is another idea, when 10...♕f2+ 11 ♔d1 ♘g4 12 ♘e4 0-0!? is unclear) 10...♗xd4 11 e5 ♗xc3+ 12 bxc3 ♘e4 13 c4 b6 14 ♗e3 ♗b7 15 ♗d3 0-0-0 16 0-0-0 ♘c3 17 ♖d2 ♘xa2+ (Black gains the advantage, but White eventually holds the draw) 18 ♔b2 ♘b4 19 ♗f5 ♗c6 20 c3 ♘a6 21 ♖a1 ♔b7 22 ♖ad1 d6 23 exd6 ♖xd6 24 ♖xd6 cxd6 25 ♖xd6 ♖e8 26 ♗d4 f6 27 g4 ♖e2+ 28 ♔a3 ♔c7 29 ♖e6 ♖xe6 30 ♗xe6 ♗d7 31 ♗g8 ♗xg4 32 ♗xh7 ♘c5 33 h4 ♗h5 34 ♗g8 ♘d3 35 ♗e3 ♔d6 36 ♗d5 ♗g4 37 ♗e4 ♘c5 38 ♗d5 ♗d7 39 ♔b4 ♘d3+ 40 ♔a3 ♘c5 41 ♗f3 ½-½, Ostermeyer-Neunhöffer, Bundesliga 1989.

7 dxe5 ♕xe5 8 ♗d2 0-0 9 0-0-0

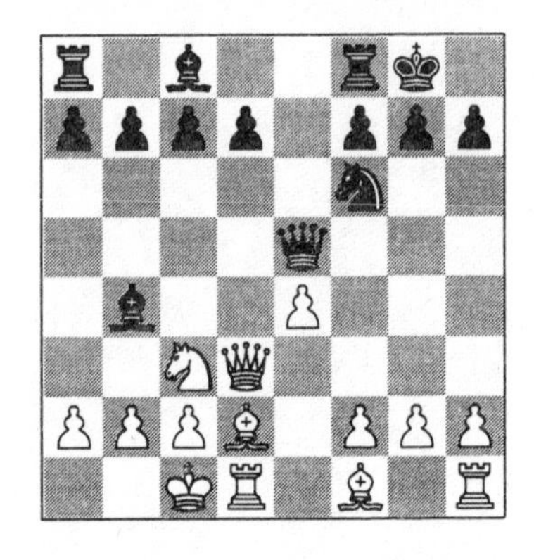

9...♗xc3

The main alternative is 9...d6 and now:

➪ 10 ♖e1 (preparing f4 avoids the problems with the e-pawn which arise after 10 f4 ♕e6) 10...♖e8 11 f4 ♕e7 12 g4?! (imaginative, but it can't really be sound) 12...♘xg4 13 ♖g1 c6 14 ♗e2 ♘f6 15 ♗d1 a5?! (a casual move, underestimating White's chances) 16 e5 dxe5 17 fxe5 ♘d5 18 ♗g5 ♕e6 19 ♗f6 g6 20 ♗g4 ♕xg4 21 ♖xg4 ♗xg4 (Black has enough for the queen) 22 ♘xd5 cxd5 23 ♖g1 ♗e6 (at this stage White is not doing badly, but he loses the thread of the game and Black quickly takes over the initiative) 24 h4 ♖ec8 25 h5 ♖c4 26 a3 ♗c5 27 ♕d2?! (27 hxg6 fxg6 28 ♖h1 is better) 27...♖c8 28 c3 ♗xg1 29 ♕h6 ♗e3+ 30 ♕xe3 ♖g4 31 hxg6 ♖xg6 32 ♕b6 a4 33 ♔d2 ♖g4

34 ♕xb7 h5 35 ♕b6 d4 36 cxd4 h4 37 d5 ♗xd5 38 ♕e3 ♖g2+ 39 ♔e1 h3 0-1, Bellon Lopez-Larsen, Las Palmas 1981.

⇨ 10 f4 ♕a5? (a horrible move, which gives White a clear advantage with absolutely no risk) 11 a3 ♗xc3 12 ♗xc3 ♕h5 13 ♗xf6 gxf6 14 ♗e2 ♕h6 15 ♖df1 ♖e8 16 g4 ♗d7 17 h4 ♗c6 18 g5 fxg5 19 hxg5 ♕g6 20 f5 ♕xg5+ 21 ♔b1 ♕e7 22 ♕g3+ 1-0, Rosen-Wiesloch, corr. 1967.

⇨ 10 f4 ♕e6 (a much better square than a5) 11 ♘d5 (11 ♖e1!? is more dangerous, although some would hesitate to sacrifice the a-pawn) 11...♗xd2+ 12 ♖xd2 ♘xe4 (a brave move, all the more so in that taking on d5 was entirely playable) 13 ♖e2 f5 14 ♘xc7 ♕xa2 15 ♖xe4 ♕a1+ 16 ♔d2 fxe4 17 ♕xd6 e3+ 18 ♔xe3 ♕c1+ 19 ♔f3 ♕xc2

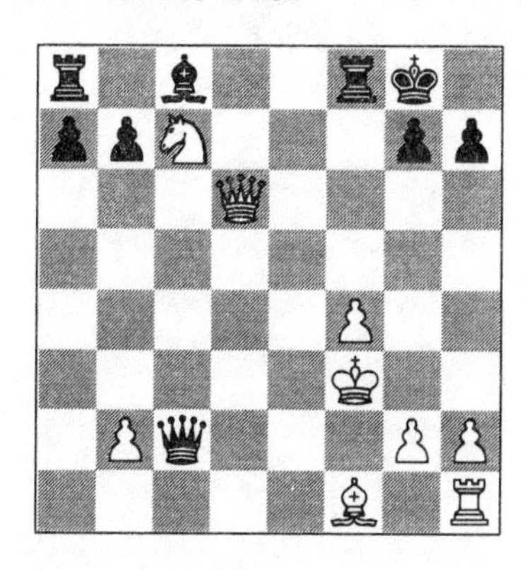

20 ♗d3 (20 ♕d5+ ♔h8 21 ♘xa8 ♗f5 22 g4 ♗g6 was also very unclear) 20...♗g4+ (20...♕b3!? was another idea, meeting 21 ♘xa8 by 21...♗f5) 21 ♔g3 ♕b3 22 ♘xa8 ♗e2 23 ♖a1 ♗xd3 24 ♖a3 ♕f7 25 ♖xd3 ♖xa8 26 h3 ♖e8 (the complications have resulted in approximate equality) 27 ♖c3 ♕g6+ (27...♕e6 is also safe) 28 ♕xg6 hxg6 29 ♔f3 ♖e6 30 ♖c8+ ♔h7 31 ♖a8 a6 32 ♖d8 ♖b6 33 ♖d2 ♖b3+ 34 ♔g4 a5 35 h4 ♖b4 36 ♔g5 a4 37 g4 ♖b5+ 38 f5 gxf5 39 gxf5 ♖b3 40 ♔g4 b5 41 ♔g5 ♖b4 42 ♖h2 ♖c4 43 h5 ♖c1 44 ♖g2 ♖b1 45 h6 b4 46 hxg7 ♔xg7 47 f6+ ♔f7 48 ♖f2 b3 49 ♔f5 ♖c1 50 ♔e5 ♖d1 51 ♖h2 ♖a1 52 ♖h7+ ♔f8 53 ♖h8+ ♔f7 54 ♖h7+ ♔g8 55 ♖g7+ ♔f8 56 ♖b7 ♖b1 57 ♔e6 ♖e1+ 58 ♔d5 ♖e2 59 ♖a7 ♖xb2 60 ♖xa4 ♖b1 61 ♖d4 ♔f7 62 ♖d2 b2 63 ♔d4 ♔xf6 64 ♔c3 ½-½, Olthof-Meszaros, Budapest Open 1989.

10 ♗xc3 ♕f4+

After 10...♕xe4 11 ♕g3! White has a dangerous initiative, but this may be no worse than the main line.

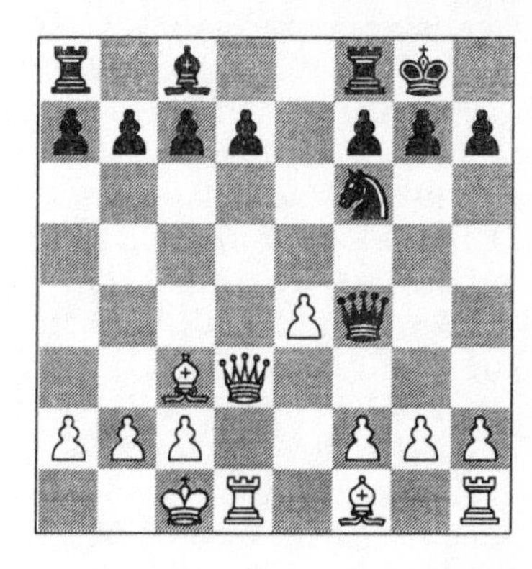

11 ♖d2

⇨ 11 ♔b1? (this is simply bad) 11...♘xe4 12 g3 ♘xc3+ 13 ♕xc3 ♕xf2 14 ♕xc7 d6 15 ♗c4 (15 ♗d3 ♕c5) 15...♗f5 16 ♗b3 ♖ac8 17 ♕xb7? (17 ♕xd6 ♗xc2+ leaves Black a pawn up for nothing, but the game is much worse) 17...♗xc2+ 18

♗xc2 ♕xc2+ 19 ♔a1 ♖b8 20 ♕xb8 ♖xb8 21 ♖b1 h5 22 a3 (Drimer obviously didn't believe in resigning) 22...♔h7 23 ♔a2 ♕b3+ 24 ♔a1 ♖c8 25 ♖hf1 ♖c2 26 h3 f6 27 ♖g1 d5 28 h4 ♖c3 29 g4 ♖g3 30 gxh5 ♖xg1 31 ♖xg1 d4 0-1, Drimer-L.Portisch, Hastings 1970.

11...♕xe4

Or 11...d5 (11...♘xe4? 12 ♕d4 wins, while 11...♖e8 12 f3 d5 13 g3 dxe4 14 gxf4 exd3 15 ♗xd3 is positionally better for White according to Portisch) and now:

➩ 12 exd5 (this is the critical line) 12...♖e8 13 b3 ♗f5 (13...♘e4 14 ♕d4 ♕h6 15 ♗b5 is good for White after 15...c6 16 dxc6 bxc6 17 ♗xc6 ♘xd2 18 ♔b2! or 15...♖e7 16 ♖e1 ♗f5 17 ♕xg7+! ♕xg7 18 ♗xg7 ♔xg7 19 ♖de2 followed by ♗d3 or f3 regaining the piece) 14 ♕f3 ♖e1+ 15 ♔b2 ♕g5?! (this only makes matters worse; 15...♕xf3 was essential) 16 h4 ♕g6 17 d6 ♘e4 18 ♖d5 ♗e6 19 ♖e5 ♗g4 20 d7 ♘f6? (20...♘d6) 21 ♕xb7 1-0, Bellon Lopez-Lukacs, Bucharest 1978.

➩ 12 ♗xf6 dxe4 13 g3 ♕f5 14 ♕d4 ♕xf6 15 ♕xe4 ♗e6 16 ♗d3 g6 17 ♗c4 ♖ae8 18 ♖hd1 ♔g7 ½-½, Topakian-Svidler, Oakham 1992.

12 ♗xf6

The dangerous move 12 ♕g3! is more promising than the tame 12 ♗xf6.

12...♕xd3 13 ♖xd3 gxf6 14 ♖f3 d6

I prefer 14...♔g7, when White has more of a fight to regain his pawn; Informator gives 15 h4 d6 16 h5 as clearly better for White, but it is hard to see the point of the h-pawn advance after 16...h6.

15 ♖xf6 ♗d7 16 ♗d3 ♖ae8 17 ♖h6 f5 18 ♔d2 ♔g7 19 ♖h4 ♖e5?

19...h6 was much safer, preventing White's next move.

20 g4!

Suddenly White has dangerous threats.

20...h6?! 21 gxf5 ♗xf5 22 ♖g1+ ♔h7 23 ♖f4

With a highly unpleasant pin.

23...c5 24 b3 d5?

A losing blunder in a very bad position.

25 ♖e1! ♖xe1 26 ♖xf5 1-0

Game 19

Evers-Schutze
corr. 1986

1 e4 e5 2 ♘f3 ♘c6 3 ♘c3 ♘f6 4 d4 ♗b4 5 ♘xe5 ♘xe4 6 ♕g4

Or 6 ♕f3 ♘f6 and now:

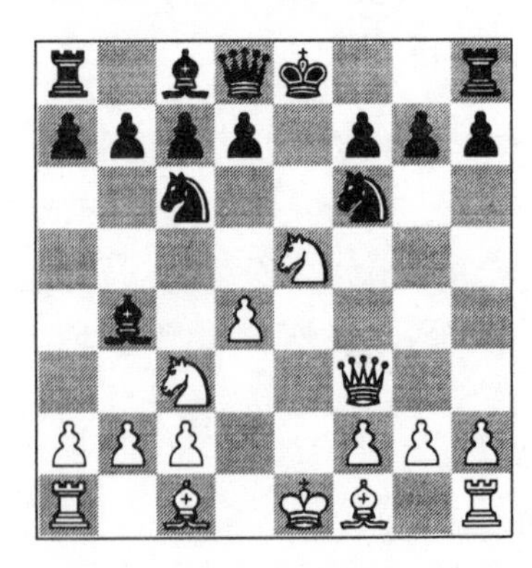

➩ 7 ♗d3 (a distinctly unsound gambit) 7...♘xd4 8 ♕g3 0-0 9 ♗g5 ♘e6 10 h4 ♗e7 11 f4 d6 12 0-0-0 dxe5 13 ♗xh7+ ♘xh7 14 ♖xd8 ♗xd8 (Black has more than enough for the queen and should win) 15 f5 ♘exg5 16 hxg5 ♗xf5 (it is safer to take first on g5 and only then on f5) 17 ♘d5

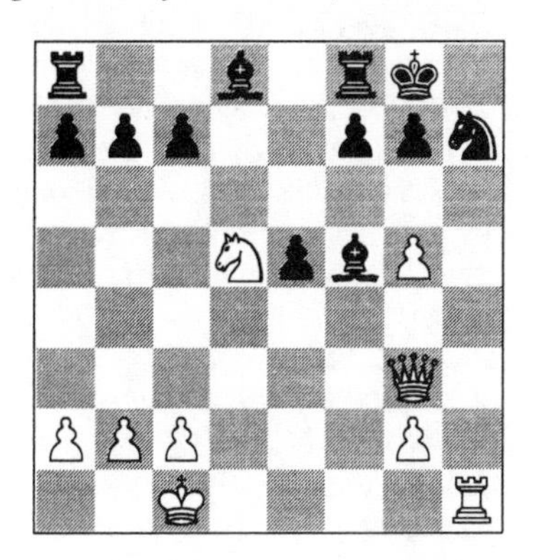

17...♗xg5+?? (an unbelievable blunder; 17...♖e8 is winning for Black) 18 ♕xg5 1-0, Berkovich-Dvoretsky, Moscow Team 1978.

⇨ 7 ♗e3 (a more sensible choice, but also promising no advantage for White) 7...0-0 8 ♗d3 ♖e8 9 ♘xc6 dxc6 10 0-0 ♗g4 11 ♕g3 ♕d7 12 h3 ♗f5 (Black is at least equal) 13 ♖ad1 ♗xd3 14 ♖xd3 ♗xc3 15 bxc3 ♘e4 16 ♕f3 ♕d5 17 ♖a1 ♖e7 (White's position is uncomfortable but over the next few moves he escapes; perhaps the simple 17...♘d6 was better, because even if White swaps his bishop for Black's knight he will still have weak pawns) 18 ♗f4 ♖ae8 19 ♖e3 ♘d6 20 ♖xe7 ♖xe7 21 ♕xd5 cxd5 22 ♗xd6 cxd6 23 ♖b1 ♔f8 24 ♔f1 b6 25 ♖b5 ♖c7 26 ♖b3 ♖c4 27 ♖a3 a5 28 ♖b3 a4 29 ♖xb6 ♖xc3 30 ♖xd6 ♖xc2 31 a3 ♖a2 32 ♖xd5 ♖xa3 33 ♖d7 ♖a2 34 ♖a7 a3 35 d5 ♖d2 36 ♖xa3 ♖xd5 37 ♔e2 g6 38 h4 ♔g7 39 g3 ½-½, Adams-Howell, London (Lloyds Bank) 1992.

6...♘xc3 7 ♕xg7 ♖f8 8 a3 ♘xd4

Black plays the sharpest line, but it is probably not the best. The alternative is 8...♗a5 9 ♘xc6 dxc6 10 ♕e5+ ♕e7 11 ♕xe7+ ♔xe7 12 ♗d2 ♗f5 and now:

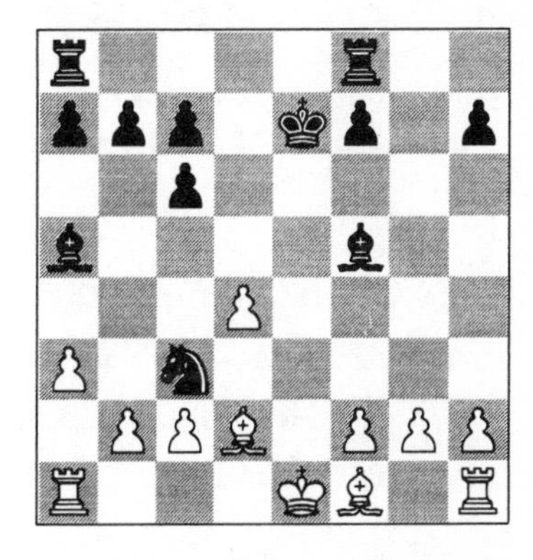

⇨ 13 ♗xc3 ♗xc3+ 14 bxc3 ♗xc2 15 ♔d2 ♗g6 16 f4 (perhaps 16 h4 is better, as in the game below) 16...♔d6 17 ♖e1 ♖ae8 18 ♗d3 (White has a microscopic advantage, but Black reaches the draw without real difficulty) 18...f6 19 g4 c5 20 ♗xg6 hxg6 21 dxc5+ ♔xc5 22 ♖xe8 ♖xe8 23 h4 ♔c4 24 h5 gxh5 25 gxh5 ♖h8 26 h6 c5 27 ♖h5 b5 28 h7 a5 29

♔c2 b4 30 cxb4 cxb4 31 axb4 axb4 32 ♖h6 f5 33 ♖h5 ♔d4 34 ♖xf5 ♖xh7 ½-½, Wolf-Neunhöffer, Bundesliga 1988.

⇨ 13 bxc3 ♗xc2 14 c4 ♗xd2+ 15 ♔xd2 ♗g6 (this is the same position as in Wolf-Neunhöffer above, but with White's pawn on c4 instead of c3; this is probably slightly to White's advantage because c3 is a good square for his king) 16 h4 (better than 16 f4 as above) 16...♔d6 (I feel that this ending shouldn't be too bad for Black, but he soon runs into serious trouble) 17 h5 ♗f5 18 ♗d3 ♗xd3 19 ♔xd3 c5 20 ♖h4 ♖ad8 21 ♖e1 ♖fe8? (21...cxd4 22 ♖xd4+ ♔c6) 22 ♖xe8 ♖xe8 23 ♖f4 (suddenly White is winning) 23...♔e6 24 ♖e4+ ♔d7 25 ♖xe8 ♔xe8 26 dxc5 ♔e7 27 ♔e4 ♔e6 28 g4 1-0, Estevez-Corujedo, corr. 1988.

9 axb4 ♘xc2+ 10 ♔d2 ♘xa1 11 ♔xc3 a5

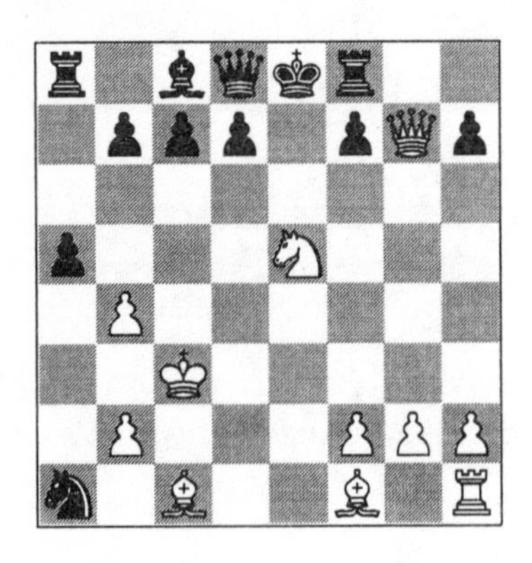

12 ♗c4

⇨ In this critical position various White moves have been tried, but current theory suggests that 12 ♗c4 offers good winning chances. The alternative 12 ♗g5 leads to a nearly forced draw after 12...axb4+ 13 ♔d3 f6 14 ♗e2 ♕e7 15 ♗h5+ ♔d8 16 ♘f7+ ♖xf7 17 ♗xf7 ♕d6+ 18 ♔e4 (after 18 ♔e2 Black can safely play 18...fxg5 because there is no perpetual check) 18...fxg5 (18...♕e5+ 19 ♔f3 ♕f5+ 20 ♗f4 ♕d3+ 21 ♔g4 is risky for Black) 19 ♕g8+ ♔e7 20 ♕e8+ (White wisely settles for the draw; 20 ♖e1 ♕d2! 21 ♖e3 d5+ 22 ♔e5 ♗e6 23 ♕xg5+ ♔d7 24 ♗xe6+ ♔c6 is good for Black) 20...♔f6 21 ♕h8+ ♔xf7 22 ♕xh7+ ½-½, Polovodin-Katalymov, 1980.

12...♕e7

The other possibility is 12...axb4+ and now:

⇨ 13 ♔d3 (this has been unjustly condemned) 13...d5 14 ♗b5+ c6 15 ♘xc6 ♗f5+ 16 ♔d2? (*Informator* gave 16 ♔e2! bxc6 17 bxc6+ ♗d7 18 ♗xa8 as unclear, but in fact White stands well, for example 18...♕xa8 19 ♗h6 ♕a6+ 20 ♔f3 ♕d3+ 21 ♔f4 ♕e4+ 22 ♔g3 or 18...♕e7+ 19 ♗e3 ♗b5+ 20 ♔f3 ♕e4+ 21 ♔g3) 16...bxc6 17 ♗xc6+ ♔e7 (now there is no check on g5) 18 ♗xa8 ♕xa8 19 ♕g5+ ♔e6 20 ♖e1+ ♗e4 21 f3 ♖g8 (21...♘b3+! is even stronger, for example 22 ♔d1 ♖c8 or 22 ♔e2 ♘xc1+) 22 ♕h6+ ♖g6 23 ♕h3+ f5 24 ♔e2 ♘c2 25 fxe4 dxe4 26 ♕b3+? (26 ♖d1) 26...♕d5? (26...♔f6! wins immediately) 27 ♕xd5+ ♔xd5 28 ♖d1+ ♔e5 29 g3 ♘d4+ 30 ♔f2 ♘f3 31 ♗f4+ ♔e6 32 ♖d8?! (after 32 h3 or 32 ♖d6+ ♔e7 33 ♖d5 White has drawing chances) 32...♘xh2 33 ♖b8 ♔d5 34 ♖xb4 ♖c6 35 ♖b7 ♘g4+ 36 ♔e1 e3 37 ♖xh7 0-1 (it isn't clear why White would resign here since Black has no simple win, for example 37...♔e4 is met by 38 ♖c7, so I imagine this was a loss on time) 0-1, Angantysson-I.Polgar, Dresden 1969. ➪ 13 ♔d2! (this appears even better) 13...d5 14 ♗b5+ c6 (14...♔e7 15 ♔d1!) 15 ♖e1 ♗e6 16 ♘xc6 bxc6 (16...♕d6 17 ♖xe6+ fxe6 18 ♘a5+ and White wins) 17 ♖xe6+ ♔d7 18 ♖xc6 ♕e7 19 ♔d1 ♖ab8 20 ♗f4 1-0, Polovodin-Rutman, Leningrad 1978.

13 ♖e1

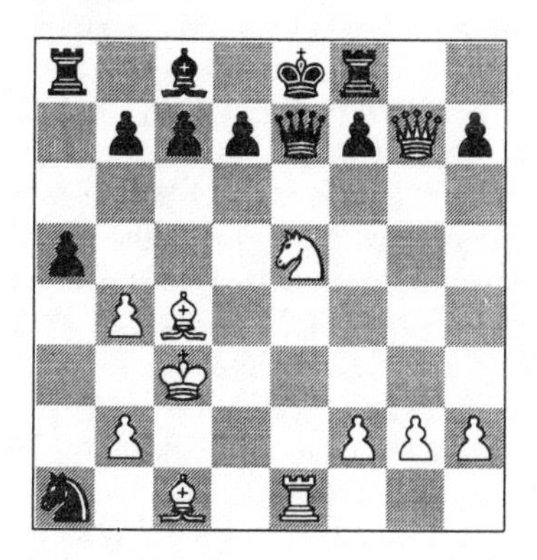

13...d5

➪ After 13...♕xb4+ (13...axb4+ 14 ♔d2 ♕d6+ 15 ♘d3+ ♔d8 16 ♔d1 ♘b3 17 ♗f4 1-0, Smith-Fauth, corr. 1981) 14 ♔d3 Black blundered by 14...d5?? in J.C.Diaz-Am.Rodriguez, Cuba 1981, and had to resign after 15 ♘xf7+! because of 15...♕xe1 16 ♘d6+ cxd6 17 ♗b5+ ♔d8 18 ♗g5+ mating. 14...♕d6+! is a clear improvement, but after 15 ♔e2 White's attack is still extremely strong.

14 ♗b5+

The next few moves are forced for both sides.

14...c6 15 ♘xc6 ♕xe1+ 16 ♗d2 bxc6

16...♕e4 17 ♘b8+ wins for White after 17...♔d8 18 ♕xf8+ ♔c7 19 ♕c5+ ♔xb8 20 ♕d6+ ♔a7 21 ♗e3+ or 17...♔e7 18 ♗g5+ ♔d6 19 ♕xf8+ ♔c7 20 ♗d8+ ♔xb8 21 ♕d6+ ♔a7 22 ♗b6 mate.

17 ♗xc6+ ♗d7 18 ♗xd7+ ♔xd7 19 ♗xe1 ♖ac8+ 20 ♔d3

Approximate material equality has been restored, but White has a clear advantage based on the continued exposure of Black's king and White's chances to create a dangerous passed h-pawn.

20...♘c2 21 ♗c3 ♘xb4+ 22 ♗xb4 axb4 23 ♕xh7 b3 24 h4 ♔e7 25 ♕g7 ♖c6 26 h5 ♖fc8 27 f4 d4 28 f5 ♖c2 29 h6 ♖d8 30 h7 ♖xb2 31 ♕e5+ ♔d7 32 ♕xd4+ ♔e7 33 ♕xd8+ ♔xd8 34 h8♕+ 1-0

After 1 e4 e5 2 ♘f3 ♘c6 3 ♘c3 ♘f6 White is not forced to play 4 d4 or 4 ♗b5, although other moves are rare. There are two significant alternatives, namely 4 ♗e2 and 4 g3. The first of these was adopted a few years ago by Van der Wiel but although the surprise element led to some early successes, the idea didn't catch on and has now disappeared again. The simple 4...d5 appears the most reliable reply, as in game 20 below. 4 g3 has been played several times by Glek. The resulting positions can also arise from the 1 e4 e5 2 ♘c3 ♘f6 3 g3 variation of the Vienna, although in that case the g1 knight is usually developed at e2. Due to lack of practical experience, it isn't possible to recommend the most effective reply, but 4...♗b4 has been chosen by most of Glek's opponents. The 4 g3 line is covered in game 21.

Game 20

Van der Wiel-Timman
Wijk aan Zee 1985

1 e4 e5 2 ♘f3 ♘c6 3 ♘c3 ♘f6 4 ♗e2 (see diagram at the top of the next column) **4...d5**

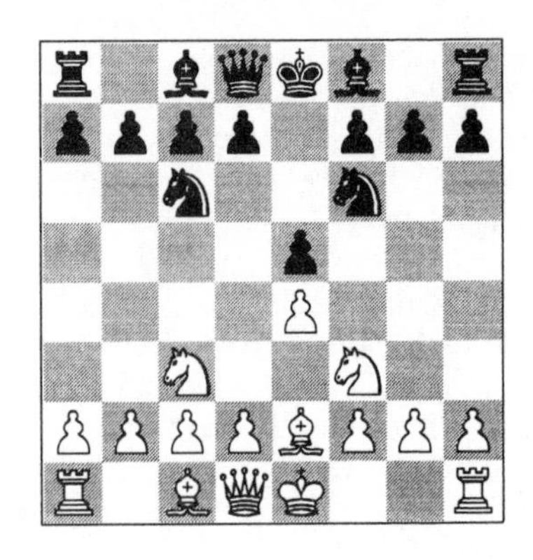

➪ 4...♗b4 5 ♘d5 ♘xe4 (a new idea; 5...♗e7 was played previously, and 5...♗a5 is a reasonable alternative) 6 ♘xb4 ♘xb4 7 d3 ♘f6 8 ♘xe5 (White has a very small but permanent advantage because of his two bishops) 8...♘c6 9 ♘xc6 dxc6 10 0-0 0-0 11 ♗g5 h6 12 ♗f4 ♘d5 13 ♗g3 ♗f5 (the aggressive 13...f5 14 ♗e5 ♗e6 is recommended by Van der Wiel, but it would require great courage to weaken e5 so seriously) 14 ♗f3 ♕d7 15 h3 ♖ad8 16 ♖e1 ♖fe8 17 ♕d2 b6 18 a3 ♖xe1+ 19 ♖xe1 ♗e6 20 ♕e2 c5 21 ♕e4 ♕c8?! (21...c6 was more solid; the move played allows White to infiltrate with his queen) 22 ♕a4 a5 23 ♕c6 ♕d7 24 ♗xd5 ♕xd5 25 ♕xd5 ♖xd5 26 ♗xc7 b5 (26...c4 27 dxc4 ♖d2 was the last chance) 27 ♗xa5 c4 28 dxc4 bxc4 29 ♗c3 ♗f5 30 ♖e8+ ♔h7 31 ♖e7 ♖d1+ 32 ♔h2 ♔g6 33 ♖c7 ♗e6 34 a4 ♖c1 35 a5 ♖xc2 36 ♔g3 ♖c1 37 a6 ♖a1 38 a7 ♖a6 39 ♗d4 ♔h7 40 ♔f4 ♗d5 41 f3 g5+ 42 ♔e5 ♗e6 43 ♗b6 ♖a1 44 ♖b7 ♔g6 45 ♖b8 ♖e1+ 46 ♔d6 ♖d1+ 47 ♔c5 c3 48 bxc3 1-0, Van der Wiel-L.Day, Grand Manan 1984.

➪ 4...♗c5 (this move is dubious) 5 ♘xe5 ♘xe5 6 d4 ♗b4 7 dxe5 ♘xe4 8 ♕d3 ♘xc3 9 bxc3 ♗e7 10 ♕g3 (by a more or less forced sequence White has gained a big lead in development) 10...g6 11 ♗h6 d5 12 0-0 c6 13 c4 ♗e6 14 cxd5 ♕xd5 15 ♖fd1 ♕e4 16 ♗f3 ♕xc2 17 ♗g7 ♖g8 18 ♗f6 (Black's king is in serious trouble) 18...♕f5 19 ♕h4 g5 20 ♕d4 ♕f4 21 ♕c3 ♕c4 22 ♕b2 ♕b4 23 ♕c2 ♗xf6 24 exf6 ♖g6 25 ♖ab1 ♕c4 26 ♕b2 ♖b8 27 ♗h5 ♕f4 (27...♖h6 loses to 28 ♕e5 attacking b8, g5 and in some lines e6, so White wins the exchange) 28 ♗xg6 hxg6 29 ♕a3 ♕xf6 30 ♕xa7 ♖c8 31 ♖xb7 ♔f8 32 a4 ♔g7 33 a5 ♖d8 34 ♖bb1 ♗d5 35 ♕d4 ♖a8 36 ♖a1 ♕xd4 37 ♖xd4 ♔f6 38 a6 ♔e5 39 ♖b4 c5 40 ♖b5 ♔d4 41 a7 1-0, Van der Wiel-R.Kuijf, Netherlands Ch. 1987.

5 exd5 ♘xd5 6 0-0 ♘xc3 7 bxc3

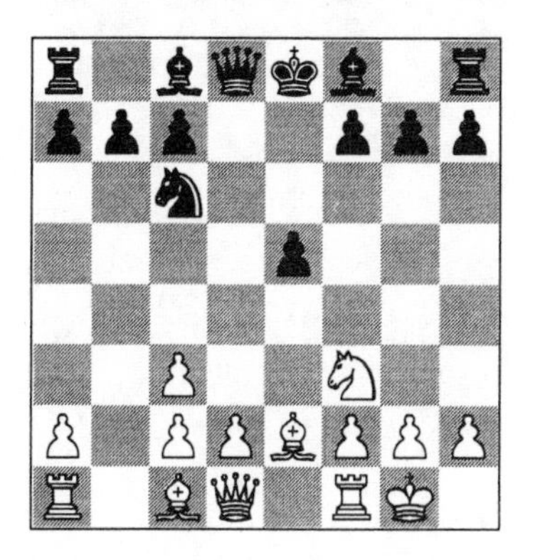

7...♗d6

⇨ 7...e4 (this is the most direct move, but White can meet it with a pawn sacrifice) 8 ♘d4 ♘xd4 9 cxd4 ♕xd4 10 c3 ♕d5 (10...♕e5 11 d4 is more risky) 11 d3 ♗d6 (11...♗c5 12 dxe4 ♕xd1 13 ♖xd1 ♗e6 14 ♗f4 ♖c8 15 a4 ♔e7 16 ♖db1 was a little better for White in Van der Wiel-Scheeren, Netherlands Team Ch. 1984/5, while 11...♗d7 and 11...♗f5 are also playable according to Van der Wiel) 12 dxe4 ♕xd1 (12...♕xe4 13 ♗b5+ is too dangerous, but after the simple 12...♕e5! 13 g3 0-0 the position is equal) 13 ♖xd1 0-0 14 ♗e3 ♗e6 (the position is slightly in White's favour; his bishops restrain Black's queenside pawns, while White has chances of a kingside initiative with f4) 15 a4 ♖fd8 16 a5 b6 17 f4 f6 18 ♔f2 ♖ab8 19 ♖d2 ♔f8 20 g4 (this allows Black to make a bid for freedom; White could have continued his kingside advance more cautiously by 20 h4) 20...bxa5 21 ♖xa5 ♖b3 22 ♖c2?! (I don't like this move; Van der Wiel's notes point out that 22 e5 fxe5 23 fxe5 ♗e7 24 ♖xd8+ ♗xd8 25 ♖xa7 is well met by 25...♗h4+!, but 25 ♗d4! is much better, defending all the pawns and maintaining an attack on a7) 22...♖a3! (a strong reply, based on the tactical point that 23 ♖xa3 ♗xa3 24 ♗xa7 ♗b3 traps the rook) 23 ♖h5 ♔g8 (in order to meet 24 ♗c5 by 24...♖a5) 24 c4 ♗b4 25 ♖b5 a5 26 c5 ♖a2? (26...♗e1+ is an immediate draw, while 26...♖b3!? is an unclear way to continue the fight) 27 ♖xa2 ♗xa2 28 ♖b7 ♖d7? (a further error in time-trouble, but even 28...c6 29 ♖b6 is clearly better for White) 29 ♗b5 ♖e7 30 ♗c6 (Black is completely tied up) 30...♔f8 31 h4 ♗f7 32 ♖b8+ ♗e8 33 ♖c8 a4 34 ♗xa4 ♖xe4 35 ♗c2 ♖e7 36 ♗xh7 ♔f7 37 h5 ♗c6 38 ♗g8 mate, Van der Wiel-Yusupov, Reykjavik 1985.

8 d4 0-0 9 ♖b1

The unlikely move 9 ♗b5 would lead to a reversed Scotch Opening.

9...h6 10 dxe5 ♘xe5 11 ♘xe5 ♗xe5 12 ♗a3?

A definite error according to Timman, who recommends 12 ♗f3 ♖b8 13 ♗a3 ♗d6 14 ♗xd6 ♕xd6 15

♕xd6 cxd6 16 ♖d1 ♖d8 with a roughly equal position. However, 12...c6 13 ♗a3 ♖e8 looks better, and White still has to find compensation for his weakened queenside pawns.

12...♖e8 13 ♗f3 ♕h4! (now Black has an extra possibility) **14 g3 ♕a4 15 ♕c1 ♗xc3 16 ♗xb7**

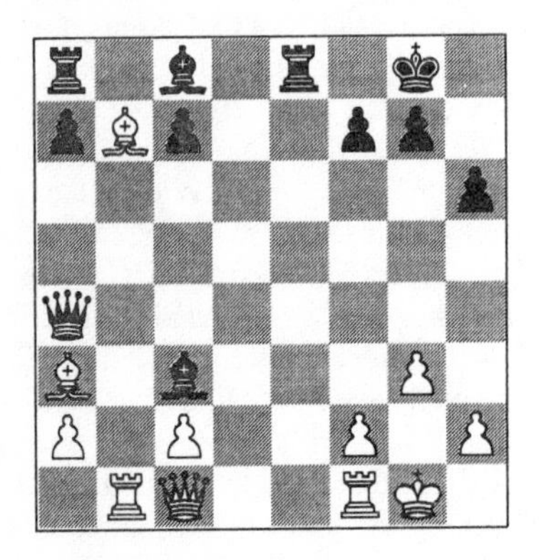

16...♗h3 (Timman gives 16...♗xb7 17 ♖xb7 ♗a5 as an improvement, and the simple 16...♗xb7 17 ♖xb7 ♕c6 18 ♖b3 ♖e2 also appears promising) **17 ♗b2** (better than 17 ♗xa8 ♖xa8 18 ♕e3 ♕xa3 and White cannot exploit the momentary lack of co-ordination between Black's pieces) **17...♗xb2** (17...♗xf1 18 ♗xc3 defends) **18 ♖xb2 ♖ad8 19 ♗g2 ♗xg2 20 ♔xg2 ♖e2** (Black still has the advantage) **21 c3 ♖de8 22 ♖d2 a5 23 ♕b2 ♕c6+ 24 ♔g1 ♕c4 25 a3?** (a blunder; 25 ♕b8+ ♔h7 26 ♕b1+ g6 27 ♕b3 ♕xb3 28 axb3 ♖b2 was a better defence, when both 29 b4 axb4 30 cxb4 ♖xb4 31 ♖c1 ♖b7 32 ♖c6 and 29 ♖d1 ♖xb3 30 ♖d7 ♖xc3 31 ♖xf7+ ♔g8 32 ♖f6 ♔g7 33 ♖a6 offer some drawing chances) **25...♖e1 26 ♖xe1 ♖xe1+ 27 ♔g2 ♕f1+ 28 ♔f3 ♕h1+ 29 ♔g4 f5+ 30 ♔h3 ♕f1+ 0-1** (it is mate in three more moves).

Game 21

Kremenietsky-Beliavsky
USSR 1982

1 e4 e5 2 ♘f3 ♘c6 3 ♘c3 ♘f6 4 g3

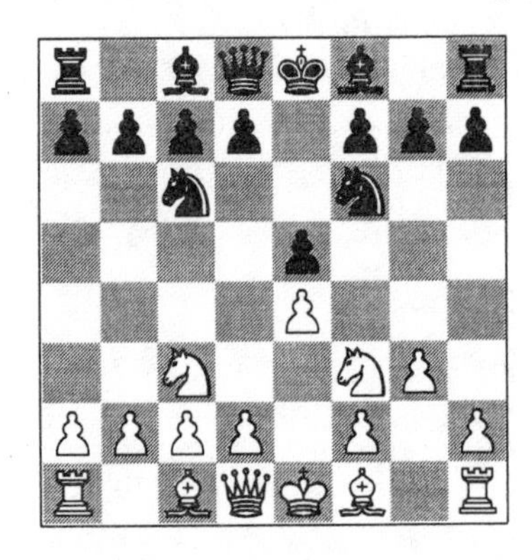

4...♗b4

⇨ 4...♗c5 5 ♗g2 d6 6 d3 a6 7 0-0 ♗g4 8 h3 ♗e6 9 ♔h2 h5 10 ♘h4 ♘g4+!? 11 ♔g1 (11 hxg4 hxg4 12 ♔g1 ♖xh4! 13 gxh4 ♕xh4 is very dangerous for White) 11...♘h6? (11...♘f6 is much sounder) 12 ♕xh5 ♕d7 13 ♘f5! (returning the pawn to activate the g2 bishop and inhibit ...0-0-0) 13...♗xf5 14 exf5 ♕xf5 15 ♕h4 ♘d4 16 ♗e3 c6 17 ♘e4 ♔d7 18 ♘xc5+ dxc5 19 ♗xd4 g5? (a tactical miscalculation, but 19...cxd4 20 f4 was very unpleasant in any case) 20 ♗e4! (winning an important pawn) 20...♕f6 21 ♗xe5 ♕xe5 22 ♕h5 f5 23 ♗g2 f4 24 ♖ae1 ♕f6 25

♖e4 ♖af8 26 ♕f3 ♘f5 27 gxf4 gxf4 28 ♖xf4 ♖hg8 29 ♖g4 ♖h8 30 c3 ♕d6 31 ♕f4 ♕e6 32 ♕e4 ♕f7 33 b4 ♘d6 34 ♕e5 ♖h5 35 ♕g3 ♘f5 36 ♕f3 cxb4 37 ♖xb4 ♔c8 38 ♖fb1 ♘d6 39 ♕g4+ ♖f5 40 ♖f4 ♖g8 41 ♖xf5 ♘xf5 42 ♕f3 ♕e6 43 ♖b4 ♘d6 44 ♔h2 ♘b5 45 d4 ♕d6+ 46 ♔h1 ♖f8 47 ♕e3 a5 48 ♖b1 a4 49 ♖d1 ♘a3 50 d5 c5 51 ♕e2 b5 52 ♕b2 b4 53 cxb4 cxb4 54 ♖c1+ ♔d8 55 ♖c6 ♕f4 56 ♕g7 b3 57 axb3 axb3 58 ♕b7 ♕f5 59 ♕b8+ ♔d7 60 ♕c7+ ♔e8 61 ♖e6+ 1-0, Glek-Borkowski, Moscow 1991.

⇨ 4...d5 5 exd5 ♘xd5 6 ♗g2 ♘xc3 7 bxc3 (this position should be slightly better for White because after 1 e4 e5 2 ♘c3 ♘f6 3 g3 d5 4 exd5 ♘xd5 5 ♗g2 ♘xc3 6 bxc3 ♗d6 Black normally develops his knight to d7 and not c6, but here Black is already committed to the inferior square) 7...♗c5 8 0-0 0-0 9 ♖e1 ♖e8 10 d4 exd4 11 ♖xe8+ ♕xe8 12 cxd4 ♗b6 (White's extra central pawn gives him the edge) 13 ♕d3 ♘b4? (a pointless manoeuvre) 14 ♕b3 ♘c6 15 ♗b2 ♗g4 16 ♖e1 ♕f8 17 ♗a3 ♕d8 18 d5 ♗xf3 19 ♕xf3 ♘d4 20 ♕d3 ♕f6 21 c4 (a brave move inviting complications, especially as the simple 21 ♗e7 is good for White with no risk) 21...♘b5 22 ♕e2 (22 c5 ♗a5 23 ♖b1 is another promising idea) 22...♗xf2+ 23 ♕xf2 ♕xf2+ 24 ♔xf2 ♘xa3 25 ♖c1 ♖b8 26 ♖c3 ♘b1 27 ♖c1 ♘a3 28 ♗f1 a6 29 ♗d3 b5 30 cxb5 axb5 31 ♖xc7 (everything has turned out well and White has a large endgame advantage) 31...♔f8 32 ♔e3 b4 33 ♔d4 ♘b5+ 34 ♗xb5 ♖xb5 35 d6 ♔e8 36 ♖e7+ ♔d8 37 ♖xf7 g5 38 ♔c4 ♖a5 39 ♔xb4 ♖xa2 40 ♖xh7 ♖c2 41 h4 ♖c6 42 h5 ♖xd6 43 ♔c5 ♖a6 44 ♔d5 ♔e8 45 ♔e5 ♔f8 46 ♔f5 ♖a5+ 47 ♔g6 g4 48 ♖f7+ ♔g8 49 ♖f4 ♖a3 50 ♖xg4 ♔h8 51 ♔g5 ♔h7 52 ♔h4 ♖a7 53 ♖b4 ♖c7 54 g4 1-0, Glek-Arkhipov, Lippstadt 1992.

5 d3

Or 5 ♗g2 and now:

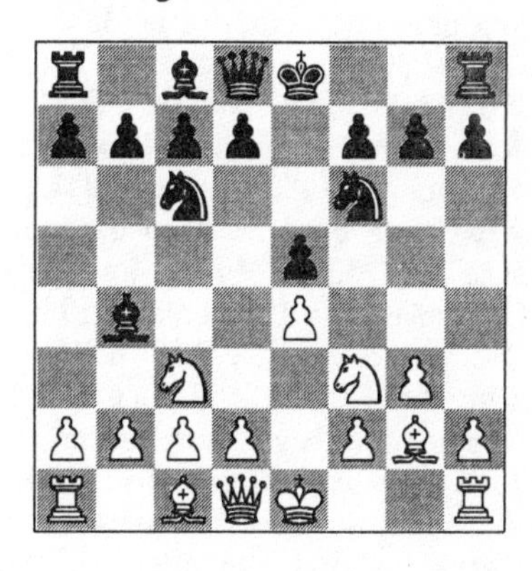

⇨ 5...d6 6 d3 ♗g4 7 h3 ♗h5 8 0-0 h6 9 ♘d5! (now the bishop on b4 appears badly placed) 9...♘xd5 10 exd5 ♘e7 11 c3 ♗c5 12 g4 ♗g6 13 d4 exd4 14 ♘xd4 (White has the advantage) 14...0-0 15 ♗e3 ♕d7 16 ♕d2 ♖ae8 17 ♖ae1 ♘c8 18 b4? (weakening the queenside for absolutely no reason; after 18 f4 Black has a difficult position) 18...♗xd4 19 ♕xd4 ♕b5 20 ♖d1 ♘b6 21 ♖fe1 ♕a4 22 ♖d2 ♖e7 23 ♖de2 ♖ee8 24 a3?! (based on the trick 24...♕xa3?? 25 ♗xh6, but in the long run it doesn't help to have the a-pawn on an undefended square; 24 f4 f5 25 ♕d3 is still unclear) 24...♕b5 25 ♖d2 ♕c4 26 ♗f1 ♕b3 (suddenly White is in big trouble; the a-pawn is attacked and ...♖e4 is threatened) 27 f3 ♖e5 28 c4 ♖fe8 (the immediate 28...♕xa3! is more accurate, preventing the defence in the game) 29 ♔f2 ♕xa3 30 ♕b2 ♕xb2 31 ♖xb2 ♘a4 32 ♖b3 ♗c2 33 ♖a3 ♘b2 34 ♗e2 a6 35 ♗d2 ♖5e7 (35...♗d1! is very strong, for example 36 ♗f1 ♖xe1 37 ♗xe1 ♗xf3!) 36 ♖c3 ♖xe2+ (this combination only leads to a draw) 37 ♖xe2 ♘d1+ 38 ♔e1 ♖xe2+ 39 ♔xe2 ♘xc3+ 40 ♗xc3 ♗b3 41 ♔d3 f6 42 ♔d4 ♔f7 43 ♗e1 ♗d1 44 ♔e3 b6 45 h4 g6 46 ♗c3 h5 47 gxh5 gxh5 48 ♗e1 ♔g6 49 ♗g3 ♔f5 50 c5 bxc5 51 bxc5 dxc5 52 ♗xc7 c4 53 f4 ½-½, Ioseliani-Gaprindashvili, Tbilisi match 1980.

⇨ 5...0-0 6 0-0 ♖e8 7 d3 (if White wanted to restrain ...d5, then 7 ♖e1 would have been more accurate) 7...♗xc3 8 bxc3 d5 9 exd5 ♘xd5 10 ♘g5! (now play becomes very sharp) 10...h6 11 ♘e4 (after 11 ♘xf7 ♔xf7 12 ♕h5+ g6 13 ♕xh6 ♘f6 White has inadequate compensation) 11...f5! 12 c4! ♘f6 13 ♘c5 (13 ♘xf6+ ♕xf6 14 ♖b1 may be slightly better for White) 13...♕d6!? 14 ♗a3 e4! (threat ...♖e5) 15 dxe4 ♕xd1 16 ♖axd1 fxe4 (White's two bishops balance the weak queenside pawns) 17 ♖fe1 ♗f5 18 ♘xb7 (18 ♗b2 was safer) 18...♘e5 19 ♗b2 ♘f3+ 20 ♗xf3 exf3 21 ♖xe8+ ♖xe8 22 ♗xf6 gxf6 23 ♖d8 ♖xd8 24 ♘xd8 ♗xc2 25 ♘e6? (time-trouble starts to affect the play; this is a serious error allowing Black to create a passed pawn, whereas 25 ♘c6 would have been unclear) 25...♗d3 26 c5 ♗c4 27 ♘xc7 ♗xa2 28 c6 ♔f8 29 ♔f1? (29 ♘b5 a5 30 c7 ♗e6 31 ♘d4 ♗h3 32 ♘xf3 is good for Black, but a much better chance than the move played) 29...♗b3? (29...♗c4+! 30 ♔e1 ♔e7 31 ♔d2 ♔d8! 32 ♘a8 ♗d5 wins easily) 30 ♔e1 ♔e7 31 ♔d2 a5 32 ♔c3 ♗f7 33 ♘b5 ♗d5 34 ♘d4 ♔d6 35 ♘f5+ ♔xc6 36 ♘xh6 ♗e6 0-1 (time), Glek-I.Zaitsev, Moscow Open 1991. In *Informator* Zaitsev claims that Black is winning in the final position because of the line 37 g4 ♔d6 38 h4 ♔e5 39 g5 fxg5 40 hxg5 ♔d6, even though the continuation 41 g6 promoting the pawn is certainly not better for Black! In fact the final position is probably not winning for Black at all, for example 37 g4 ♔d6 38 h4 ♔e7 39 ♘f5+ ♗xf5 40 gxf5 ♔f7 is drawn because 41 ♔b3 ♔g7 42 ♔a4 ♔h6 43 ♔xa5 ♔h5 44 ♔b4 ♔xh4 45 ♔c4 ♔g4 46 ♔d3 ♔xf5 47 ♔e3 ♔g4 48 ♔e4 is a position of reciprocal zugzwang with Black to move, and is therefore a draw.

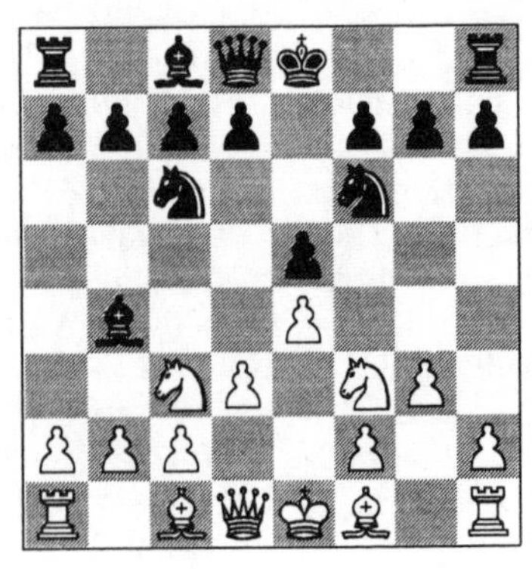

5...d5

Attempting to exploit White's move-order; after 5...d6 6 ♗g2 play transposes to Ioseliani-Gaprindashvili above, while 5...0-0 will almost certainly lead to Glek-Zaitsev.

6 exd5 ♕xd5

This is a kind of Ruy Lopez with colours reversed.

7 ♗g2 ♗g4 8 h3

8 0-0 ♗xc3 9 bxc3 e4 10 dxe4 ♕xd1 11 ♖xd1 ♘e5 is fine for Black.

8...♗xf3 9 ♗xf3 e4 10 ♗g2

10 dxe4 ♕xd1+ 11 ♔xd1 ♗xc3 12 bxc3 0-0-0+ 13 ♔e2 ♖he8 is slightly better for Black.

10...♗xc3+ 11 bxc3 0-0-0 12 0-0 ♖he8

White has two potentially powerful bishops, but Black has a large lead in development.

13 ♖b1 ♖e6 14 ♗e3 ♕f5 15 g4 ♕a5 16 c4 h6 17 ♕c1 exd3 18 cxd3 ♖xd3

The bishops provide some compensation for the pawn, but I doubt if it is sufficient.

19 ♕c2 ♕c3 20 ♕a4 ♘e4 21 ♖b3 ♕c2 22 ♕a3 ♖dd6?

Kremenietsky gives 22...♖xb3 23 axb3 a5 as slightly better for Black.

23 ♗xa7 ♕xc4 24 ♗e3 ♕a6 25 ♕b2 ♘a5 26 ♖b4 ♘f6 27 ♖b1

The threats start to become dangerous.

27...b6 28 ♖c1 ♘d5 29 ♗xd5 ♖xd5 30 ♗xb6

Why not 30 ♕xg7 ♘c6 31 ♕xf7 winning material?

30...♘c6 31 ♖b3 ♖ed6

31...cxb6 32 ♖xb6 gives White a dangerous attack after 32...♕a8 33 ♕xg7 or 32...♕a4 33 ♖b8+ ♔d7 34 ♕b7+ ♔d6 35 ♖d8+.

32 ♗e3 ♖d1+ 33 ♔h2 ♕f1 34 ♖xd1 ♖xd1 35 ♔g3 ♕g1+

35...g5 was probably better, when 36 f3 is unclear.

36 ♔h4

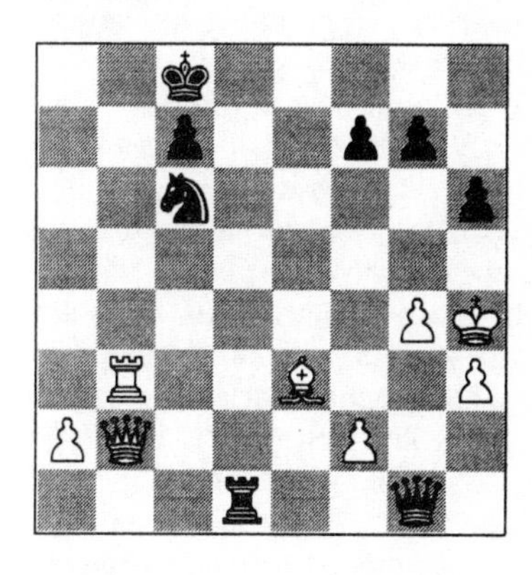

36...f6

36...g5+ 37 ♔h5 ♕g2!? is a tougher defence.

37 ♕c2! ♘e7 38 ♕e4

Surprisingly Black's king is more exposed than White's.

38...♔d7 39 ♖d3+ ♖xd3 40 ♕xd3+ ♔e8 41 ♗c5 ♕c1 42 ♕e3 ♕xe3 43 fxe3

The outside passed a-pawn and White's active king prove too much for Black.

43...g6 44 ♗d4 f5 45 a4 ♔d7? 46 ♗c5 fxg4 47 ♗xe7 1-0

After 47...gxh3 48 ♔xh3 ♔xe7 49 a5 ♔d7 50 a6 ♔c8 51 e4 c5 52 e5 c4 53 e6 c3 54 e7 ♔d7 55 a7 White will promote with check.

The two main replies to 4 ♗b5 are 4...♘d4 and 4...♗b4, but there are other playable moves. 4...♗c5 is a reasonable choice, when White has a number of possibilities. He can play positionally by continuing with d3, either before or after exchanging on c6, or he can head for tactics based on ♘xe5, either immediately or after both sides castle.

The first plan is probably objectively weaker, but it leads to positions like those in the Delayed Exchange Variation of the Ruy Lopez, and White players who like the long-term chances associated with such positions may prefer it to the more tactical variations based on ♘xe5. The first plan is covered in game 22 and the second in game 23. Other Black fourth moves are much less common. 4...a6 is possible, but current theory suggests that White can retain at least a slight plus. This is game 24. 4...d6 leads to a type of Ruy Lopez after 5 d4, so we do not consider it in this book.

Game 22

Psakhis-Barua
Calcutta 1988

1 e4 e5 2 ♘f3 ♘f6 3 ♘c3 ♘c6 4 ♗b5 ♗c5

⇨ 4...♗e7 is a rare alternative. After the obvious reply 5 d4 play is similar to the Steinitz variation of the Ruy Lopez, so we content ourselves with a single example: 4...♗e7 5 d4 exd4 6 ♘xd4 0-0 7 0-0 ♘xd4 8 ♕xd4 d6 9 ♗g5 ♗e6 10 ♖ad1 a6 11 ♗e2 ♘d7 12 ♗c1 f5 (Black makes a bid for activity, but he has to be careful because this does weaken the kingside) 13 ♘d5 fxe4 14 ♗c4 ♔h8 15 ♕xe4 ♗xd5 16 ♗xd5 c6 (here or next move Black should exchange the white-squared bishop) 17 ♗e6 d5?! 18 ♕g4 ♘f6 19 ♕h3 ♗c5 20 ♗f5 ♕c7 21 g4?! (over-aggressive; the simple 21 ♗g5 would have been slightly better for White) 21...g6 22 ♗xg6 ♖g8! (22...♘xg4 23 ♕xg4 hxg6 24 ♖d3 is good for White) 23 ♗f5 ♘xg4 24 ♔h1 (24 ♗xg4 ♕g7) 24...♘xf2+?? (24...♕g7 is unclear) 25 ♖xf2 ♗xf2 26 ♗f4 (26...♕g7 27 ♗e5) 1-0, Janowski-Burn, Ostend 1905.

5 ♗xc6

⇨ 5 d3 d6 6 ♗e3 ♗b6 7 ♘d5 ♗xe3 8 fxe3 0-0 9 ♘c3 (White's ineffective opening has allowed Black to equalise, but he is gradually outplayed) 9...♘e7 10 ♕d2 ♘g6 11 0-0 ♗d7 12 ♗c4 ♗e6 13 ♗b3 ♗xb3 14 axb3 c6 15 ♔h1 a6 16 ♘g1 d5 17 exd5 ♘xd5 18 e4 ♘df4 19 ♘ge2 f6 20 ♘g3 ♘h4 21 ♖f2 ♕d7 22 ♘f1 ♘e6 23 ♘e3 ♘d4 24 ♘a4 ♖ae8 25 ♖af1 ♖f7 26

♘c5 ♕c7 27 b4 ♕b6 28 ♕c3 ♘b5 29 ♕b3 ♘d6 30 ♕a3 ♘g6 31 c3 ♘f4 32 ♖f3 ♘e6 33 ♘b3 ♕d8 34 ♕a2 ♕b6 35 ♖d1 ♖ee7 36 ♘a5 ♕c7 37 ♖ff1 ♔h8 38 ♘b3 ♕b6 39 ♖fe1 ♔g8 40 ♘f5 ♖d7 41 d4 exd4 42 ♘bxd4 ♘f8 43 e5 fxe5 44 ♘xd6 ♖xd6 45 ♘f3 ♖xd1 46 ♖xd1 ♕e3 47 ♖f1 ♕d3 48 ♕xf7+ 1-0, Wahls-Wegner, Hamburg (SKA) 1991.

The advantage of the immediate ♗xc6 is that taking back with the b-pawn is dubious (because of ♘xe5), so White reaches an Exchange Ruy Lopez structure by force.

5...dxc6 6 d3

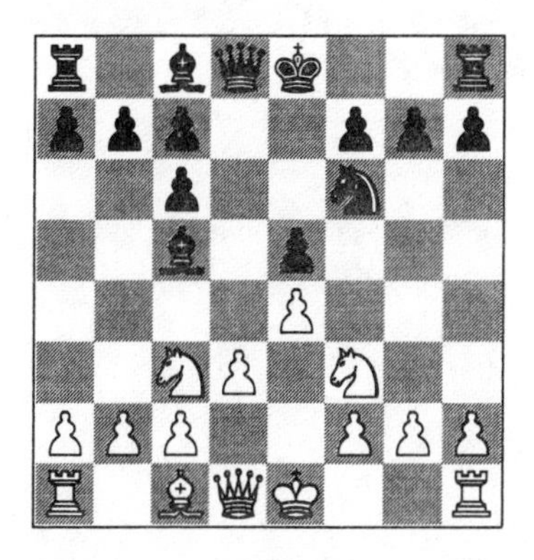

White's modest plan resembles the line 1 e4 e5 2 ♘f3 ♘c6 3 ♗b5 a6 4 ♗a4 ♘f6 5 ♗xc6 dxc6 in the Ruy Lopez. Perhaps the only real difference is that here Black's bishop is already committed to c5, which may not be the best square. However, this is probably not enough to seriously tip the balance in White's favour.

6...0-0

This may be a slight inaccuracy as it gives White a clear target to aim at if he decides to castle queenside.

⇨ 6...♗g4 7 h3 ♗h5 8 ♗e3 ♕e7 9 ♗xc5 ♕xc5 10 ♕e2 ♘d7 11 g4 ♗g6 12 0-0-0 ♘f8 13 h4 (if White wants to play for the advantage he has to try 13 d4 exd4 14 ♘xd4 0-0-0 15 ♘f5) 13...h5 14 ♕e3 ♕xe3+ 15 fxe3 ♘d7 16 g5 0-0 17 ♖hg1 ♖fe8 18 ♘e2 ½-½, Hug-An.Fernandes, Thessaloniki Ol. 1988.

7 h3

For the moment White would like to leave open the option of castling on either side, hence the semi-waiting move 7 h3. 7 ♕e2 is another move with the same idea. In *Informator* Psakhis gives 7 ♘xe5? ♕d4 as winning for Black, but in fact 8 ♗e3 ♕xe5 9 d4 ♕e7 10 dxc5 ♘xe4 is equal.

7...♖e8 8 ♘e2 ♗f8 9 g4!?

White reveals that he intends to castle queenside. His slow-motion attack is more dangerous than it might appear, because Black's lack of pawn breaks makes it hard to generate counterplay. However, there was no need for White to commit himself so soon and 9 ♗g5 was sounder.

9...h5

This offends against general principles but it is not necessarily bad! Psakhis suggests that the plan of ...♘d7 followed by ...c5 and ...♘b8-c6-d4 was the best way of activating Black's pieces, even though this idea is very slow.

10 ♗g5

White offers a pawn to accelerate his attack. After 10...hxg4 11 hxg4 ♗xg4 12 ♘g3 followed by ♖h4 Black faces dangerous threats with no real counterplay in sight.

10...♕d6!? 11 ♘g3 hxg4 12 hxg4 ♘xg4

Taking with the knight is much better because White cannot immediately drive the knight away.

13 ♕e2 a5?

A strange move. The idea is that if White plays 14 0-0-0, then ...a4-a3 will create counterplay, but it allows White to gain time on the kingside. Instead 13...♕g6! would have both prevented ♘h4 and prepared a counterattack against f2 by ...♗c5, and then White would have had more problems developing his attack.

14 ♘h4 g6 15 f3 ♘f6 16 0-0-0 ♗g7 17 ♖dg1

The storm clouds gather; indeed there is an immediate threat of 18 ♘hf5 gxf5 19 ♗xf6 ♕xf6 20 ♘h5.

17...♔f8 18 ♕d2! ♘g8 19 ♘e2!

Now the idea is 20 f4 exf4 21 ♘xf4 lining up for a sacrifice on g6.

19...♕b4 20 c3 ♕a4 21 ♔b1 ♗e6 22 ♘c1

Black has sent his queen to the far edge of the board and now faces a new threat of 23 f4 exf4 24 ♕xf4 when g6 collapses.

22...♖ed8?! 23 ♗xd8 ♖xd8

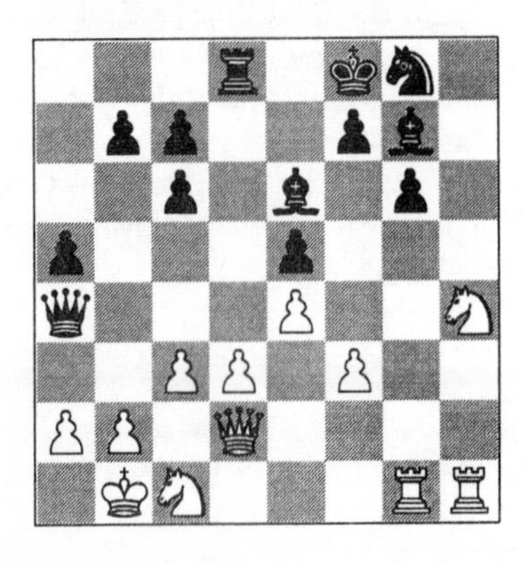

24 ♘xg6+! (not 24 f4? ♕xe4!) **24...fxg6 25 ♖xg6 ♗f6** (there is no real defence, for example 25...♗f7 26 ♖xg7) **26 ♖hh6! ♔e7** (or 26...♔f7 27 ♕g2 followed by ♖xf6+) **27 ♖h7+ ♗f7 28 ♕h2 ♕b5 29 ♕h5** (Black is helpless against the threats of 30 ♖xg8 and 30 ♖xf6) **1-0**

Game 23

Short-Adams
Final, English Ch. 1991

1 e4 e5 2 ♘f3 ♘c6 3 ♘c3 ♘f6 4 ♗b5 ♗c5

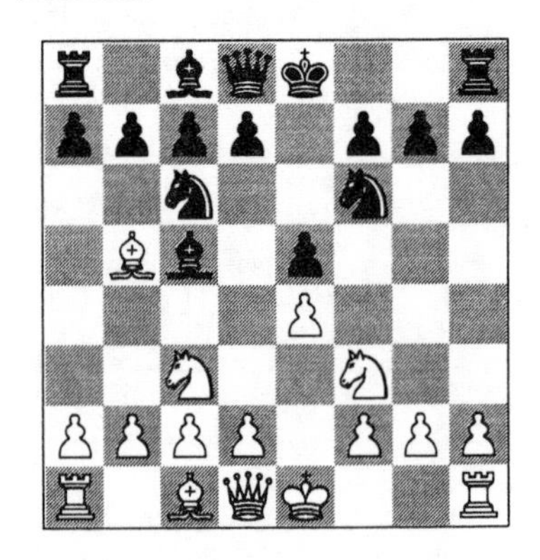

5 0-0

The alternative is to play ♘xe5 immediately. After 5 ♘xe5 ♘xe5 6 d4 ♗d6 7 f4 Black can play:

➪ 7...♗b4 8 fxe5 ♘xe4 9 ♕f3 (the move-order 9 0-0 ♘xc3 10 ♕f3 is also possible) 9...♘xc3 10 0-0 0-0 (10...♘e2+ 11 ♗xe2 0-0 12 ♗c4 d6 13 ♕b3 ♗a5 14 ♖xf7 ♖xf7 15 ♗xf7+ ♔h8 16 ♗f4 ♗b6 17 c3 dxe5 18 ♗xe5 was winning for White in the game Haskamp-H.Bastian, Bundesliga 1990/1) 11 bxc3 ♗e7 12 ♗c4 ♕e8 13 ♗f4 d6 14 ♖ae1 (with a massive lead in development for White) 14...♕d8 15 ♕e4 dxe5 16 ♗xe5 ♗h4 17 ♗xc7! (a nice combination) 17...♕xc7 18 ♖xf7 ♗d7 19 ♖xf8+ ♔xf8 20 ♕d5 (unfortunately White misses the instantly decisive 20 ♕f3+ ♗f6 21 ♕d5, when Black has to give up his queen, although it makes no difference to the final result) 20...♗e6 21 ♖f1+ ♔g8 22 ♕xe6+ ♔h8 23 ♖f7 ♕d8 24 g3 ♗f6 25 ♗d3 ♕g8 26 ♕f5 b5 27 ♖b7 ♖f8 28 ♕xb5 ♕e6 29 ♔g2 ♕e1 30 ♕h5 ♕d2+ 31 ♔h3 ♕h6 32 ♕xh6 gxh6 33 ♖xh7+ ♔g8 34 ♖xa7 ♖c8 35 ♖a3 ♔f7 36 ♖b3 ♖a8 37 ♗c4+ ♔g6 38 ♖b6 ♔g5 39 ♖c6 ♖b8 40 ♗b3 ♔f5 41 a4 ♖a8 42 ♖c5+ ♔g6 43 a5 h5 44 ♗d5 ♖a7 45 ♗e4+ ♔h6 46 ♖c6 ♔g5 47 a6 1-0, Almasi-S.Farago, Budapest Festival 1991.

⇨ 7...♘g6 8 e5 c6 9 ♗c4 (9 ♗a4 has been suggested as an improvement) 9...♗c7 10 exf6 ♕xf6 11 0-0 d5 12 ♗xd5 (it is not surprising that White chose this sacrifice, because after 12 ♗e2 Black has a clear advantage due to the weakening move f4, which also blocks in the c1 bishop) 12...cxd5 13 ♘xd5 ♕d6 14 ♕e2+ ♘e7 15 ♖e1 ♗d8? (15...♗e6 appears better, since 16 ♘xe7 ♔xe7 17 f5 loses to 17...♕xh2+ 18 ♔f1 ♕h1+ 19 ♔f2 ♕h4+ 20 ♔f1 ♗g3) 16 c4 f6 17 ♗d2 a5 18 ♕h5+ g6 19 c5 ♕a6 20 ♕h6 ♗e6 21 ♘xf6+?! (after 21 ♕g7 ♗xd5 22 ♕xh8+ ♔d7 23 ♕xh7 White has a material advantage but the d5 bishop is extremely powerful; the position is unclear) 21...♔f7 22 ♘e4 ♘f5 23 ♕h3 ♗e7 24 ♗c3 ♗d5 25 g4 ♘h4 26 ♘d6+ ♔f8 27 ♖xe7 ♘f3+ 28 ♕xf3 ♗xf3 29 ♖f7+ ♔g8 30 d5 ♗xd5 31 ♖g7+ ♔f8 32 ♖e1 ♕c6 33 b4 ♖d8 34 ♗d4 ♖xd6 35 cxd6 ♗h1 0-1, Janowski-Em.Lasker, Cambridge Springs 1904.

⇨ 7...♘c6 8 e5 ♗b4 9 d5 (*ECO* gives 9 exf6 ♕xf6 10 d5 ♗xc3+ 11 bxc3 ♕xc3+ 12 ♗d2 ♕c5 as good for Black, which seems correct) 9...♘e4 10 ♕d3 ♘xc3 11 bxc3 ♗e7 12 dxc6 dxc6 with equality is *ECO's* line, but 10...f5! is probably much better since both 11 exf6 ♘xc3 12 bxc3 (12 fxg7 ♘xb5+) 12...♕xf6 13 ♗b2 ♘e7 and 11 dxc6 dxc6 lead to a decisive gain of material for Black.

5...0-0 6 ♘xe5

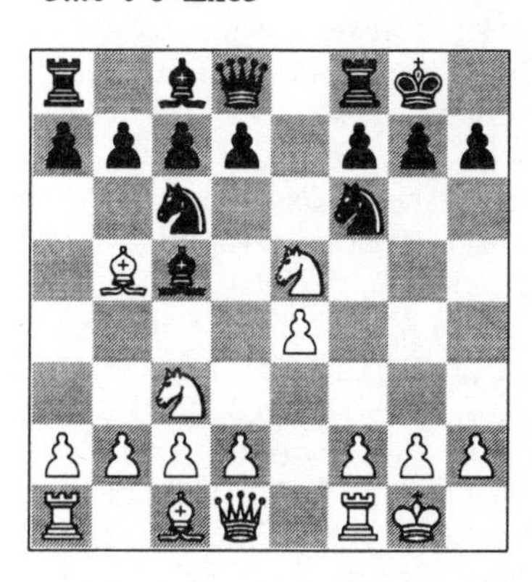

6...♘xe5

The pawn sacrifice 6...♖e8 was popular in the last century and it appears occasionally even today:

⇨ 7 ♘xc6 (this was played in one of Morphy's most famous games) 7...dxc6 8 ♗c4 b5 9 ♗e2 ♘xe4 10 ♘xe4 ♖xe4 11 ♗f3 ♖e6 12 c3? (an incredibly bad move) 12...♕d3 13 b4 ♗b6 14 a4 bxa4 15 ♕xa4 ♗d7 16 ♖a2 ♖ae8 17 ♕a6 ♕xf3! (obvious but still attractive) 18 gxf3 ♖g6+ 19 ♔h1 ♗h3 20 ♖d1 (20 ♕d3 f5 21 ♕c4+ ♔f8 doesn't help) 20...♗g2+ 21 ♔g1 ♗xf3+ 22 ♔f1 ♗g2+ 23 ♔g1 ♗h3+ (here Morphy overlooked a mate in four by 23...♗e4+ 24 ♔f1 ♗f5, but it doesn't change the result) 24 ♔h1 ♗xf2 25 ♕f1 ♗xf1 26 ♖xf1 ♖e2 27 ♖a1 ♖h6 28 d4 ♗e3 0-1, Paulsen-Morphy, New York 1857.

➪ 7 ♘f3 (the best reply, ensuring some advantage for White) 7...♘xe4 8 d4 ♘xc3 9 bxc3 ♗e7 10 d5 (10 ♖e1 ♗f6 11 ♗g5 ♖xe1+ 12 ♕xe1 ♗xg5 13 ♘xg5 h6 14 ♘f3 d6 15 ♕e4 d5 16 ♕e3 ♗f5 was slightly better for White in Wagman-B.Finegold, Steinweg 1991, but Maroczy's line appears stronger) 10...♘b8 11 ♗f4 a6 12 ♗a4 ♗f6 13 d6 c6 14 ♗b3 (this looks like a game from a simultaneous display and it is hard to imagine that the great Pillsbury was Black) 14...b5 15 ♕d2 ♗b7 16 ♘g5 ♖f8 17 ♘e4 a5 18 a3 ♘a6 19 ♖ae1 c5 20 ♗d5 ♗xd5 21 ♕xd5 b4 22 ♖e3 ♗xc3 23 ♖xc3! bxc3 24 ♗g5 (with ♘f6+ to come) 24...♘c7 25 ♕c4 ♕e8 26 dxc7 ♕e5 27 ♖d1 ♖fe8 28 ♖xd7 ♔h8 29 ♕xf7 ♕xg5 30 f4 ♕g4 31 h3 ♕xd7 32 ♕xd7 ♖xe4 33 c8♕+ 1-0, Maroczy-Pillsbury, Nürnberg 1896.

7 d4 ♗d6

➪ 7...♗b4 (a weak alternative) 8 dxe5 ♗xc3 9 bxc3 ♘xe4 10 ♕d4 ♘g5 (10...d5 11 ♗a3) 11 ♗a3 ♖e8 12 ♖ad1 (with a crushing lead in development) 12...c6 13 ♗d3 d5 (desperation, but otherwise 14 ♗d6) 14 exd6 ♗d7 15 f4 ♘e6 16 ♕f2 ♕b6 17 f5 ♕xf2+ 18 ♖xf2 ♘g5 19 ♖f4 f6 20 c4 ♘f7 21 c5 b5 22 ♗b2 ♘e5 23 ♗e4 ♔f7 24 ♗d4 g5 25 fxg6+ hxg6 26 ♖df1 f5 27 g4 ♘c4 28 ♖1f2 ♖g8 29 gxf5 gxf5+ 30 ♔f1 ♖g5 31 h4 ♖g3 32 ♗xf5 ♗xf5 33 ♖xf5+ ♔e6 34 ♖g5 ♖xg5 35 hxg5 ♖g8 36 ♖e2+ ♔d5 37 ♗f6 ♘a5 38 d7 ♘b7 39 ♖e8 ♖g6 40 ♖b8 1-0, Najdorf-Pilnik, New York 1948.

8 f4 ♘c6 9 e5

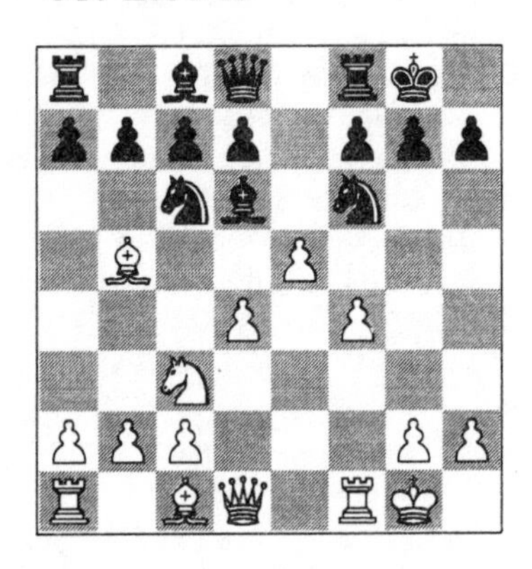

9...a6

It isn't clear who benefits from the interpolation of ...a6 and ♗e2. The alternative is 9...♗e7 10 d5 and now:

➪ 10...♘b8 (very passive) 11 d6 (even 11 exf6 ♗xf6 12 ♘e4 should be slightly better for White, but the move played is much stronger) 11...cxd6 12 exf6 ♗xf6 13 ♘d5 ♘c6 14 c3 b6 15 ♖f3 (the simple 15 ♗d3 ♗b7 16 ♗e3 also looks good for White) 15...♗b7 16 ♖d3 ♖e8 17 ♗e3 ♗e7 18 ♗f2 ♗f8 19 ♕g4 ♖e6 20 ♗h4 ♕c8 21 ♘f6+?! (White throws away part of his advantage by premature aggression; 21 ♖ad1 is very strong) 21...♔h8 22 ♖g3 ♘e7 23 ♘xd7 ♖g6 24 ♕e2 ♘f5 25 ♖xg6 hxg6 26 ♗f2 d5 27 ♘xf8 ♕xf8 28 ♖e1 ♔g8 29 ♕e8? (a complete misjudgment; White should keep the queens on) 29...♖xe8 30 ♖xe8 ♕xe8 31 ♗xe8 ♘d6 32 ♗d7 ♔f8 33 ♗g4 ♔e7 34 ♔f1 ♗a6+ 35 ♔e1 ♗d3 36 ♗d4 f6 37 b3 ♗e4 38 g3 ♗b1 39 ♔d2 ♗f5 40 ♗e2 ♘e4+ 41 ♔c1 ♔d6 42 ♔b2 ♘c5 43 b4 ♘e6 44 ♗f2 g5 45 fxg5 ♘xg5 46 a4 ♘f7 ½-½, Marco-Showalter, Nürnberg 1896.

⇨ 10...♘b4 11 d6?! (this is still an interesting idea but Black is much better off with the knight on b4) 11...cxd6 12 exf6 ♕b6+ 13 ♔h1 ♗xf6 14 ♗a4 d5 15 ♘xd5 ♘xd5 16 ♕xd5 ♗xb2 (16...d6 is also possible, and if White replies 17 f5 then Black can take on b2) 17 ♖b1 (after 17 ♗xb2 ♕xb2 18 ♖ae1 ♕f6 it is hard to see how White's attack may be continued) 17...♕d4 18 ♕xd4 ♗xd4 19 ♗a3 ♖d8 20 ♖bd1 ♗f6 21 ♖fe1 a6? (the simple 21...d5 22 ♖xd5 ♗e6 is slightly better for Black) 22 ♗b3 g6 23 ♗d6 ♔g7 24 g4 h6 25 ♖e2 (now Black has severe problems freeing herself) 25...♖g8 26 g5 hxg5 27 fxg5 ♗xg5 28 ♖f1 f5 29 ♗xg8 ♔xg8 30 ♖g2 ♗e3, Dekic-Jo.Chaves, Manila Women's Ol. 1992, and now 31 ♖xf5 would have been easily winning for White. In the game White eventually won in 93 moves.

⇨ 10...♘b4 11 exf6 ♗xf6 12 a3 ♗xc3 13 bxc3 ♘xd5 14 ♕xd5 c6 15 ♕d3 cxb5 16 f5 f6!? (a new idea; 16...♖e8 17 f6 forces further black-squared weaknesses and gives White good compensation for the pawn) 17 a4 (the idea is to switch the queen's rook into the attack; 17 ♗e3 was a reasonable alternative, simply depositing the bishop on the active square d4) 17...bxa4 18 ♖xa4 d5 19 ♖h4? (looking for a non-existent mate; the simple 19 ♖d4 would have regained the pawn with a slight advantage because the c8 bishop cannot be easily developed) 19...♖e8! 20 ♕d1 (a further step along a disastrous path) 20...♖e5 21 ♕h5 ♕b6+ 22 ♔h1 ♗xf5 (end of game) 23 ♗f4 ♕f2 24 ♕d1 ♕xh4 25 ♗xe5 fxe5 26 ♖xf5 ♕e4 27 ♖f1 ♖f8 28 ♖xf8+ ♔xf8 29 h3 ♔g8 30 ♕b1 b6 31 ♕a2 a5 32 ♕b3 h6 33 ♕xb6 a4 0-1, Nunn-J.M.Hodgson, English Ch. 1991.

10 ♗e2

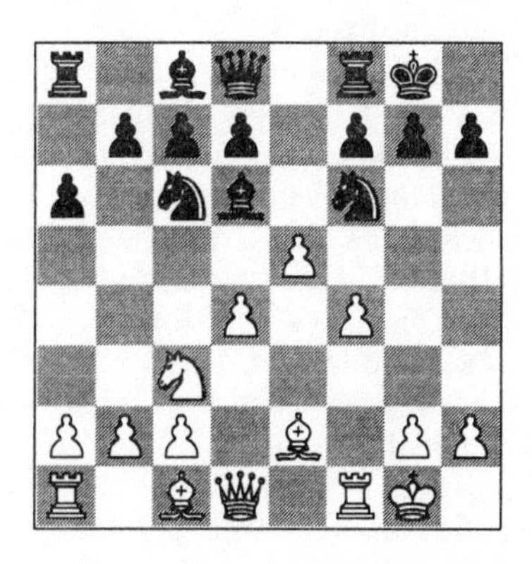

10...♗b4

⇨ 10...♗e7 (in the play-off Adams preferred this to his earlier choice of 10...♗b4, but the consequences were even worse) 11 d5 ♘xd5 12 ♘xd5 d6 13 ♘xe7+ ♕xe7 14 exd6 cxd6 15 f5 f6 (Black has to stop f6) 16 ♗c4+ ♔h8 17 ♗d2 d5 18 ♗d3 ♘e5 19 ♖f4! (threatening ♗b4 and at the same time making a move towards an attack starting with ♕h5) 19...♗d7? (overlooking the main threat) 20 ♗b4 ♕d8 21 ♗xf8 ♕b6+ 22 ♔h1 ♖xf8 23 b3 g5 24 fxg6 hxg6 25 ♖h4+ ♔g7 26 ♕d2 ♘g4 27 ♖f1 d4 28 ♖f4 f5 29 h3 ♕d8 30 ♖fxg4 fxg4 31 ♕h6+ ♔f6 32 ♕xg6+ ♔e5 33 ♖h5+ ♔f4 34 ♔h2 ♔e3 35 ♕h6+ ♖f4 36 ♖e5+ ♔d2 37 ♕xf4+ ♔c3 38 ♖c5+ ♔b2 39 ♕xd4+ ♔xa2 40 ♖d5 ♕c7+ 41 ♔g1 1-0, Short-Adams, English Ch. Play-Off (15 minute game) 1991.

11 d5 ♗c5+ 12 ♔h1 ♘xd5 13 ♘xd5

Not necessarily best. After 13 ♕xd5 d6 14 f5! ♘xe5 15 ♘e4 White has an extremely dangerous attack for the sacrificed pawn.

13...d6 14 ♗d3

White's play in this game is typical Short. He makes no attempt to launch an immediate attack, but contents himself with a liquidation in which he has long-term chances due to Black's more exposed king.

14...dxe5

14...♗e6 15 ♘c3 dxe5 16 f5 ♗d7 17 ♘e4 gives White a very dangerous initiative.

15 fxe5 ♘xe5

15...♗e6 16 ♘f6+! gxf6 17 ♗xh7+ is a winning attack for White.

16 ♗xh7+ ♔xh7 17 ♕h5+ ♔g8 18 ♕xe5

Threat 19 ♘f6+.

18...♗d6

It is surprisingly hard to shift the knight from d5, for example 18...♕d6 19 ♕h5 (Short suggests 19 ♕xd6 ♗xd6 20 ♗f4 with an endgame edge for White) 19...♗e6 20 ♘f6+ gxf6 21 ♗h6 ♕e5 22 ♕h4 ♖fd8 23 ♖f3 with a very dangerous attack, so 18...♕d6 19 ♕h5 ♗g4 20 ♕xg4 ♕xd5 21 ♗h6 ♕d4 is probably best, although White can keep a small plus by 22 ♕g5 threatening ♗xg7.

19 ♕h5 f6

To prevent a deadly ♘f6+, but this further exposes Black's king.

20 ♗f4 ♗e6 21 ♖ad1 ♗f7 22 ♕f3 ♗xf4 23 ♘xf4 ♕c8 24 ♘d5 ♗xd5 25 ♕xd5+ ♖f7 26 ♖d3 (heading for the h-file) **26...c6 27 ♕h5 ♖e7 28 ♖h3 ♕f8 29 ♕h7+** (there is no immediate win, but White has time to build up his attack) **29...♔f7 30 ♖g3 ♔e8?!** (it is better to play 30...♖d8 or 30...♖ae8, since in neither case does 31 ♖xf6+ ♔xf6 32 ♕g6+ ♔e5 lead to mate; perhaps 31 h4 is the best reply, giving White's king some air and threatening 32 ♕g6+) **31 ♖d1!** (taking the open file; Black cannot reply 31...♖d8 because of 32 ♕h5+ ♕f7 33 ♕h8+) **31...g5?!** (this is a forced loss, so 31...♔f7 was the last chance)

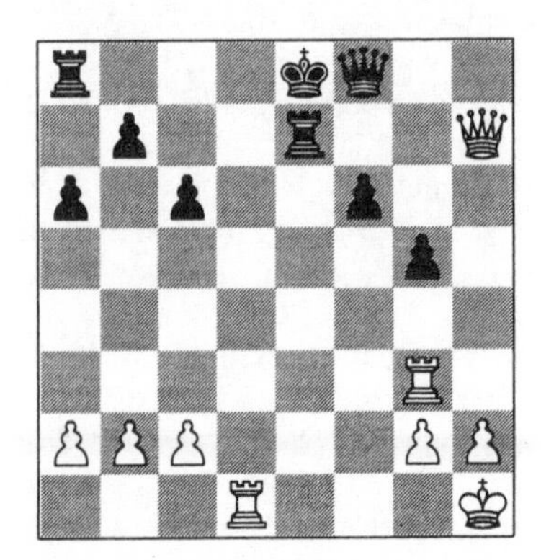

32 ♕h5+ (missing the instantly crushing 32 ♖e3!, but the move played is sufficient for victory) **32...♕f7 33 ♕h8+ ♕f8 34 ♕h5+ ♕f7 35 ♕h8+ ♕f8 36 ♖h3! ♖g7 37 ♖e3+** (37...♔f7 38 ♖d7+ ♔g6 39 ♖xg7+ wins the a8 rook, while 37...♖e7 38 ♖xe7+ ♔xe7 39 ♕h8+ ♕f7 40 ♖d7+ wins the queen) **1-0**

Game 24

Znosko-Borovsky–Rubinstein
Ostend B 1907

1 e4 e5 2 ♘f3 ♘c6 3 ♘c3 ♘f6 4 ♗b5 a6

This move entails a loss of time and White should be able to gain the advantage, but it is not as easy as one might expect. There are two reasonable plans. White can either continue with ♗xc6 and d3, as in Game 22 above with an extra tempo, or he can open the position with ♗xc6 and ♘xe5, hoping to exploit Black's centralised king. Both plans are promising.

5 ♗xc6 dxc6

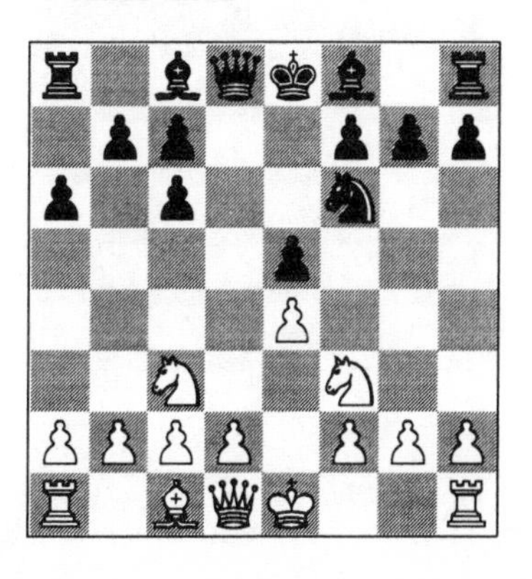

6 ♘xe5

➪ 6 0-0 (Capablanca prefers the positional continuation; a more modern interpretation of this plan would be 6 d3, as in Psakhis-Barua above, keeping open the option of castling queenside) 6...♗g4 7 h3 ♗h5 8 ♕e2 ♗d6 9 d3 ♕e7 10 ♘d1!? 0-0-0 11 ♘e3 ♗g6 12 ♘h4 (Black will eventually be forced to take a knight landing on f5, forfeiting the two bishops) 12...♖hg8 13 ♘ef5 ♕e6 14 f4 ♗xf5 15 ♘xf5 (now Black has no compensation for his inferior pawn structure) 15...exf4 16 ♗xf4 ♗c5+ 17 ♗e3 ♗f8 18 ♕f2 (Black has a wretched position and it is no surprise that White eventually grinds his opponent down) 18...♖d7 19 ♗c5 ♗xc5 20 ♕xc5 ♔b8 21 ♖f2 ♘e8 22 ♖af1 f6 23 b3 ♘d6 24 ♖f4 ♘xf5 25 ♕xf5 ♕xf5 26 ♖xf5 ♖e8 27 g4 b6 28 b4 ♔b7 29 ♔f2 b5 30 a4 ♖d4 31 ♖b1 ♖e5 32 ♔e3 ♖d7 33 a5 ♖e6 34 ♖bf1 ♖de7 35 g5 fxg5 36 ♖xg5 ♖h6 37 ♖g3 ♖he6 38 h4 g6 39 ♖g5 h6 40 ♖g4 ♖g7 41 d4 ♔b8 42 ♖f8+ ♔b7 43 e5 g5 44 ♔e4 ♖ee7 45 hxg5 hxg5 46 ♖f5 ♔c8 47 ♖gxg5 ♖h7 48 ♖h5 ♔d7 49 ♖xh7 ♖xh7 50 ♖f8 ♖h4+ 51 ♔d3 ♖h3+ 52 ♔d2 c5 53 bxc5 ♖a3 54 d5 1-0, Capablanca-Janowski, New York 1913.

6...♘xe4 7 ♘xe4 ♕d4 8 0-0 ♕xe5 9 ♖e1 ♗e6 10 d4 ♕f5

After 10...♕d5 White can either head for a better ending by 11 ♘g5 0-0-0 12 ♘xe6 fxe6 13 ♕g4 ♕xd4 14 ♕xe6+ ♕d7 15 ♕xd7+ ♖xd7 16 ♖e8+ ♖d8 17 ♖xd8+ ♔xd8 18 b3 ♗c5 19 ♗b2 ♖f8 20 ♖d1+ ♔c8 21 ♖d2, as in Réti-Spielmann, Vienna 1914, or play for an attack by 11

♗g5 ♔d7 12 ♖c1!? intending c4. Only a very brave player would meet this by taking the a-pawn!

11 ♗g5

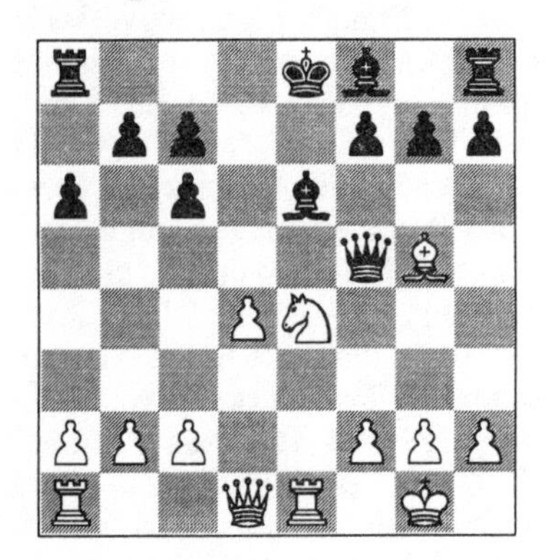

11...♗d6

This is normally given a question mark, but the real error only comes next move. The usual line is 11...h6 12 ♕d3 (this move, threatening ♘d6+, has been preferred in practice, but there is an argument for the immediate 12 ♗h4, when 12...♔d7 13 ♘c5+ is good for White) and now:

⇨ 12...♔d7 13 ♗h4 ♖e8 14 ♖e3 (I prefer 14 ♗g3, when 14...♗d6 loses to 15 ♗xd6 cxd6 16 ♕g3, while 14...♗e7 15 c4 gives White attacking chances) 14...♗d6 15 ♖ae1 ♕b5 16 ♘xd6 cxd6?! (Black should have taken the chance to exchange queens) 17 ♕a3 a5 18 c3 (now Black has to retreat in order to meet the threat of ♗g3) 18...♕b6 19 ♗g3 ♕c7 20 c4 (20 b3 would have been slightly better for White; the move played leads to a clear draw) 20...♗xc4 21 ♖xe8 ♖xe8 22 ♖xe8 ♔xe8 23 ♗xd6 ♕d7 24 ♕e3+ ♗e6 25 ♗c5 f6 26 a3 ♔f7 27 ♕g3 ♗d5 28 h3 ♕e6 29 f3 ♕e3+ 30 ♕f2 ♕b3 31 ♔h2 b6 32 ♗d6 ♗e6 33 ♕d2 h5 34 ♗c7 a4 35 ♗g3 b5 36 ♗e1 ♗f5 37 ♕f2 ♕c2 38 ♕xc2 ♗xc2 39 ♔g1 ♔e6 40 ♔f2 ♔d5 41 ♔e3 ♔c4 42 g3 ♗d3 43 ♗c3 ♗f1 44 h4 ♗h3 ½-½, Schlechter-Tarrasch, Hastings 1895.

⇨ 12...♕h7 13 ♗h4 ♗d6 14 c4?! (14 ♕c3 is very unpleasant because 14...0-0 loses a pawn after 15 ♘xd6 cxd6 16 ♗e7) 14...♔f8? (why not 14...0-0?) 15 ♕b3 b5 16 ♘xd6 cxd6 17 ♕b4 ♕f5 18 ♕xd6+ ♔g8 19 ♖e5 ♕d3 20 d5?! (20 ♕xc6 is simple and strong; instead White gradually relinquishes his advantage) 20...cxd5 21 cxd5 ♔h7 22 ♗e7 ♗f5 23 ♖e3 ♕d4 24 ♕e5 ♕xe5 25 ♖xe5 ♔g6 26 ♗c5 ♖he8 27 ♖ae1 ♖xe5 28 ♖xe5 a5 (the winning chances have gone) 29 f3 ♖c8 30 d6 f6 31 ♖d5 ♗e6 32 d7 ♗xd7 33 ♗b6 ♖c1+ 34 ♔f2 ♖c2+ 35 ♔g3 ♗c6 36 ♖c5 ♖xc5 37 ♗xc5 a4 38 ♔f4 ♗d5 ½-½ V.Meier-Pirrot, Bundesliga 1989/90.

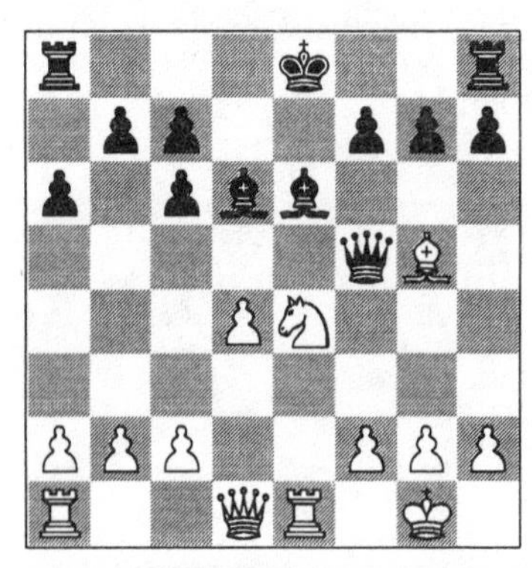

12 g4

This is probably less effective than the simple 12 ♕d2, when White has the same type of slight advantage as in the examples given in the note to Black's 11th move.

12...♕g6?

A serious error. After 12...♕d5 or 12...♕b5 White has no forcing continuation, and the weakening of his kingside resulting from the move g4 improves Black's long-term chances for counterplay.

13 f4!

Now Black is crushed, for example 13...h6 14 f5 ♗xh2+ 15 ♔h1! ♕h7 16 ♗h4 and Black loses material. The rest is a nightmare for Black.

15...f5 14 ♘xd6+ cxd6 15 d5 0-0 16 ♖xe6 ♕f7 17 ♕e2 fxg4 18 ♕xg4 cxd5 19 ♖ae1 ♖ac8 20 ♕g2 ♕f5 21 ♗h6 ♖c7 22 ♖e7 ♖f7 23 ♖e8+ ♖f8 24 ♖1e7 ♕f6 25 ♕xd5+ ♔h8 26 ♖xf8+ ♕xf8 27 ♖xc7 1-0

This chapter deals with one of the two main defences against 4 ♗b5, the dynamic continuation 4...♘d4. In game 25 we cover the innocuous White reply 5 ♘xd4. This is normally the prelude to an early draw offer, although there are occasional decisive results. The main line of game 25 shows that no matter how drawish the position, it is still possible to lose by playing badly.

These days the move 5 ♗a4 is by far the most common reply (for other moves see standard opening books). Black has three reasonable alternatives. The first is 5...♘xf3+ when 6 ♕xf3 probably gives White a slight advantage, but the interesting 6 gxf3!? is also possible. The second possibility is the pawn sacrifice 5...c6, a favourite with Hebden. At present no clearly promising antidote has emerged, although Chandler-Hebden is marginally better for White. These two lines are covered in game 26.

The main line is undoubtedly 5...♗c5 6 ♘xe5 0-0 7 ♘d3 ♗b6 8 e5 ♘e8. We deal with earlier deviations from this line in games 27 and 28. Game 27 covers the dubious line 6...♕e7, while game 28 analyses the White alternatives 7 d3 and 7 ♘d3 ♗b6 8 ♘f4. The new idea which has been largely responsible for the sudden surge in popularity of the Four Knights arises in the position after 8 e5 ♘e8. Instead of the old continuation 9 0-0 (see game 29), the new plan involves the manoeuvre 9 ♘d5 d6 10 ♘e3, which blocks the b6-f2 diagonal and clears the way for the move c3 expelling the d4 knight. If White can also succeed in moving the d3 knight then he can play d4 and complete his development. The sequence of moves ♘d5, ♘e3, 0-0, c3, ♘e1 and d4 represents White's dream plan. After 10 ♘e3 Black's best strategy is far from clear; he has tried 10...dxe5, 10...c6, 10...♕g5, 10...♕h4 and 10...♕e7. We deal with 10...dxe5 and 10...c6 in game 30 and the remaining possibilities in game 31.

Game 25

Van de Oudeweetering-Van der Wiel
Netherlands Team Ch. 1987

1 e4 e5 2 ♘f3 ♘c6 3 ♘c3 ♘f6 4 ♗b5 ♘d4 5 ♘xd4 exd4 6 e5 dxc3 7 exf6

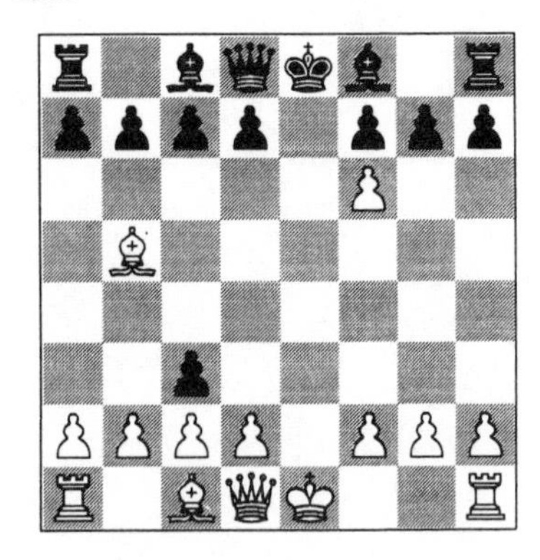

7...♕xf6

⇨ 7...cxd2+ (this is too greedy) 8 ♗xd2 ♕xf6 9 0-0 ♗e7 10 ♗c3 ♕g5 11 ♖e1 ♕xb5 (Black decides to accept the offer; after the alternative 11...0-0 White may continue 12 ♖e5

♕f6 13 ♗d3 g6 and now the tempting 14 ♖h5 ♕c6 15 ♖xh7 is dubious because of 15...♗f6!, but 14 ♕e2! was very good for White in Milev-Fuderer, Amsterdam Ol. 1954) 12 ♕g4 ♖g8 (12...d5 13 ♕xg7 ♖f8 14 ♖xe7+ ♔xe7 15 ♗f6+ ♔e8 16 ♖e1+ ♗e6 17 ♖xe6+ fxe6 18 ♕e7 mate)

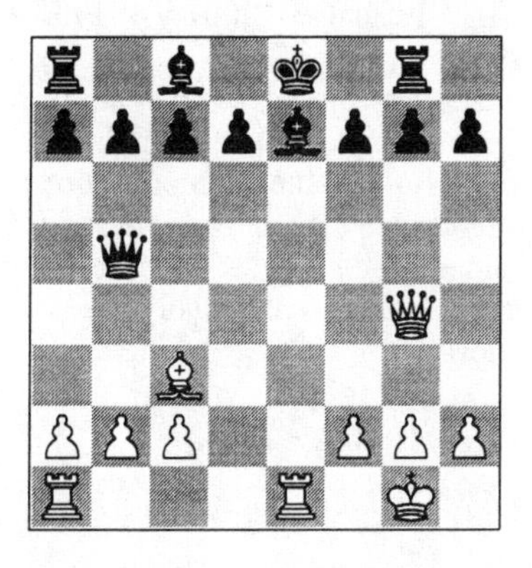

13 ♖xe7+! (not 13 ♗f6? d6! 14 ♖xe7+ ♔f8 and there is nothing clear) 13...♔xe7 14 ♕e4+ ♔d8 (14...♔f8 15 ♖e1 mates) 15 ♕h4+ f6 16 ♗xf6+ ♔e8 17 ♖e1+ ♔f7 (17...♔f8 18 ♗xg7+! ♔xg7 19 ♖e7+ ♔g6 20 ♕xh7+ mates in another five moves) 18 ♖e7+ ♔g6 19 ♗e5! d6 (after 19...♕e2 20 ♖xg7+! the reply 20...♖xg7 21 ♕f6+ leads to mate in three more moves, while 20...♔f5 21 ♕xh7+ ♔xe5 22 ♖e7+ results in decisive material gain) 20 ♕g3+ (the quickest win was by 20 ♕e4+ forcing mate in nine, but the method chosen by White is also adequate) 20...♔h5 21 ♕f3+ ♔h6 22 ♕f4+ g5 (22...♔h5 23 ♕f7+ is mate in a further six moves) 23 ♕f6+ ♖g6 24 ♖xh7+ ♔xh7 25 ♕h8 mate, Shipman-Weber, New York 1985.

8 dxc3 ♗c5

The normal line is 8...♕e5+, when 9 ♕e2 is usually followed by a few optional moves and a handshake. White can continue the game by 9 ♗e2, but objectively he has no advantage, for example 8...♕e5+ 9 ♗e2 ♗c5 10 0-0 0-0 11 ♗d3 and now:

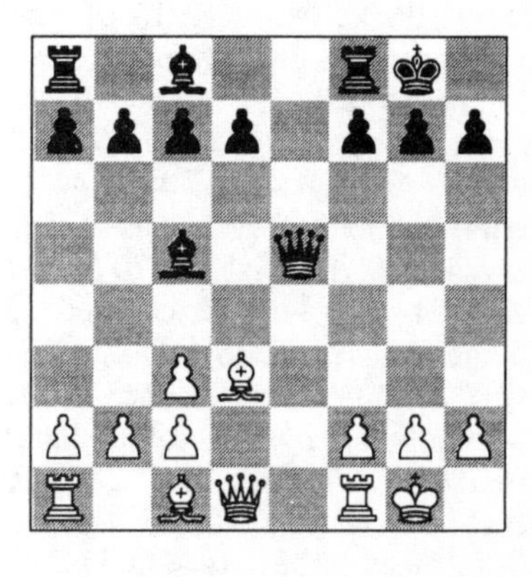

➪ 11...d5 (the most reliable defence) 12 ♕f3 ♗d6 13 g3 c6 14 ♗d2 ♕e6 15 ♕h5 ♕h3! (effectively forcing the draw) 16 ♗xh7+ ♔h8 17 ♗g6+ ♔g8 18 ♗h7+ ½-½, Wittmann-Greenfeld, Thessaloniki Ol. 1984.

➪ 11...d6 (this is more risky) 12 ♕f3 ♗e6 13 ♕xb7 ♗d5 14 ♕a6 (14 ♕xc7 is too greedy and gives Black a dangerous initiative after 14...♕e6, threatening both 15...♗b6 and 15...♕g4) 14...f5 15 ♗c4 f4 16 ♗xd5+ ♕xd5 17 ♕d3 ♕h5 18 ♕c4+ ♔h8 19 ♗xf4 ♕g4 20 g3 ♖f5 21 ♖ae1 ♖af8 22 ♕e4 (22 ♔g2 followed by h3 would have been good for White) 22...h5 (not 22...♖xf4?? 23 ♕xf4, but now the bishop is genuinely attacked) 23 ♕g2 h4 24 ♔h1?! (this makes life harder; after

24 h3! ♕g6 25 ♔h2 Black has little to show for the two pawns) 24...h3 25 ♕c6? (25 ♕e4 d5 26 f3! was still good for White) 25...g5 26 ♗e5+ ♖xe5 (26...♔h7!? would have been good for Black according to Pliester) 27 ♖xe5 dxe5 (it is perpetual check by White) ½-½, Shabanov-Mark Tseitlin, Leningrad 1986.

⇨ 11...d6 12 ♕f3 ♗e6 13 c4 (this also appears to give White the edge) 13...c6 14 ♗d2 d5 (taking the b2 pawn appears very risky) 15 ♖fe1 ♕c7 16 cxd5 ♗xd5 17 ♕h5 g6 18 ♕h4 ♖fe8 19 ♗c3 (White has a clear advantage) 19...♖xe1+ 20 ♖xe1 ♕d8 21 ♗f6 ♕f8 22 c4 ♗e6 23 ♗xg6 fxg6 24 ♖xe6 ♕f7 25 ♕e4 ♕d7 26 ♗h4? (after 26 ♗c3 White is simply a pawn up for nothing) 26...♕d1+ 27 ♕e1 ♕d4 28 ♗f6 ♕xc4 29 b3 ♕g4 30 h3 ♕f5 31 ♖e8+ ♖xe8 32 ♕xe8+ ♗f8 33 ♗e5 ♕f7 34 ♕a8 ♕e7 35 ♗g3 a6 36 ♕c8 ♔f7 37 ♔h2 ½-½, Odeev-Frolov, USSR Junior Qualifier 1989.

Another possibility is 8...c6, which was popular in the early part of this century, but is probably less reliable than 8...♕e5+. Here is one recent example:

⇨ 8...c6 9 ♗d3 ♕e5+ 10 ♗e3 d5 11 ♕f3 ♗c5 12 0-0 ♗xe3 13 ♖fe1 0-0 14 ♖xe3 ♕d6 15 ♖ae1 (White has gained time and thanks to his control of the e-file he can claim some advantage) 15...♗d7? (15...♗e6 was better) 16 ♗f5 ♖ad8 (after this Black gets into real trouble, but 16...♖ae8 17 ♖xe8 ♖xe8 18 ♖xe8+ ♗xe8 19 ♕e3 ♕b8 is also uncomfortable) 17 ♗xd7 ♖xd7 18 ♕f5 g6 19 ♕g5 ♖fd8 20 h4 (there is no way to break White's grip) 20...♕f8 21 ♖e7 h5 22 ♖1e6! ♔h8?! 23 ♖xg6 fxg6 24 ♕e5+ ♔g8 25 ♕e6+ ♔h8 26 ♖xd7 ♖xd7 27 ♕xd7 ♕f4 28 ♕e8+ ♔g7 29 ♕e7+ ♔g8 30 ♕g5 ♕e4 31 ♕d8+ ♔h7 32 ♕c7+ ♔h6 33 ♕b8 ♕xh4 34 ♕h8+ ♔g5 35 ♕d8+ ♔g4 36 ♕d7+ ♔g5 37 ♕e7+ ♔g4 38 f3+ 1-0, Imanaliev-Thipsay, Frunze 1985.

Readers should not imagine from these examples that this line's reputation for extreme boredom is unjustified, since the relatively interesting games given above were selected from dozens of totally tedious draws.

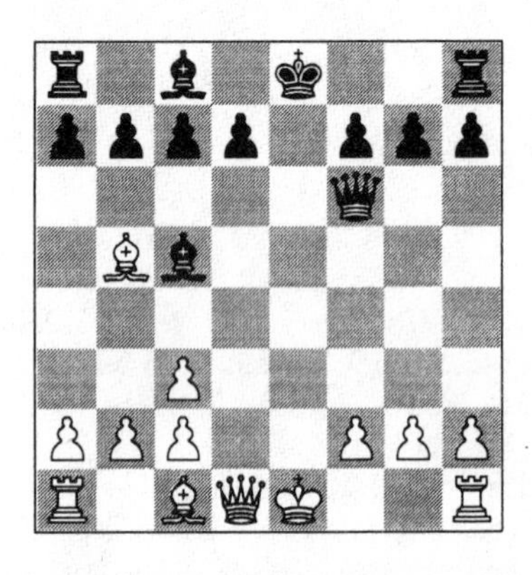

9 0-0 0-0 10 ♕h5 (if White wanted a draw, then 10 ♗xd7 ♖d8 11 ♕h5 ♗xd7 12 ♕xc5 ♗c6 was the simplest method) **10...d6 11 ♕g5 ♕xg5 12 ♗xg5 a6 13 ♗d3 h6 14 ♗d2 ♗d7 15 ♖fe1 ♖fe8 16 ♖xe8+ ♖xe8 17 ♖e1** (it is hard to imagine that White could lose this position) **17...♖e6 18 ♔f1 ♔f8 19 ♖e2 ♔e7 20 ♗c4 ♗b5 21 ♗xb5 axb5 22 f3 d5 23 ♗f4 ♗d6 24 ♗xd6+ ♔xd6 25 ♔f2 ♖xe2+ 26 ♔xe2 ♔e5 27 ♔e3**

h5 28 ♔d3 ♔f4 29 ♔e2 f5 30 ♔f2 h4 31 ♔e2 ♔e5 32 ♔e3 f4+ 33 ♔f2 h3 34 g4?! (34 gxh3 looks like a draw) **34...fxg3+ 35 ♔xg3 ♔f5 36 ♔xh3?! ♔f4 37 ♔g2 ♔e3 38 h4 c5 39 ♔g3 d4 40 f4 ♔d2 41 h5 ♔xc2 42 h6 gxh6 43 cxd4 cxd4 44 f5 d3 45 f6 d2 46 f7 d1♕ 47 f8♕** (the queen ending is lost for White) **47...♕g1+ 48 ♔h3 ♕e3+ 49 ♔h4 ♕d4+ 50 ♔h5 ♔xb2 51 ♔xh6 ♕h4+ 52 ♔g7 ♕g3+ 53 ♔h6 ♕h3+ 54 ♔g5 ♕g2+ 55 ♔h4 ♔xa2 56 ♕f7+ ♔a3 57 ♕f8+ b4 58 ♕c5 ♕e4+ 59 ♔g3 ♔a4 60 ♔h2 b3 61 ♕a7+ ♔b5 62 ♕f2 ♕c2 63 ♔h1 ♕e4+ 64 ♔g1 b6 65 ♕f6 ♕b1+ 66 ♔h2 ♕c2+ 67 ♔h3 b2 68 ♕f1+ ♕c4 69 ♕f5+ ♔b4 70 ♔h2 ♕e2+ 71 ♔h3 ♔c3 72 ♕f6+ ♔c2 0-1**

Game 26

Short-Beliavsky
Linares 1992

1 e4 e5 2 ♘c3 ♘f6 3 ♘f3 ♘c6 4 ♗b5 ♘d4 5 ♗a4

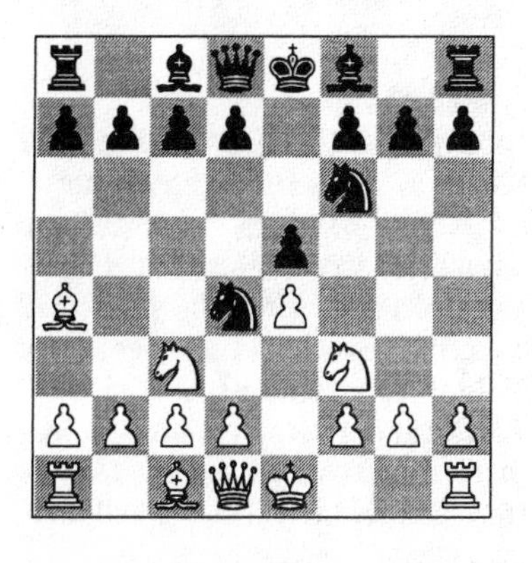

5...♘xf3+

Or 5...c6 (Hebden's idea) and now there are two plans:

1) 6 d3 (6 0-0 is a similar quiet alternative) and now:

⇨ 6...b5 7 ♗b3 d5 8 exd5 ♗g4 9 dxc6 ♕c7 10 ♗g5 (10 0-0 is possible) 10...♗b4 11 ♗xf6 gxf6 12 ♗d5 ♖d8 13 0-0 ♖g8 14 ♔h1 ♗xc3 15 bxc3 ♖xd5 16 cxd4 ♖xd4 17 ♖b1 (17 ♖e1! is stronger, preventing 17...♕xc6 because of 18 ♘xd4) 17...♕xc6 18 ♖e1 (not 18 ♘xd4? ♗h3! and wins) 18...♖f4 19 ♖e4 ♖xf3 20 ♖xg4 ♖xg4 21 ♕xf3 ♕xf3 22 gxf3 ♖a4 with a drawn rook ending, Poulsen-J.O.Pedersen, corr. 1986.

⇨ 6...d6 (if Black takes on f3 then play will probably transpose to the main line of Short-Beliavsky) 7 ♘xd4 exd4 8 ♘e2 ♕a5+ (8...d5!?) 9 c3 dxc3 10 bxc3 ♗e7 11 ♗c2 (White's extra central pawn gives him the advantage) 11...♕h5? 12 f3 (now Black's queen is going to be driven away with further loss of time, so he adopts desperate measures) 12...g5 13 ♗e3 ♗e6 14 a4 d5 15 e5 ♘d7 16 ♘g3 ♕h4 17 d4 f6 18 exf6 ♗xf6 19 0-0 0-0-0 20 a5 ♖de8 21 ♗f2 ♕h6 22 ♕b1 (the switch to a direct attack on Black's king is justified because the enemy queen is totally out of play) 22...♗d8 23 ♕b3 ♗c7 24 ♖fb1 b6 25 axb6 axb6 26 ♖a7 g4 27 ♕a4 ♘b8 28 ♖xc7+ ♔xc7 29 ♕a7+ ♔d6 30 ♘e4+ 1-0, Lanc-Im.Horvath, Stary Smokovec 1986.

2) 6 ♘xe5 d6 7 ♘f3 ♗g4 8 d3 ♘d7 9 ♗e3 ♘xf3+ 10 gxf3 ♗h5 11 d4 (11 ♖g1!? is interesting, because

11...♘e5 12 ♖g3 ♕f6 13 ♘d5! looks good for White, while after 11...♕h4 12 ♕e2 ♕xh2 13 0-0-0 White has a big lead in development) 11...♕f6 12 ♖g1 ♕xf3 13 ♕xf3 ♗xf3 and now:

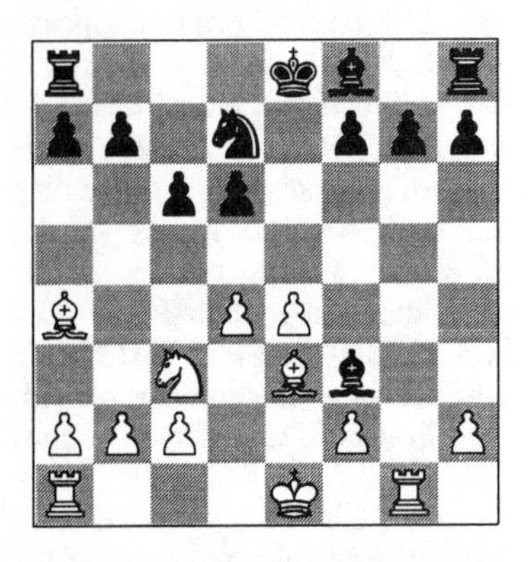

➪ 14 d5 c5 15 ♔d2 0-0-0 16 ♗xd7+ ♔xd7 (Black has no problems) 17 ♖g3 ♗h5 18 ♖b1 a5 19 a3 g6 20 b4 axb4 21 axb4 c4 22 b5 ♗g7 23 ♖b4 ♖he8 24 ♖xc4 ♖c8 25 ♖xc8 ♔xc8 26 ♗f4 ♔d7 27 b6 ♗d4 28 ♗e3 ♗e5 29 ♖g1 ♗f3 30 ♖a1 ♗xe4 31 ♖a7 ♗xc3+ 32 ♔xc3 ♗xd5 33 ♔d4 ♗c6 34 c4 ♖e4+ 35 ♔d3 ♖h4 36 ♖a8 ♗g2 37 ♖d8+ ♔xd8 38 ♗g5+ ♔d7 39 ♗xh4 ♔c6 40 ♗e7 ♔c5 41 ♗f6 ♗f1+ 42 ♔e4 ♔xc4 43 f4 ♗g2+ 44 ♔e3 ♗h3 45 ♔e4 ♗f5+ 46 ♔e3 ♔d5 47 ♔f3 ♔c5 48 ♗e7 ♔xb6 49 ♗xd6 ♔b5 50 ♔e3 ♔c4 51 ♗e5 b5 52 h4 b4 0-1, P.Wells-Hebden, Hastings B 1991.

➪ 14 ♖g3 (better) 14...♗h5 15 f3 0-0-0 16 0-0-0 ♘b6 17 ♗b3 (White has only a very slight plus; later in the game Chandler developed a more significant advantage, but Black held a complicated rook ending) 17...d5 18 exd5 cxd5 19 ♗f4 f6 20 ♘b5 a6 21 ♗c7 axb5 22 ♗xb6 ♖d7 23 ♗c5 ♔c7 24 ♗xf8 ♖xf8 25 ♖e1 ♖e8 26 ♖xe8 ♗xe8 27 ♔d2 ♔d6 28 c3 ♗g6 29 ♖g1 ♖e7 30 ♗d1 ♗f5 31 ♗e2 ♔c6 32 h4 g6 33 ♖g2 h6 34 ♖h2 ♖e6 35 a3 g5 36 ♖h1 ♔b6 37 ♖h2 ♔c6 38 hxg5 fxg5 39 ♗d3 ♗xd3 40 ♔xd3 ♔d7 41 ♔c2 ♔e7 42 ♔b3 ♔f7 43 ♔b4 ♔g6 44 ♔xb5 ♖e3 45 ♖f2 h5 46 c4 dxc4 47 ♔xc4 ♔f5 48 d5 h4 49 d6 ♔e6 50 ♖d2 ♔d7 51 ♖d5 ♖xf3 52 ♖xg5 ♔xd6 53 ♖h5 h3 54 a4 ♖f2 55 ♖h6+ ♔c7 56 ♖h7+ ♔c6 57 ♖h6+ ♔c7 58 ♖h7+ ♔c6 59 ♖h6+ ♔c7 ½-½, Chandler-Hebden, London (Lloyds Bank) 1992.

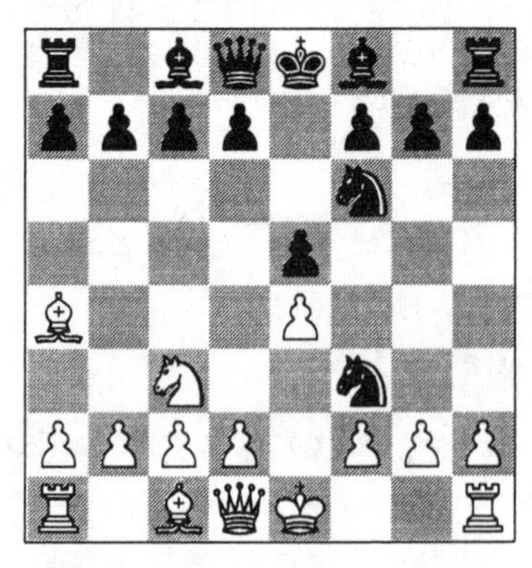

6 ♕xf3

➪ 6 gxf3!? c6 (after 6...♗c5 7 f4 ♕e7 8 d3 White is slightly better) 7 d4 exd4 8 ♕xd4 d6 9 ♗b3 b5? (an unjustified weakening of the queenside) 10 a4 c5 11 ♕d1 b4 (11...c4 12 ♗a2 b4 13 ♘d5 is also good for White) 12 ♘d5 ♗e6 13 ♖g1 (now Black cannot complete his development) 13...♘xd5 14 ♗xd5 ♖c8 15 f4 (the advance of the f-pawn will force an exchange on d5, when Black will be unable to displace White's queen) 15...g6 16 f5 ♗xd5 17 ♕xd5 ♗g7 18 ♗g5 ♗f6 19 h4 ♕e7 20 0-0-0 ♖d8 21 e5! ♗xg5+ 22 hxg5 dxe5 23 ♕c6+ ♔f8 24 f6 1-0, Nunn-L.Cooper, Walsall Kipping Jubilee 1992.

6...♗c5

Or 6...c6 7 d3 d6 (Adams gives 7...♗e7 8 ♕g3 d6 9 ♕xg7 ♖g8 10 ♕h6 ♖xg2 as an improvement for Black; this line is indeed promising, so White should prefer simple development by 8 ♗b3 followed by 0-0 with a likely transposition to the examples below) and now:

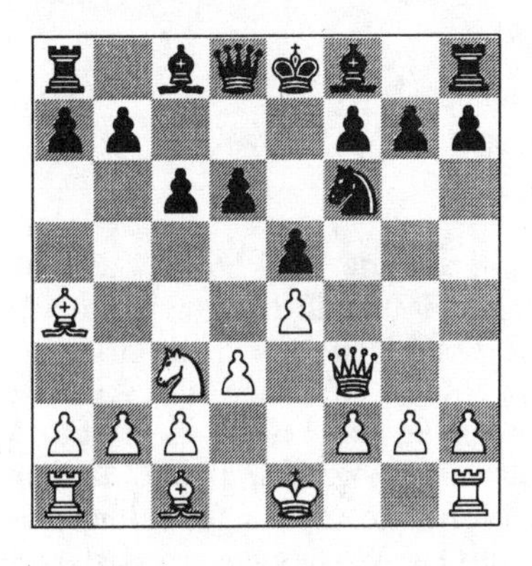

➪ 8 ♗b3 ♗e7 9 ♕e2 0-0 10 f4 ♗g4 11 ♕f2 ♗e6 12 0-0 (after 12 fxe5 dxe5 13 ♗xe6 fxe6 the unfortunate position of White's queen gives Black counterplay along the f-file) 12...exf4 13 ♗xf4 d5 14 ♖ae1 dxe4 15 ♘xe4 (*Informator* gives 15 ♗xe6 fxe6 16 ♘xe4 ♘xe4 17 ♖xe4 g5 as winning for Black, but 18 ♕g3 is at least equal for White, for example 18...♕b6+ 19 ♗e3 ♖xf1+ 20 ♔xf1 ♖f8+ 21 ♔g1 ♕xb2 22 ♗xg5) 15...♗xb3 16 axb3 ♕d7 17 ♘xf6+ (17 ♘c5!?) 17...♗xf6 18 ♗e5 ♗xe5 19 ♖xe5 f6! 20 ♖e4 ♖fe8 21 ♖xe8+ ♖xe8 22 ♕xa7 ♖e2 23 ♖f2 ♖e1+ 24 ♖f1 ♖e2 ½-½, Anand-Ivanchuk, Dortmund 1992.

➪ 8 0-0 ♗e7 9 ♕e2 0-0 10 ♔h1 a6?! (Black doesn't achieve much with his queenside pawn advance) 11 ♗b3 b5 12 a4 b4 13 ♘d1 ♖e8 14 f4 exf4 15 ♗xf4 (this game looks completely modern and it is hard to believe that it was played over a century before the other examples in this section) 15...♗e6 16 ♗xe6 fxe6 17 e5 ♘d5 18 ♗g3 dxe5 19 ♗xe5 ♗d6 20 ♘f2 ♗xe5 21 ♕xe5 ♘f6 22 ♖ae1 (22 ♘e4! was a simple route to a clear advantage, but the move played is not bad) 22...♕d5 23 b3 ♖ad8 24 ♘h3 ♘d7?! (it is very risky to abandon the kingside) 25 ♕g3 e5 26 ♘g5 ♖f8 27 ♕h3 (27 ♕g4! attacks b4 and threatens ♘e6) 27...♖xf1+ 28 ♖xf1 ♘f6 29 ♖xf6 gxf6 30 ♕xh7+ ♔f8 31 ♕h8+ ♔e7 32 ♕g7+ ♔e8 33 ♕xf6 ♖d6 34 ♘e4?? (a really horrible blunder; 34 ♕h8+ ♔d7 35 h4 intending ♘e4 is very good for White) 34...♕xe4 35 ♕h8+ ♔f7 0-1, Paulsen-Mason, Nürnberg 1883.

➪ 8 0-0 ♗e7 9 ♘d5! (the exclamation mark is from Adams) 9...♘d7 (9...♘xd5? 10 exd5 b5 11 dxc6 bxa4 12 c7 wins for White) 10 ♘xe7 ♕xe7 11 c3 (the bishops give White a small but permanent advantage) 11...0-0 12 ♕g3 ♘c5 13 ♗c2 ♘e6 14 ♗e3 c5 15 ♖ad1 b6 16 ♗b3 ♗b7 17 f4 exf4 18 ♗xf4 ♘xf4 19 ♖xf4 (White has exchanged the two bishops for pressure down the f-file) 19...♗c8 20 ♗d5 ♖b8 21 ♖df1 ♗e6 22 h4 ♖be8 (22...♗xd5 23 exd5

♖be8 was more accurate, when White's advantage is microscopic) 23 c4 ♗xd5 24 cxd5 ♔h8 25 ♕f2 ♔g8 26 g4 ♕d7 27 g5 ♖e5 28 ♔h2 ♕e7 29 ♕f3 (threatening 30 b4 cxb4 31 d4) 29...♕d7 30 ♖f2 b5 31 b3 a5 32 ♖g2 ♕e7 33 ♕g4 ♖e8 34 ♖gf2 ♖f8 35 ♖2f3 g6 36 ♖f2 (White cannot make progress and the game soon reduces to equality) 36...♔g7 37 ♔g1 h6 38 ♖f6 h5 39 ♕f3 c4 40 ♖f4 cxd3 41 ♕xd3 b4 42 ♔g2 ♔g8 43 ♕f3 ♕c7 44 ♔g3 ♖e7 45 ♔g2 ♕d7 46 ♖f6 ♖fe8 47 ♖e2 ♖c8 48 ♕h3 ♕e8 49 ♕f3 ♖c3 50 ♕f4 ♕c8 51 ♖xd6 ♖ec7 52 ♔f2 ♖c2 53 ♖b6 ♕h3 54 ♖c6 ♖2xc6 55 dxc6 ♖xc6 56 ♖d2 ½-½, Kamsky-Adams, Dortmund 1992.

7 d3 c6

⇨ 7...h6 (this is probably a mistake) 8 ♕g3 ♕e7 9 ♕xg7 (not bad, but 9 0-0! would have left Black with no natural way to defend the g7 pawn) 9...♗xf2+ 10 ♔xf2 ♖g8 11 ♘d5 ♖xg7 12 ♘xe7 ♔xe7 13 c3?! (the two bishops give White a definite edge, for example after the obvious 13 ♗d2) 13...b6! (Black spots a weakness on d3; thanks to the tempo spent on c3 White's development is too poor to keep Black's piece activity under control) 14 ♗d1 ♗a6 15 c4 ♘g4+! 16 ♗xg4 ♖xg4 17 ♗xh6 f5 18 exf5 ♗b7 (Black has enough compensation for the sacrificed material) 19 ♖hg1 ♖ag8 20 g3 ♖h8 21 h3 ♖gg8 22 ♗d2 ♖xh3 23 ♖af1 (the result should be a draw, but White loses his way and eventually the game) 23...♖g4 24 ♔e2 ♔f6 25 ♗e1 c5 26 ♔d1 ♗c6 27 b3 a6 28 ♔c2 b5 29 a3 d5 30 cxd5 ♗xd5 31 b4 c4 32 ♖f2 cxd3+ 33 ♔xd3 ♖gxg3+ 34 ♖xg3 ♖xg3+ 35 ♔c2 ♖xa3 36 ♗c3 a5 37 ♖e2 ♖a2+ 38 ♗b2 axb4 39 ♔b1 ♖xb2+ 40 ♖xb2 b3 41 ♖d2 ♗c4 42 ♔b2 e4 43 ♖d8 e3 44 ♖e8 e2 0-1, Howell-Gretarsson, Hafnarfirdi 1992.

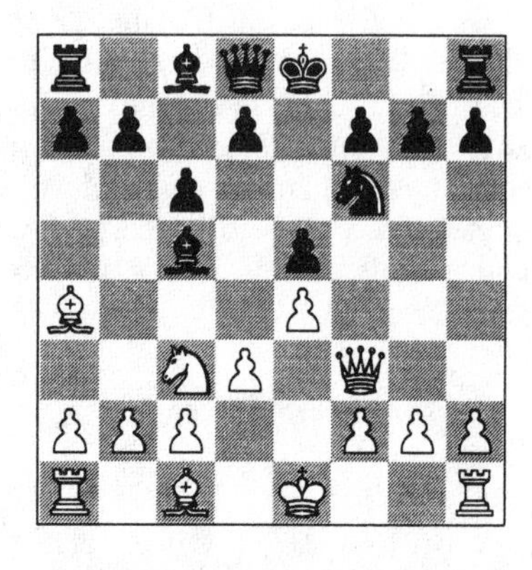

8 ♗b3 d6 9 0-0 h6 10 ♗e3 ♗b6 11 h3 0-0 12 ♖fd1 (now White will force through d4, with the guarantee of a small advantage) **12...♗xe3 13 ♕xe3 b5 14 a4 b4 15 ♘e2 ♕b6 16 d4 a5 17 ♘g3 ♖a7 18 ♖d2 ♖e7 19 ♖ad1 d5** (causing a general liquidation, but White's edge persists) **20 exd5 cxd5 21 dxe5 ♕xe3 22 fxe3 ♖xe5 23 ♗xd5 ♖xe3 24 ♗f3 ♖e5 25 ♘e2 ♖c5 26 ♘d4 ♗d7 27 ♘b3 ♖c7 28 ♘xa5 ♗xa4 29 b3 ♗b5 30 ♖e1 ♖fc8 31 ♖e5 ♗d7 32 ♘c4 ♗e6 33 ♘e3 ♖b8 34 ♖a5 g6 35 ♖d4 ♖d7 36 ♖xd7 ♗xd7 37 ♔f2 ♔g7 38 ♖a7 g5 39 ♔e2 ♗b5+ 40 ♔d2 ♔g6 41 ♖b7 ♖xb7 42 ♗xb7 h5 43 c4 bxc3+ 44 ♔xc3 h4 45 ♗f3 ♘h5 46 ♔d4 ♘g7 47 ♗e4+ ♔h5 48 ♔e5 ♘e8 49 ♘g4** (with skilful play White has increased his advantage to dangerous proportions; now 49 b4 would have been very unpleasant for Black) **49...♗d7 50 ♗f5 ♗c6 51 ♗e4 ♗d7 52 ♗f5 ♗c6 53 ♘e3 ♔h6 54 b4 ♔g7 55 ♗d3 ♔f8 56 b5 ♗b7 57 ♘d5 f6+ 58 ♔e6??** (a tragic blunder; after 58 ♘xf6 ♘xf6 59 ♔xf6 White wins in the two lines 59...♗xg2 60 ♗f5 ♔e8 61 ♔xg5 ♔d8 62 ♔xh4 ♔c7 63 ♔g5 ♔b6 64 h4 and 59...g4 60 hxg4 ♗xg2 61 g5 h3 62 g6 ♗d5 63 g7+ ♔g8 64 b6 h2 65 b7; therefore Black must try 58...♗xg2, but even then 59 ♘h7+ and 60 ♘xg5 gives White good winning chances) **58...♗c8 mate.**

Game 27

Liu Wenzhe-Shu Yimin
China 1987

1 e4 e5 2 ♘f3 ♘f6 3 ♘c3 ♘c6 4 ♗b5 ♘d4 5 ♗a4 ♗c5 6 ♘xe5 ♕e7

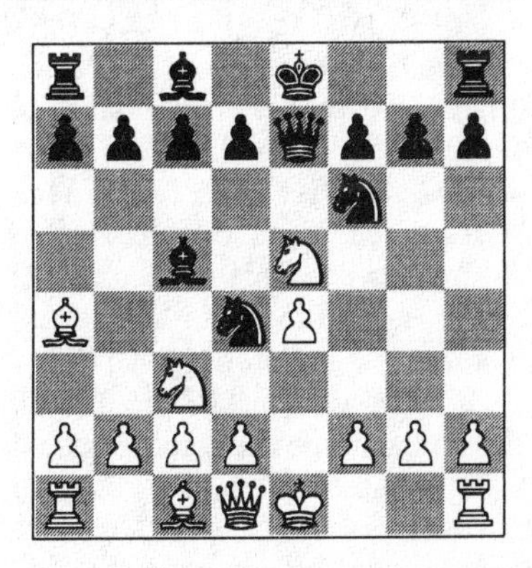

This variation has been played a number of times in recent games, perhaps because Black players have wanted to avoid the theory of the main lines. However, the practical results have been very favourable for White and Black players should avoid 6...♕e7.

7 ♘d3 ♘xe4

➩ 7...b5 8 ♘xc5 ♕xc5 (8...bxa4 9 ♘5xa4 ♘xe4 10 0-0 ♘xc3 11 ♘xc3 0-0 12 d3 ♗b7 13 ♗e3 ♘f5 14 ♕d2 a5, Nikitin-Estrin, USSR 1958, and now 15 ♖ae1 would have been good for White) 9 ♗b3 a5 10 a3 0-0 11 0-0 ♗a6 12 d3 ♘xb3 13 cxb3 b4 14 ♘e2 ♖fe8 15 ♖e1 h6 16 d4 ♕b6 17 ♘g3 (Black has no compensation for the lost pawn) 17...♖ab8 18 f3 d6 19 ♗e3 ♗c8 20 d5 c5 21 dxc6 ♕xc6 22 axb4 axb4 23 ♕d4 ♗e6 24 ♗xh6 ♕c5 25 ♗e3 ♕xd4 26 ♗xd4 ♗xb3 27 ♘f5 ♖e6 28 ♗a7 ♖a8 29 ♗f2 ♗a2 30 ♗h4 ♘d7 31 ♘e7+ ♔h7 32 ♘c6 b3 33 ♘d4 ♖ee8 34 ♘f5 ♖a6 35 ♖ad1 ♘c5 36 ♘xd6 ♖b8 37 ♘xf7 ♘a4 38 ♖e2 ♖c8 1-0, Armas-Antunes, Capablanca Mem-B 1992.

8 0-0 ♘xc3

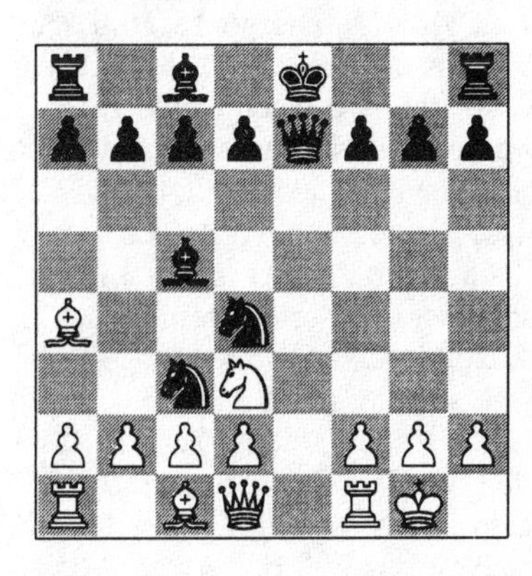

9 bxc3

Both captures are very promising for White. After 9 dxc3 ♘e6 10 ♘xc5 ♕xc5 11 ♗e3 Black has tried:

➩ 11...♕e7 12 f4 f5 13 ♕f3 0-0 14

♖fe1 ♖b8 15 ♖ad1 b6 16 ♗f2 ♔h8 17 ♕h3 ♖f7 18 b4 h6 (White's superior development and pressure along the central files, especially against the weak d7 pawn, amount to a substantial advantage) 19 ♕h5 ♖f8 20 ♗h4 ♕f7 21 ♕xf7 ♖xf7 22 c4 a6 23 ♖e5 ♔h7 24 ♗g3 ♔g6 25 a3 c5 26 c3 ♔h7 27 ♖d6 g6 28 ♗d1 ♔g7 29 ♗f3 ♔f8 30 ♗h4 g5 31 fxg5 hxg5 32 ♗g3 ♔e7 33 ♖d2 f4 34 ♗f2 ♔f6 35 ♖ed5 ♖g7 36 ♗g4 ♖b7 37 ♖d6 ♔e7 38 h4 cxb4 39 cxb4 ♖c7 40 c5 bxc5 41 ♗xe6 dxe6 42 bxc5 ♖d7 43 hxg5 ♖xd6 44 ♖xd6 ♔f7 45 ♖d8 ♗b7 46 ♗d4 ♖h7 47 ♖d6 ♗d5 48 c6 ♔g6 49 ♗b6 ♖h8 50 c7 ♖c8 51 ♗a5 ♔xg5 52 ♖xa6 ♔g4 53 ♖d6 f3 54 ♖d8 ♗b7 55 gxf3+ ♔xf3 56 ♔f1 e5 57 ♔e1 e4 58 ♔d2 ♔f2 59 ♔c3 e3 60 ♔d4 e2 61 ♖xc8 ♗xc8 62 a4 1-0, Botvinnik-Veresov, USSR Ch. 1940.

➪ 11...♕f5 12 c4 0-0 13 c3 d6 14 ♗c2 ♕f6 15 ♕h5 g6 16 ♕h6 ♕g7 17 ♕h4 f5 18 ♗h6 ♕f6 19 ♕xf6 ♖xf6 (the two bishops and Black's weakened dark squares give White a permanent advantage) 20 h4 ♗d7 21 ♖fe1 ♖e8 22 b4 ♘f8 23 ♗b3 c5 24 ♖xe8 ♗xe8 25 ♖d1 a5 26 ♗f4 (the d6 pawn is in serious trouble) a4 27 ♗c2 ♖e6 28 ♖xd6 ♖e1+ 29 ♔h2 ♖a1 30 ♗d1 ♖xa2 31 ♗f3 ♘d7 32 ♗xb7 ♖xf2 33 ♗h6 ♘e5 34 ♔g3 ♖e2 35 ♖a6 ♘g4 36 ♗f3 ♖c2 37 ♗d5+ ♔h8 38 ♗f8 ♖xc3+ 39 ♔f4 ♘e3 40 ♗xc5 ♘xd5+ 41 cxd5 ♖c4+ 42 ♔e5 ♔g7 43 ♖a7+ ♗f7 44 ♗d4 ♖c8 45 d6 ♖e8+ 46 ♔f4+ ♔h6 47 ♗f6 1-0, A.I.Ivanov-Kakageldyev, USSR Ch. Qualifier, Ashkhabad 1990.

9...♘e6 10 ♘xc5 ♕xc5 11 ♕f3

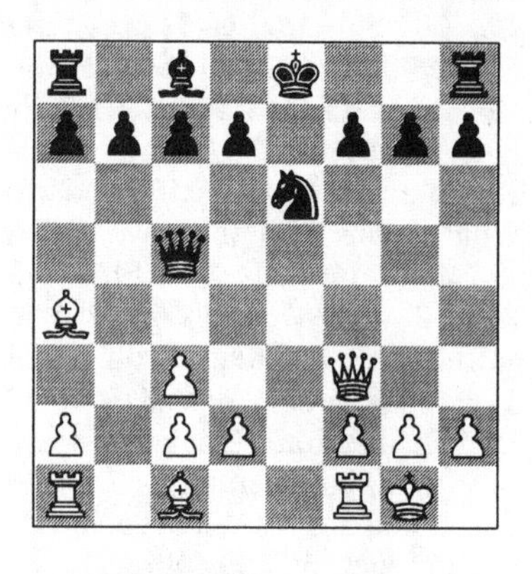

11...c6

➪ 11...0-0 12 d4 ♕a5 13 ♗b3 d6 14 ♖d1 (at the moment both ♖e1 and ♗d2 are impossible because of ...♘xd4, so White prepares to expand by ♗d2 and c4) 14...♖b8 15 ♗d2 ♘d8? (this move is unfortunate because it allows White to imprison the knight) 16 d5 ♕b5 17 ♖e1 ♕d7 18 ♖e4 f5 19 ♖e2 ♘f7 20 ♗f4 (preventing the re-emergence of Black's knight) 20...♕d8 21 ♕g3 ♔h8 22 ♖ae1 g5 (suicide) 23 ♗e3 f4 24 ♗d4+ ♔g8 25 ♕f3 ♗f5 26 ♖e7 ♕c8 27 ♖1e6! c5 28 dxc6 bxc6 29 ♖f6 ♖xb3 30 cxb3 c5 31 ♕h5 cxd4 32 ♖fxf7 1-0, R.Mainka-Schwekendiek, Bad Wörishofen Open 1992.

12 d4 ♕a5 13 ♗b3 d5 (Black tries to barricade the white-squared bishop, but the demolition squad moves in) **14 c4 0-0** (14...♘xd4 15 ♕e3+ ♘e6 16 cxd5 cxd5 17 ♖d1 wins back the pawn with a strong initiative) **15 c3 dxc4 16 ♗xc4 ♗d7 17 ♕g3 g6?** (the further weakening of the black squares is too much) **18 ♖b1 ♖ab8 19 ♗h6 ♖fe8 20 ♖fe1**

♕h5 21 ♗d2 b5 22 ♗b3 ♕f5 23 ♖bd1 a5 24 ♖e5 ♕f6 25 ♖de1 a4 26 ♗c2 ♖bc8 27 h4 ♕g7 28 h5 ♘c7 29 ♖e7 (after 29...♖ed8 Black's position is terrible but White has no forced win, so the early resignation is rather surprising) **1-0**

Game 28

Fediashin-Poleschuk
corr. 1986

1 e4 e5 2 ♘f3 ♘c6 3 ♘c3 ♘f6 4 ♗b5 ♘d4 5 ♗a4 ♗c5 6 ♘xe5 0-0

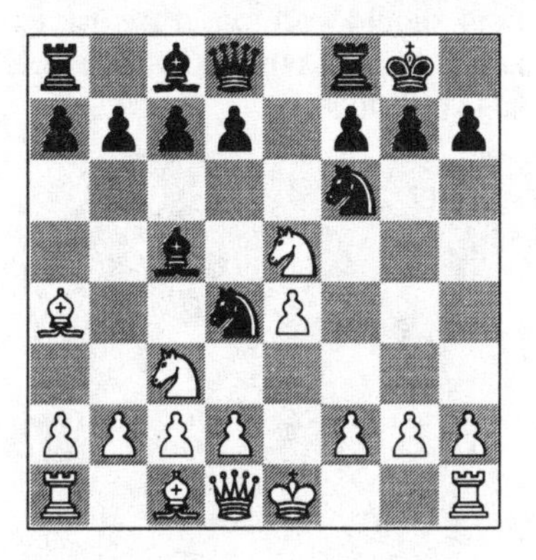

In order to avoid giving the pawn back immediately White usually plays 7 ♘d3, gaining time by attacking Black's bishop. However, this blocks the d-pawn and makes it hard for White to develop his queenside. The subsequent struggle often revolves around White's attempts to move the d3 knight and complete his development.

7 ♘d3

⇨ 7 d3 d6 (7...d5 8 ♗g5 c6 9 ♕d2 ♖e8 10 f4 b5 11 ♗b3 h6 12 ♗h4 ♘xe4! was good for Black in Tarrasch-Rubinstein, San Sebastian 1912) 8 ♘f3 ♗g4 9 ♗e3 c6 10 h3 ♗xf3 11 gxf3 d5 (Sokolov's plan has given him sufficient compensation for the pawn; White's queen cannot move and there is no obvious way to safeguard the white king) 12 ♗g5 h6 13 ♗h4 ♕d6 14 ♗g3 ♕e6 15 ♔f1 ♖ad8 16 ♔g2 (finally freeing the queen from the defence of f3, but White's king is still not secure) 16...b5 17 ♗b3 a5 18 a3 ♘xb3 19 cxb3 ♘h5 20 exd5 ♕g6! 21 ♔h2 (21 d4 ♘f4+ 22 ♔h2 ♕f5 23 ♕f1 ♗xd4 24 dxc6 ♗xc3 25 bxc3 ♖c8 is fine for Black) 21...cxd5 22 d4 ♗d6 23 ♖g1 f5 24 ♕d3 ♕f6 25 f4 ♘xf4 26 ♕f3 ♘e6 27 ♘xd5 ♕f7 28 ♗xd6 ♖xd6 29 ♘f4 ♘xd4 (material equality is restored, but White's position is a wreck) 30 ♕c3 b4 31 axb4 axb4 32 ♕d3 ♖fd8 33 ♖ae1 ♘xb3 34 ♕g3 ♘d4 35 ♘h5 g6 36 ♘f4 g5 37 h4 g4 38 f3 h5 39 fxg4 hxg4 40 h5 ♔h7 41 ♖ef1 ♕f6 42 ♔h1 ♖6d7 43 ♖g2 ♘f3 44 ♘g6 ♖d1 45 ♖gf2 ♖xf1+ 46 ♖xf1 ♖d2 47 ♕c7+ ♔h6 48 ♕f4+ ♕g5 49 ♕xg5+ ♔xg5 0-1, Kamsky-I.Sokolov, Brussels SWIFT Rapid 1992.

7...♗b6 8 ♘f4

This is the old main line, which has been played a few times recently even though it has been largely superseded by 8 e5.

8...d5 9 d3 ♗g4

This is not the only move. The alternatives are:

⇨ 9...dxe4 (dubious) 10 dxe4 ♗g4 11 ♕d3 (Black's premature pawn swap has given White this extra possibility) 11...♕e7 12 ♗e3 ♖ad8 13

♘fd5 ♘xd5 14 ♘xd5 ♕e5? (Black should have tried 14...♖xd5 15 exd5 ♕b4+, when 16 c3 is just slightly better for White after 16...♕xb2 17 0-0 ♕xc3 18 ♕xc3 ♘e2+ 19 ♔h1 ♘xc3 20 ♗b3 or 16...♕xa4 17 ♗xd4 ♗xd4 18 ♕xd4 ♖e8+ 19 ♔f1 and now *Informator* gives 19...♕c2, even though this loses immediately after 20 ♕xg4) 15 ♗xd4 ♗xd4 16 f4 ♕h5 17 ♕xd4 c6 18 ♗b3 cxd5 19 ♗xd5 ♗f5 20 ♕c4 (not 20 exf5 ♖fe8+ 21 ♔f2 when 21...♕e2+ 22 ♔g3 ♖e3+ 23 ♔h4 h5! is unclear) 20...b5 21 ♕e2 ♗g4 22 ♕d3 ♖fe8 23 ♔f2 ♕h6 24 ♖he1 ♕xh2? (Black should have taken on f4, when White must still work hard to exploit his extra pawn) 25 ♕g3 ♕h5 26 ♖e3 ♖d6 27 ♖ae1 ♖g6 28 f5 ♖g5 29 ♕f4 ♖c8 30 ♖c3 ♖f8 31 ♖h1 ♕xh1 32 ♕xg5 ♕d1 33 f6 g6 34 ♕h6 ♕d4+ 35 ♔g3 ♕xf6 36 ♔xg4 1-0, Estrin-Moldavsky, USSR 1968.

⇨ 9...c6 (this is just as good as the main line) 10 ♗e3 (10 h3 ♖e8 11 0-0 dxe4 12 dxe4 ♘xe4 13 ♘xe4 ♖xe4 14 c3 ♘f5 15 ♕xd8+ ♗xd8 16 ♗c2 ♖e7 17 ♗d2 ♗d7 was equal in Böök-Spielmann, Helsinki 1935) 10...♘g4 11 ♕d2 ♘xc2+ (this combination wasn't necessary because 11...dxe4 12 dxe4 ♘xe3 13 fxe3 ♘e6 would have been fine for Black) 12 ♗xc2 d4 13 ♗xd4 ♗xd4 14 0-0 f5 15 h3 ♘e5 16 ♔h1 ♕g5 17 ♘ce2 ♗b6 18 d4 ♘g6 19 ♗b3+ ♔h8 20 ♘xg6+ ♕xg6 ½-½, Estrin-Antoshin, USSR 1969. In the final position Black has enough play for the pawn because 21 e5 f4 22 f3 ♕h6 threatens to sacrifice on h3, forcing White to defend passively.

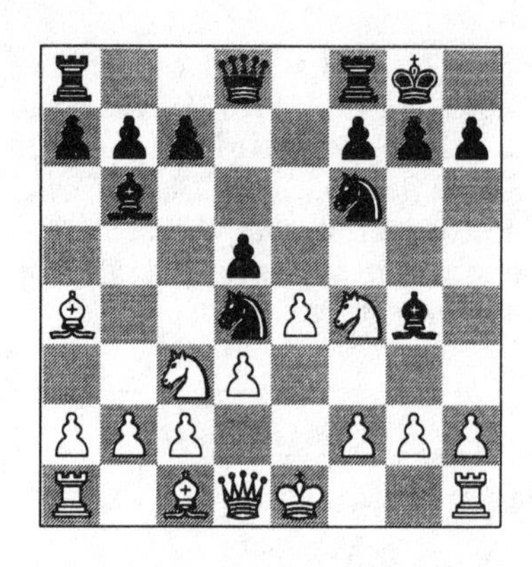

10 f3 ♘h5 11 ♘xh5

This is the first main decision point for White. The alternative 11 fxg4 should lead to a draw, for example 11 fxg4 ♕h4+ 12 g3 ♘xg3 13 ♘g2 and now:

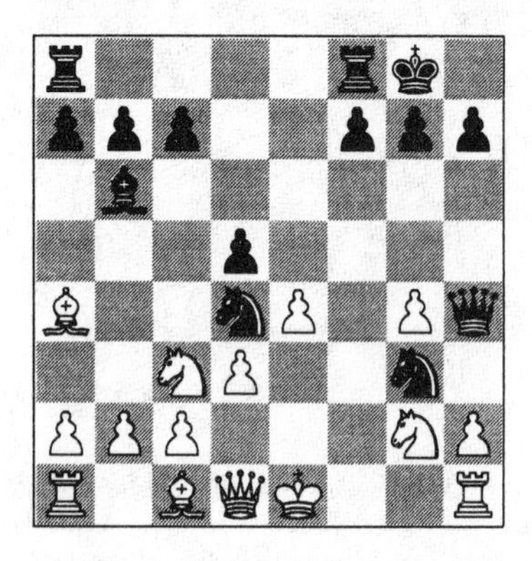

⇨ 13...♕f6 14 ♗f4! (the only way to continue the game, because the alternative 14 hxg3 ♘f3+ 15 ♔e2 ♘d4+ 16 ♔e1 ♘f3+ 17 ♔e2 ♘d4+ ½-½, G.Röder-F.Röder, Bavaria 1985, is an immediate draw) 14...♘xh1 15 ♘xd5 ♕d8 16 ♗e3 c6?! (16...♕d6 17 ♔d2 c6 18 ♘xb6 axb6 19 c3 is also good for White, but this is a better chance than the game) 17 ♘xb6 axb6 18 c3 ♘e6 19 ♔f1 (White has emerged from the complications with a decisive advantage because the h1 knight is doomed) 19...♕d6 20 ♔g1 ♘g3 21 ♗c2 ♖fe8 22 ♕f3 ♘xe4 23 dxe4 b5 24 ♘h4 g6 25 ♕f2 ♕c7 26 ♘f3 c5 27 ♘g5 c4 28 ♘xe6 fxe6 29 ♗h6 e5 30 ♖f1 ♕e7 31 a3 ♖a6 32 ♗g5 ♕e6 33 h3 ♖aa8 34 ♗h6 ♕e7 35 ♔h2 ♖a6 36 ♔g3 ♖d8 37 h4 ♖c8 38 ♗d1 ♖aa8 39 ♗e2 ♖a6 40 ♔h3 ♖ac6 41 ♗g5 ♕c7 42 ♗d1 ♖a6 43 ♗c2 ♖aa8 44 ♗h6 ♕e7 45 ♕b6 ♕d7 46 ♕f6 ♖e8 47 a4 ♕e7 48 ♕xe7 ♖xe7 49 axb5 ♖ee8 50 ♖f2 ♖a5 51 b3 ♖xb5 52 bxc4 ♖b2 53 c5 ♖c8 54 ♗c1 ♖b5 55 ♗a3 ♖a5 56 ♗b4 ♖a1 57 ♗b3+ ♔h8 58 ♗d5 ♖h1+ 59 ♔g3 h5 60 gxh5 gxh5 61 ♖f5 ♖a8 62 ♖xh5+ ♔g7 63 ♖xe5 ♖aa1 64 ♖g5+ ♔h6 65 ♖f5 ♖ag1+ 66 ♔f4 ♖xh4+ 67 ♔e5 1-0, Heidrich-H.Meyer, Bundesliga 1984/5.

➪ 13...♕h3 (this seems to be the way to force a draw) 14 ♘f4 ♕h4 15 ♘g2 ♕h3 ½-½, G.Röder-Seyb, Bavarian Ch. 1986.

11...♗xh5 12 ♘xd5

➪ 12 ♗f4 c6 13 ♖f1 (defending f3 in preparation for ♕d2; 13 ♗e5?! ♕g5 is dubious, but 13 ♗g3!? intending ♗f2 and 0-0 is interesting) 13...dxe4 14 dxe4 (14 ♘xe4 f5 15 ♘g3 ♖e8+ 16 ♔d2 ♘e6 is not so clear after 17 ♗b3, but 15...♕e7+! is very strong because 16 ♔d2 fails to 16...♘xf3+! followed by ...♕b4+ picking up one of White's bishops) 14...♕f6 15 ♕c1 (15 ♕d2 ♖ad8 16 ♗g5 fails to 16...♘xc2+) 15...♘e6 16 ♗g3 ♗d4 17 e5 ♗xe5 18 ♘e4 ♗xg3+ 19 hxg3 ♕e5 (material is equal but White's king is still stuck in the centre) 20 ♗b3 ♗g6?! (20...f5 21 ♕f4 ♕xb2 22 ♗xe6+ ♗f7 23 ♗xf7+ ♖xf7 is very good for Black because 24 ♕c1 gives him the pleasant choice between 24...♕e5 and 24...♕xc1+ 25 ♖xc1 fxe4 26 fxe4 ♖e8) 21 ♕e3 ♗xe4 22 0-0-0 ♕g5? (a very strange move; 22...♕xg3 is an extra pawn) 23 ♕xg5 ♘xg5 24 fxe4 ♖ad8 25 ♖d3 ♖xd3 26 cxd3 ♘e6 27 ♔d2 ♖d8 28 ♔e3 ♖d7 29 ♗xe6 fxe6 30 b4 (with equality) 30...♖f7 31 ♖c1 ♔f8 32 a4 ♔e7 33 ♖c5 ♖f1 34 b5 ♔d6 35 ♖h5 h6 36 bxc6 ♔xc6 37 ♖e5 ♔d6 38 ♖b5 b6 39 a5 ♔c6 40 ♖e5 ♖f6 41 ♔d4 ♖g6 42 ♖b5?? (horrible) 42...♔xb5 0-1, Jongman-Di Bucchianico, corr. 1987.

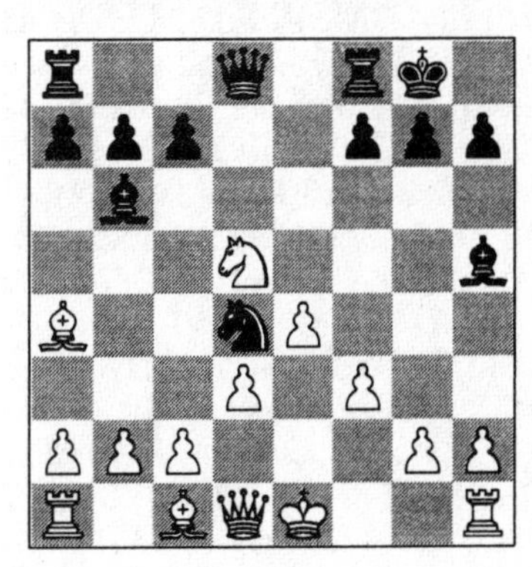

12...f5!

➪ 12...c6 (an inferior move, as is 12...♕h4+ 13 g3 ♘xf3+ 14 ♕xf3 ♗xf3 15 gxh4 ♗xh1 16 ♔e2! c6 17 ♘f4 ♗c7 18 ♗e3 ♗xf4 19 ♗xf4 ♗g2 20 ♖g1 ♗h3 21 ♗h6, which was very good for White in Canal-Eliskases, Kecskemet 1933) 13 ♘xb6 axb6 14 ♗b3 (14 c3 ♕h4+ 15 ♔f1 ♘xf3 16 gxf3 ♖xa4 17 ♕xa4 ♕h3+ 18 ♔g1 ♗xf3 19 ♕c2 ♕g4+

20 ♔f1 ♗xh1 is better for Black) 14...♕h4+ 15 ♔f1 ♘xb3 16 cxb3 f5 17 ♕e1 (Estrin won twice from this position in top-level correspondence chess, so the evidence is that White is better, although I must add that one of the games wasn't very convincing) 17...♕d8 18 ♕e2 c5 19 a4 ♖f7 20 ♗d2 ♖d7 21 exf5 ♗f7 (21...♖e7 22 ♗g5 ♖xe2 23 ♗xd8 ♖c2 24 ♗xb6 ♖e8 25 ♖g1 ♖ee2 26 ♗xc5 ♖ed2 27 b4 ♗e8 28 b3 ♗d7 29 g4 ♖xh2 30 ♖g3 h5 31 gxh5 ♗xf5 32 ♔g1 ♖hd2 33 ♗d4 ♖xd3 34 ♖xg7+ ♔f8 35 ♖g5 ♗e6 36 ♗c5+ 1-0, Estrin-Kletsel, 10th World corr. Ch. 1978) 22 ♗c3 ♗xb3 23 h4 b5 24 ♖e1 b4 25 ♗e5 ♗xa4 26 d4 cxd4 27 ♕c4+ ♖d5 28 ♕xb4 d3 29 ♕d2 ♖xe5? (I don't understand this move; why not 29...♖c8?) 30 ♖xe5 ♖c8 31 ♖e1 ♖c2 32 ♕b4 b5 33 b3 ♖b2 34 ♕c3 ♖xb3 35 ♕c6 ♔f7 36 ♕b7+ 1-0, Estrin-Karker, 6th World corr. Ch. 1968.

13 ♗f4

13 ♘xb6 ♕h4+ 14 ♔f1 (14 g3 ♕h3 is also promising for Black) 14...fxe4! 15 ♗b3+ ♔h8 16 ♕e1 ♖xf3+ 17 gxf3 ♕h3+ 18 ♔g1 ♘xf3+ 19 ♔f2 ♘xe1 20 ♖xe1 ♖f8+ 21 ♔g1 ♕g4+ 22 ♔h1 ♕f3+ 23 ♔g1 ♕f2+ 24 ♔h1 ♗f3 mate, Gorelik-Chashichin, corr. 1982.

13...fxe4 14 dxe4 ♘xf3+! (this combination leads to a forced win) **15 gxf3 ♖xf4 16 ♖f1** (desperation, but 16 ♘xf4 ♕h4+ 17 ♔d2 ♕xf4+ 18 ♔c3 ♕f6+ 19 ♔b3 ♖d8 gives Black a crushing attack) **16...♖xe4+** (the final blow seals White's fate) **17 fxe4 ♕h4+ 18 ♔d2 ♕xh2+ 19 ♔d3 ♗xd1 20 ♖axd1 ♔h8 0-1**

Game 29

Stertenbrink-Omelchenko
corr. 1987

1 e4 e5 2 ♘f3 ♘c6 3 ♘c3 ♘f6 4 ♗b5 ♘d4 5 ♗a4 ♗c5 6 ♘xe5 0-0 7 ♘d3 ♗b6 8 e5 ♘e8 9 0-0

This is the old way to continue after 8 e5, but it is now rarely seen. White needs to move his knight from d3 to complete his development, but this gives Black time to develop a dangerous initiative. The active knight on d4 and the weakness of f2 combine to make White's defensive task very difficult.

9...d6 10 exd6

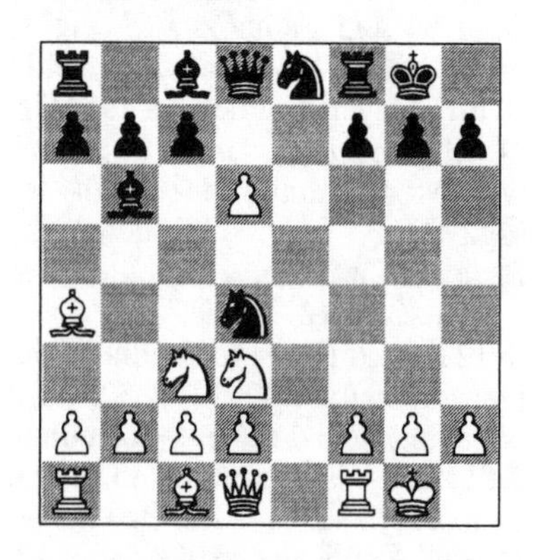

10...♘f6

This is the key move. Black's knight is heading for g4, where it targets the weak squares f2 and h2. The recapture on d6 is much less effective:

⇨ 10...♘xd6 11 ♘e1 (*ECO* recommends 11 ♔h1 c6 12 ♘f4, but 11 ♔h1 ♕h4 is more dangerous)

11...h5!? 12 ♕xh5 g6 13 ♕e5 (after 13 ♕d1 Black can play 13...♔g7 followed by ...♖h8 and ...♕h4) 13...f6 14 ♕g3 ♔g7 15 d3 ♘6f5 16 ♕f4 c6 17 ♕d2 ♖h8 18 ♘e4 ♕c7 19 g3 ♘h4! 20 gxh4 ♖xh4 21 ♘g3 ♕d7 22 ♕e3 ♘xc2? (winning White's queen is a mistake; 22...♕h3 would force White to take a draw by 23 ♕e7+; *New in Chess* suggests 22...♘e6 23 ♕e2 ♖xa4, but 23 d4! saves the piece) 23 ♗xc2 ♗xe3 24 fxe3 ♕h3 25 ♖f2 (the attack is over and once White's pieces co-ordinate for an attack on f6 the game is over too) 25...♗e6 26 ♗d2 ♖ah8 27 ♗c3 ♖f8 28 ♘f3 ♖g4 29 ♖af1 ♗d5 30 e4 ♗e6 31 ♘e1 ♔g8 32 ♖xf6 ♖xf6 33 ♖xf6 ♗f7 34 ♘g2 ♕h6 35 ♖f1 ♕f8 36 ♗b3 1-0, Franzoni-Bhend, Berne 1987.

11 d7

Universally adopted. Nobody has felt like giving Black yet another tempo by 11 dxc7 ♕d6, with the deadly threat of ...♘g4. The move played returns one pawn in order to exchange the ineffective bishop on a4 for one of Black's main attacking pieces.

11...♗xd7 12 ♗xd7 ♕xd7 13 ♘e1

White frees his d-pawn and, more importantly, prepares ♘f3 exchanging the dangerous d4 knight.

13...♖ae8 14 ♘f3

14 d3 is too slow and allows 14...♘g4 15 ♘f3 ♘xf3+ 16 ♕xf3 ♘xf2 17 ♘d5 ♘xd3+! (much stronger than 17...♕xd5 18 ♕xd5 ♘h3+ with perpetual check, Jansa-Pachman, Prague 1966) 18 ♘xb6 ♕d4+ 19 ♔h1 ♘xc1 with a definite advantage for Black, as pointed out by Hübner.

14...♘g4 15 h3 f5!

This piece sacrifice poses serious problems for White, and it is much better than other moves:

⇨ 15...♘xf2 16 ♖xf2 ♖e6 (or 16...♘xf3+ 17 ♕xf3 ♕d4 18 g3, with advantage for White in Sterten-brink-Gromotka, corr. 1983) 17 ♘g5! ♖g6 18 d3 h6 19 ♘ge4 ♕xh3 20 ♗g5 ♕e6 21 ♗e3 f5 22 ♗xd4 ♗xd4 23 ♕f3 c6?! (23...♖e8 24 ♘d2 is better for White, but still a fight) 24 ♘e2! ♗xb2 25 ♖af1 ♖g4 26 ♕xg4 fxg4 27 ♖xf8+ ♔h7 28 c3 ♕xa2 29 ♖8f7 ♗a3 30 ♘2g3 ♔g6 31 ♖xb7 a5 32 ♘f5 1-0, Sterten-brink-Vukcevich, corr. 1986.

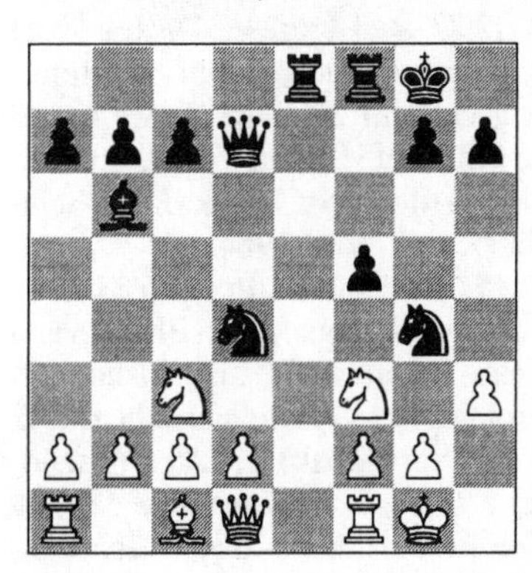

16 d3

White cannot take the piece because 16 hxg4 fxg4 17 ♘xd4 ♕xd4 18 ♔h1 ♖e5 gives Black a crushing attack.

16...♕d6

Now acceptance is forced.

17 hxg4 ♘xf3+ 18 ♕xf3

Or 18 gxf3 ♕g3+ 19 ♔h1 ♕h3+ 20 ♔g1 fxg4 with a decisive attack.

18...fxg4

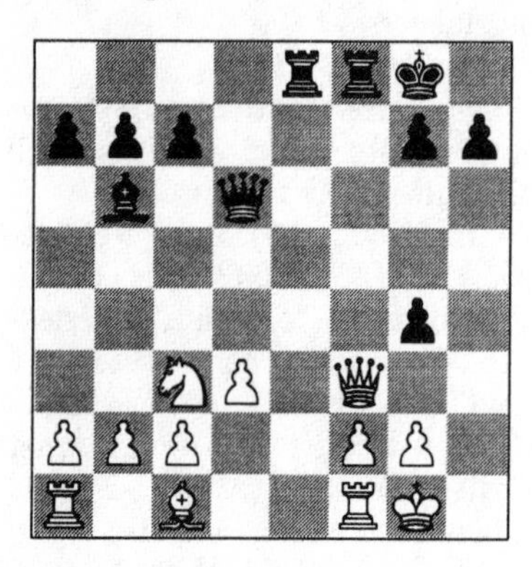

19 Bf4

⇨ 19 Qd5+ (19 Qxg4 Rxf2 wins for Black) 19...Qxd5 20 Nxd5 Bxf2+! 21 Kh1 (21 Rxf2 Re1+ 22 Kh2 Rxf2 23 Be3 Rxg2+ 24 Kxg2 Rxa1 is better for Black, but this is White's best chance) 21...Re5 22 Nf4 Bg3 23 Bd2 Ref5 24 Rae1 g5 with a winning position for Black, Rüfenacht-Chebeniuk, corr. 1984.

19...gxf3 20 Bxd6 cxd6 21 Rfe1 (material is equal, but Black has a clear advantage; his bishop is stronger than White's knight and f2 is still very weak) **21...Rc8** (intending ...Rc5-g5) **22 Rac1 Rc5 23 Ne4 Re5 24 c4** (not 24 Nxd6? Rg5 winning at once, while after 24 g3 d5 both 25 Nc3 Rg5 26 Kf1 Rh5 27 Kg2 Rh3 and 25 Nd2 Re2 are also winning) **24...Re6** (threat 25...Rg6 26 g3 Rf5, followed by doubling rooks on the h-file) **25 gxf3 Rxf3 26 Kg2 Rxd3** (the rest is purely technical) **27 Ng5 Re5 28 Rxe5 dxe5 29 c5 Bd8 30 Ne4 Bc7 31 c6 bxc6 32 Rxc6 Bb6 33 Re6 Bd4 34 Re8+ Kf7 35 Nd6+ Kf6 36 Nc4 Rd1 37 Rc8 h5 38 Rc6+ Kg5 39 Rd6 Kf4 40 Rd7 g6 41 Rf7+ Kg4 42 Rf3 Rg1+ 43 Kxg1 Kxf3 44 Kf1 e4 45 b4 h4 0-1**

Game 30

Bosch-Ciolac
Leukerbad Open 1992

1 e4 e5 2 Nc3 Nf6 3 Nf3 Nc6 4 Bb5 Nd4 5 Ba4 Bc5 6 Nxe5 0-0 7 Nd3 Bb6 8 e5 Ne8 9 Nd5 d6

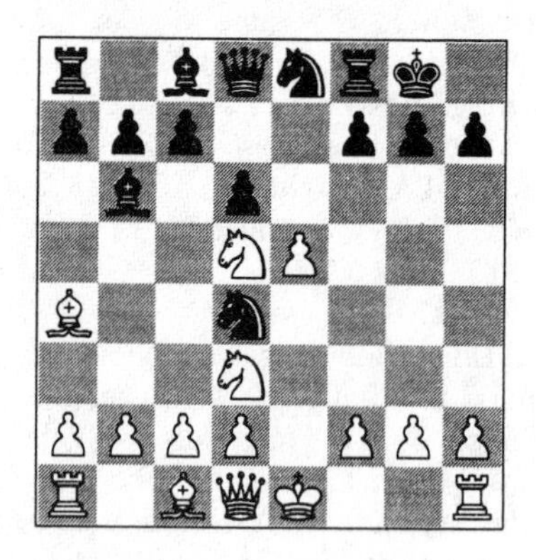

10 Ne3

The alternative 10 c3 is distinctly inferior:

⇨ 10...Bf5 11 N3b4 c5 12 Nxb6 axb6 13 cxd4 cxb4 14 0-0 (14 Bc2 looks better, preventing the bishop settling on d3) 14...Bd3 15 Re1 Qh4 (Pytel suggests 15...dxe5 16 dxe5 Nc7 17 Bc2 Ne6 as an improvement) 16 Bc2 Bxc2 17 Qxc2 Qxd4 18 exd6 ½-½, Bednarski-Pytel, Dortmund 1975.

⇨ 10...Qh4! (10...dxe5?! 11 Nxb6 axb6 12 cxd4 Qxd4 13 Bc2 Bf5 offers some compensation for the piece, but White might be able to escape by 14 ♘b4!?) 11 ♘e3 ♕e4 12 ♘b4 dxe5 13 cxd4 exd4 14 ♕c2?! (14 ♗c2 ♕e5 15 ♘d3 ♕e7 16 0-0 is better, with approximate equality) 14...♕e5 15 f4?! (15 0-0 is best, but then Black is slightly better) 15...♕xf4 16 ♘c4 ♕h4+ 17 ♔f1 (17 g3 ♕e7+) 17...d3! 18 ♘xd3 ♗f5 19 ♘xb6 axb6 20 ♗b3 ♖d8 (21 ♗c4 ♖d4! followed by ...♖f4+) 0-1, Tylor-Milner-Barry, Hastings 1938/9.

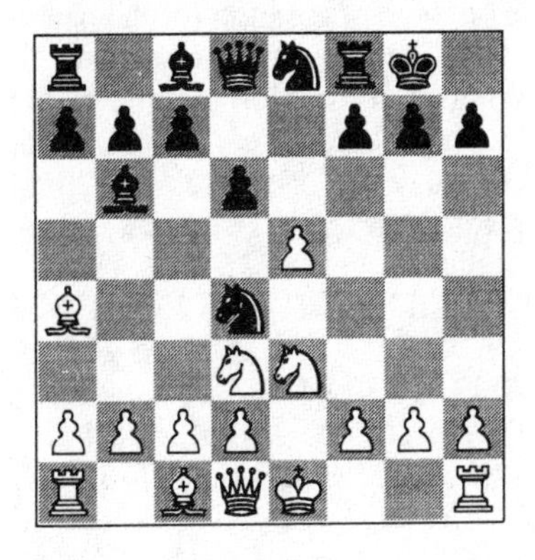

10...dxe5

Or 10...c6 (for other 10th moves, see game 31) and now:

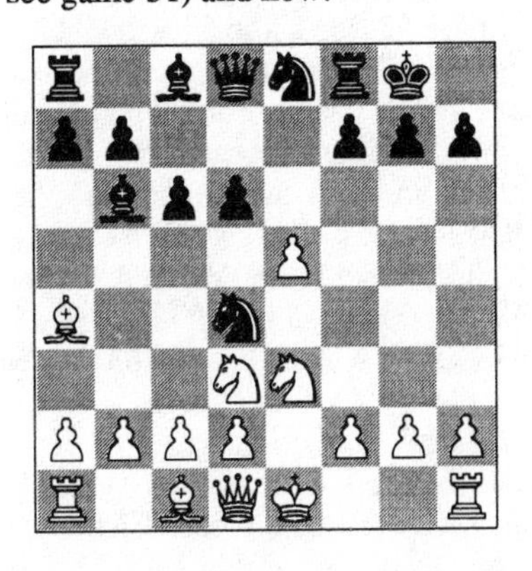

⇨ 11 c3 ♘f5 (Makarychev suggests 11...♘e6 12 0-0 ♗c7, transposing to the Short-Speelman play-off game given below, which was just very slightly better for White; if White wants to avoid this, then he has to find an alternative to 12 0-0) 12 0-0 ♗c7 13 f4 dxe5 14 ♘xe5 ♘xe3 15 dxe3 ♕e7 16 ♗c2 ♘f6 17 e4 ♖e8! 18 ♘f3? (18 ♕f3! ♗xe5 19 fxe5 is good for White after 19...♘g4 20 ♗f4! or 19...♕xe5 20 ♗f4 followed by e5) 18...♘xe4! 19 ♖e1 (Short had overlooked that 19 ♗xe4 ♕c5+! followed by ...♖xe4 is good for Black) 19...♗f5 20 ♗e3 ♖ad8 21 ♘d4 ♗g6 (Black is slightly better) 22 ♕f3 ♘f6! 23 f5!? ♗h5 24 ♕h3 c5 25 ♗g5! (25 ♘b5 ♗f4! is strong) 25...♕xe1+ 26 ♖xe1 ♖xe1+ 27 ♔f2 ♖de8 28 ♗xf6 cxd4 29 ♕xh5 gxf6 30 ♗b3 (both sides were in time-trouble) 30...♖1e2+!? ½-½, Short-Speelman, London match 1991.

⇨ 11 0-0 ♗c7 12 c3 ♘e6 13 f4 dxe5 14 ♘xe5 ♘xf4 15 d4 ♗xe5 (15...♘g6 16 ♘xg6 hxg6 17 ♗b3 is a little better for White) 16 dxe5 ♕xd1 17 ♗xd1 ♘d3 18 ♘c4 ♗e6 (18...b6 may be better, keeping the knight out of a5) 19 ♘a5 (this knight proves surprisingly hard to dislodge) 19...♘xc1 20 ♖xc1 ♖b8 21 ♗f3 ♘c7 22 c4 (in contrast Black's knight never finds a good square) 22...♘a6 23 a3 (White is slightly better) 23...♘c5 24 ♖cd1 ♖fc8 25 ♖fe1 ♔f8 26 b4 ♘a4 27 ♖d6 ♔e8 28 ♖e3 ♘b6 29 ♖e4 ♔e7 30 ♔f2 ♖c7 31 ♔e3 ♘d7 32 c5 ♖bc8 33 ♗g4 ♗xg4 34 ♖xg4 g6 35 ♔d4 b6 36 ♘b3 ♘f8 37 ♔c4 ♘e6 38 ♘d4 bxc5 39 ♘xe6 fxe6 40 bxc5? (White has patiently increased his advantage and now 40 ♔xc5 would have given him good winning chances) 40...♖f8 41 g3 ♖f1 42 ♖h4 h5 43 ♖f4 ♖c1+ 44 ♔d4 ♖d1+ 45 ♔e4 ♖e1+ 46 ♔d4 ♖d1+ ½-½, Short-Speelman, London match rapid play-off 1991.

11 ♘xe5 ♕g5

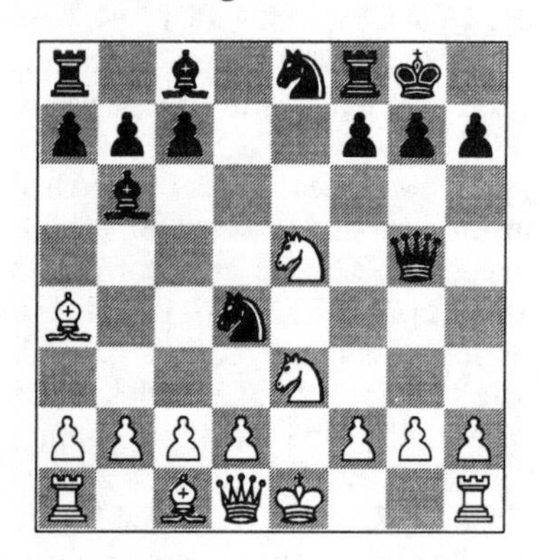

12 ♘5c4

The alternatives are inferior:

⇨ 12 ♘d7 (a bad choice) 12...♗xd7 13 ♗xd7 f5 14 c3 f4 (14...♘f6 may be even better) 15 cxd4 fxe3 16 dxe3 ♕xg2 17 ♖f1 ♘f6 18 ♗e6+ ♔h8 (this position is better for Black; the extra pawn is of no value because Black can regain it any time he likes by taking on h2, and meanwhile White's king is trapped in the centre) 19 ♗d2 ♖ad8 20 d5 ♘e4 (taking on d5 guarantees a clear advantage, but the move played is also promising) 21 ♕e2 ♕xh2 22 ♗c3 ♘xc3 23 bxc3 c6 24 ♖d1 cxd5 25 ♗xd5 ♗xe3? (25...♕e5 is dangerous for White, which makes this sacrifice all the more strange) 26 fxe3 ♖xf1+ 27 ♔xf1? (what's wrong with 27 ♕xf1?) 27...♖f8+ 28 ♗f3 ♕g3 29 ♕f2 ♕xf3 30 ♕xf3 ♖xf3+ 31 ♔e2 ♖f8 (Black reaches an ending a pawn up, but White's active rook provides enough compensation for a draw) 32 ♖d7 ♖b8 33 e4 ♔g8 34 ♔e3 ♔f8 35 ♔f4 a5 36 e5 ♖c8 37 ♖xb7 ♖xc3 38 e6 ♖c5 39 ♖f7+ ♔g8 40 ♖a7 ♔f8 41 ♖f7+ ♔g8 42 ♖d7 ½-½, Franzoni-Godena, Manila Ol. 1992.

⇨ 12 ♘d3 ♗f5 13 0-0 ♗xd3 14 cxd3 ♘d6 (this line gives Black more than enough compensation for the pawn) 15 b4 (an unfortunate necessity if White is to develop his queenside) 15...♕g6 16 ♗c2 c6 17 ♗b2 ♖ad8 18 ♖c1 ♘xc2 19 ♕xc2 ♘c8 20 d4 ♗xd4 21 ♕xg6 hxg6 (already Black is slightly better) 22 ♗c3 ♘b6 23 ♖fe1 ♖d7 24 ♔f1 ♖fd8 25 ♖c2 f6 26 ♔e2 ♔f7 27 ♖b1 a6 28 g3 ♖e8 29 ♔f3 ♘a4 30 h4 ♗a7 31 ♔e2 ♖ed8 32 ♖e1 ♖d3 33 ♖b1 ♖3d7 34 ♖e1 ♘b6 35 ♖b1 ♘c8 36 a4 ♘d6 37 ♔f3 ♖e8 38 ♔e2 ♗b6 39 ♔f3 ♗d8 40 ♔e2 f5 41 ♔f3 ♗f6 42 ♔e2 ♘e4 43 b5 ♗xc3 44 dxc3 cxb5 45 axb5 a5 46 b6 ♘xg3+ 47 fxg3 ♖de7 48 ♔f2 ♖xe3 49 ♖d1 ♖3e6 50 ♖b2 ♖c6 51 ♖b3 a4 52 ♖a3 ♖xb6 53 ♖xa4 ♖b2+ 54 ♔f3 (Black has maintained his advantage, but there is still no forced win) 54...♖ee2 (perhaps 54...♖ae2 offers more winning chances) 55 ♔f4 ♖g2 56 ♖d3 ♖bd2 57 ♖ad4 ♖xd3 58 ♖xd3 (now White defends) 58...♔e6 59 ♔g5 ♔e5 60 ♖e3+ ♔d5 61 ♖f3 ♔e4 62 ♖f4+ ♔e3 63 ♔xg6 ♖xg3+ 64 ♔xf5 ♔d3 65 ♖b4 ♔xc3 66 ♖xb7 ♔d2 67 h5 ♔e2 68 ♖b4 ♔f2 69 ♖a4 ♔g2 70 ♖b4 ♔h3 71 ♖a4 ♔g2 ½-½, I.Sokolov-Chandler, Brussels SWIFT Rapid 1992.

12...f5

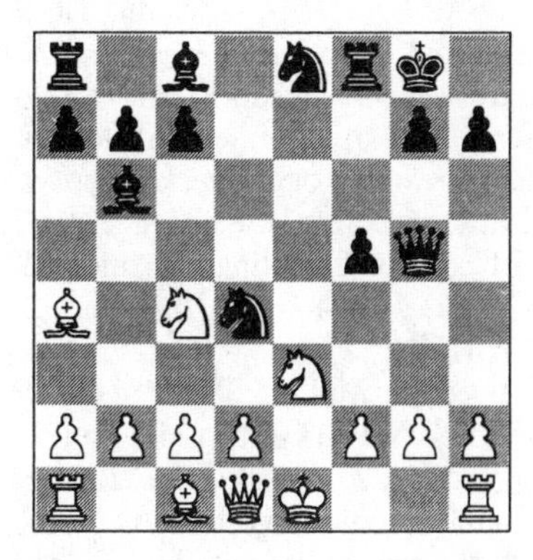

13 f4!

➪ Better than 13 c3 f4 14 cxd4 fxe3 15 ♘xe3 ♗xd4, as played in Bogaerts-Geenen, Belgium 1991, and now 16 0-0 ♗h3 17 ♕b3+ ♔h8 18 ♕d5 ♗xe3 19 ♕xg5 ♗xg5 20 gxh3 is given in *Informator* as good for Black. However, the critical question is whether White can play 18 ♕xb7!?, meeting 18...♘d6 by 19 f4, when the position is absolutely unclear.

13...♕xf4 14 c3 ♘e6 (14...♕h4+ 15 g3 ♕e4 is refuted by 16 0-0) **15 d4 c6 16 g3 ♕e4 17 ♖f1** (17 0-0 ♘g5 18 ♕h5 followed by ♗c2 is also very good for White) **17...♘g5?** (bad, but even 17...♘c7 18 ♘e5 ♘d5 19 ♕e2 is excellent for White) **18 ♘e5!** (suddenly there is no escape for Black's queen) **18...f4 19 ♗c2** (Black could have given up here) **19...♕xe5 20 dxe5 fxe3 21 ♗b3+ ♗e6 22 ♖xf8+ ♔xf8 23 ♗xe6 ♘xe6 24 ♗xe3 ♗xe3 25 ♕f3+ ♔g8 26 ♕xe3 ♘8c7 27 0-0-0 c5 28 ♕e4 ♖b8 29 ♖d6 b5 30 ♕c6 ♖b6 31 ♕d7 1-0**

Game 31

Short-Timman
Linares 1992

1 e4 e5 2 ♘f3 ♘c6 3 ♘c3 ♘f6 4 ♗b5 ♘d4 5 ♗a4 ♗c5 6 ♘xe5 0-0 7 ♘d3 ♗b6 8 e5 ♘e8 9 ♘d5 d6 10 ♘e3

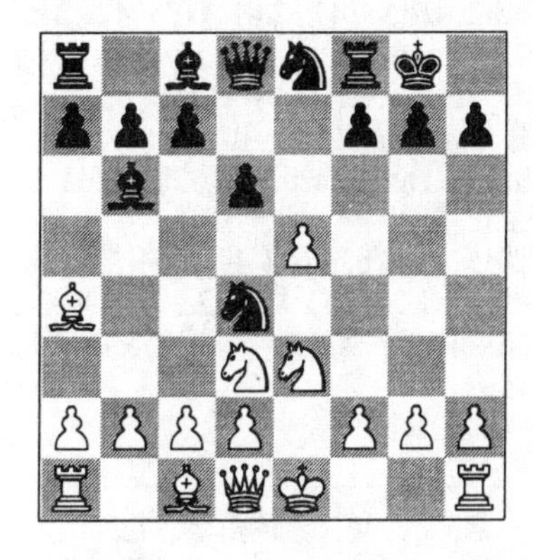

10...♕g5

➪ 10...♕e7 11 exd6 ♘xd6 12 0-0 c6 13 c3 ♘4f5 14 ♘e1 ♘e4 15 ♗c2 ♖e8 16 d4 (16 ♘f3 ♘xe3 17 fxe3 ♗g4 18 ♕e1 ♖ad8 19 ♘d4 ♗c7 is assessed as unclear by Makarychev) 16...♗c7 17 ♘d3 (a critical moment; Makarychev gives 17 ♘xf5 ♗xf5 18 ♘f3 ♖ad8 19 ♖e1 ♕f6 and 17 ♘f3 ♘xe3 18 ♗xe3 ♗g4 19 h3 ♗h5 20 ♖e1 ♕f6! as unclear, but perhaps 17 ♕f3!? is an improvement) 17...♕h4 18 ♘e5 ♗xe5 19 dxe5 ♖xe5 20 f3? (White could have kept an edge by 20 ♘c4 ♖e8 21 ♕f3 ♘f6 22 ♘e3 ♘xe3 23 ♗xe3 ♗g4 24 ♕g3) 20...♘xe3 21 ♗xe3 ♘xc3 22 ♕e1 ♕e7 23 ♕xc3 ♖xe3 24 ♖fe1 ♖xe1+

25 ♖xe1 ♗e6 26 ♗b3 (White has lost a pawn, but he may have enough compensation to draw) 26...♖d8 27 ♕e3 a6 28 f4 ♕f6 29 ♕b6 ♗xb3 30 axb3 h5 31 ♕xb7 ♕d4+ 32 ♔h1 ♕e4 33 ♖g1 h4 34 h3 f5 35 ♕xa6 ♖d3 36 ♔h2? (in time-trouble White misses 36 ♕c4+ drawing) 36...♕xf4+ 37 ♔h1 ♕e4 38 ♔h2? ♕e5+ (38...♖xb3 would have been winning for Black) 39 ♔h1 ♕d5 40 ♔h2 ♕d6+ 41 ♔h1 ♕d5 42 ♔h2 ♔h7 (now 42...♖xb3 may be met by 43 ♕c8+ ♔h7 44 ♕e8!) 43 ♕c4 ♕e5+ (Black is still slightly better but he cannot win) 44 ♔h1 ♕e4 45 ♔h2 ♖d4 46 ♕c3 ♕e5+ 47 ♔h1 ♕d5 48 ♔h2 ♖d2 49 ♕b4 ♖d4 50 ♕c3 c5 51 ♖f1 ♖d2 52 ♕f3 ½-½, Nikolenko-Makarychev, USSR Ch. 1991.

➪ 10...♕h4

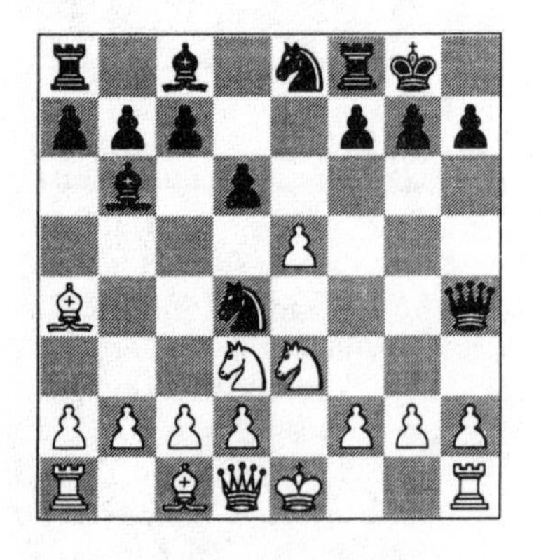

11 0-0 ♗e6 12 c3 (12 f4!? is a reasonable alternative) 12...♘e2+ 13 ♔h1 ♗xe3 14 dxe3 ♘xc1 15 ♖xc1 ♖d8 (15...dxe5 16 ♘xe5 ♖d8 is wrong because of 17 ♘f3!) 16 ♗b3 dxe5 17 ♗xe6 fxe6 18 ♕c2 (if White can consolidate then he will have a clear advantage, so Black must launch a speedy bid for counterplay) 18...♖f5! 19 ♖cd1 (after this Black can hold the balance; 19 f4 exf4 20 exf4 is better, when White can defend his king while still leaving Black with one weak e-pawn) 19...♘d6 20 ♕b3 ♖e8 21 ♘c5 ♖xf2 (21...e4 is tempting because 22 ♘xe6? fails to 22...♖b5, but 22 ♘xb7! ♖b5 23 ♕a4 is the refutation) 22 ♘xe6 ♔h8 23 ♖xf2 ♕xf2 24 ♘xc7 ♖f8 25 h3 ♘f5? (25...♘e4! 26 ♘e6 ♕g3 27 ♘xf8 ♘f2+ 28 ♔g1 ♘xh3+ would have forced a draw; Black can try to win by 29 ♔h1 ♘f2+ 30 ♔g1 ♘g4 31 ♕f7 ♕e3+ 32 ♔h1 ♘f2+ 33 ♔h2 ♘xd1, but the result will be a draw all the same after 34 ♕e8) 26 ♘e6 ♘xe3 27 ♕xb7 ♖g8? (in *Informator* I gave 27...♕f6 28 ♖d6 ♕g6 29 ♘xf8 ♕b1+ 30 ♔h2 ♘f1+ as a draw, but now I see that 27...♕f6 28 ♘xf8 ♘xd1 29 ♘d7 ♕f1+ 30 ♔h2 ♕f4+ 31 g3 ♕d2+ 32 ♕g2 is good for White) 28 ♖g1 ♕f6 29 ♕f3?! (after 29 ♘c5 Black has little to show for his minus pawn) 29...♕xe6 30 ♕xe3 ♕xa2 31 b4 ♖e8 32 ♖d1 (White keeps an advantage because his pieces are more active and Black's pawns are weak) 32...♕f7 33 ♖a1 ♖e7 34 ♕e4 (now White is ready to push his c-pawn) 34...h6 35 c4 ♕f4 36 ♕xf4 exf4 (this ending is lost for Black; the outside passed pawn is one factor, but equally important is the exposed pawn on f4) 37 c5 ♔g8 38 b5 ♔f7 39 b6 axb6 40 cxb6 ♔f6 41 ♖b1 ♖b7 42 ♔g1 g5 43 ♔f2 ♔e7 (Black has no time for ...h5 and ...g4) 44 ♔f3 ♔d8 45 ♔g4 ♔c8 46 ♖c1+ ♔b8 47 ♖c6

♖d7 48 ♖xh6 ♖d2 49 ♔xg5 ♖xg2+ 50 ♔xf4 ♖f2+ 51 ♔g3 ♖b2 52 ♖f6 ♖b3+ 53 ♔g4 ♖b4+ 54 ♔g5 ♖b5+ 55 ♖f5 ♖xb6 56 h4 ♔c7 57 h5 1-0, Nunn-Christiansen, Bundesliga 1991/2.

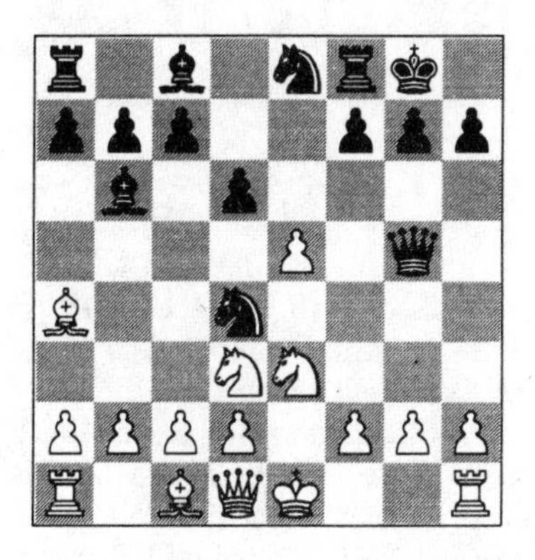

11 f4

The alternative is 11 exd6 ♘xd6 12 0-0 and now:

➪ 12...c6 13 c3 ♘e6? (13...♘4f5 is the only reasonable move) 14 ♗c2 f5 15 f4 (stopping Black's attack and leaving White a pawn up with the better position) 15...♕f6 16 g3 h6 17 ♘e5 g5 18 d4 gxf4 19 gxf4 ♔h8 20 ♔h1 ♖g8 21 ♗d2 c5 22 ♘d5 ♕g7 23 ♖g1 ♕xg1+ 1-0, Chandler-McMahon, London (Lloyds Bank) 1992.

➪ 12...♘6f5? (Hübner recommends 12...♘4f5 13 ♘e1 ♘xe3 14 fxe3 ♗g4 15 ♘f3 ♕h5 16 ♕e1 c6 followed by ...♖ae8, with an unclear position) 13 c3 (13 ♘e1!? is good for White after 13...♘h4 14 c3 ♘e6 15 d4 ♘f4 16 ♔h1 or 13...♘xe3 14 dxe3 ♘c6 15 ♗xc6 bxc6 16 ♕f3 followed by ♘d3, according to Hübner's analysis) 13...♘xe3 14 dxe3 ♗h3 (after 14...♗g4 15 exd4 ♗xd1 16 ♗xg5 ♗xa4 17 ♖fe1 White has good winning chances) 15 ♘e1 (after 15 ♘f4?! ♗g4 16 f3 ♘f5! 17 fxg4 ♘xe3 18 ♕f3 ♘xf1+ 19 ♔xf1 ♕c5 20 ♘e2 ♖ad8 the position is rather unclear) 15...♘c6 16 e4? (16 ♗xc6 bxc6 17 ♔h1 ♗e6 18 ♕e2 would have left Black with very little for the sacrificed pawn) 16...♕g6 17 ♔h1 ♗e6 18 ♕e2 ♘e5 (Black's active pieces provide enough play for the pawn) 19 ♗b3 ♗xb3 20 axb3 ♖fe8 21 f3 ♖ad8 22 ♗f4 ♕e6 23 ♗xe5 (23 ♕c2 ♘g6 24 ♗g3 ♕d7 25 ♗f2 ♘f4 26 ♗xb6 axb6 27 ♖f2 f5 28 exf5 ♕e7 is also unclear) 23...♕xe5 24 ♘c2 f5 25 ♖ae1 fxe4 26 fxe4 c6 27 ♘a3 ♗c7 28 g3 ♕e6 29 b4 ♖d7 30 ♘c2 ½-½, Nunn-Hübner, Munich 1991.

Short's move is more aggressive. He intends keeping the pawn on e5, even if this means weakening the b6-g1 diagonal.

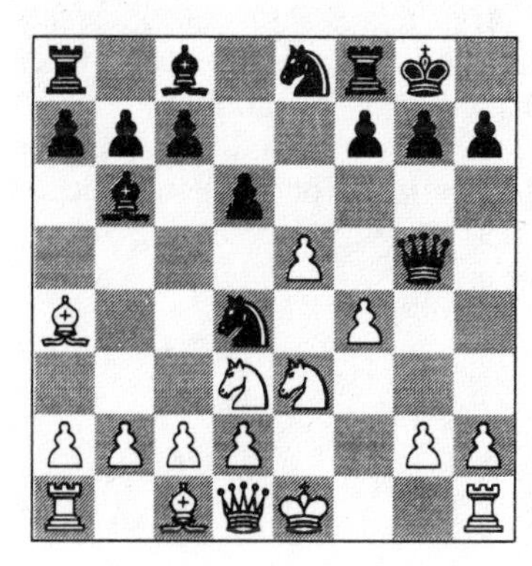

11...♕g6

In *Informator* Makarychev gave the line 11...♕h4+ 12 g3 ♕h3 13 c3 (13 ♘f2 ♕e6) 13...♘f5 14 ♘f2

♘xe3 15 dxe3 ♕h6! (15...♕g2? 16 ♗c2 threatening ♗e4 is good for White) 16 exd6 ♘xd6 17 0-0 ♗f5, assessing this position as unclear. However, 13 ♘f2 ♕e6 14 c3! looks very good for White, for example 14...dxe5 15 fxe5 ♘f5 16 d4 and White consolidates.

12 0-0 f6 13 exd6?!

White should not bring the e8 knight back into play unless there is absolutely no choice. 13 ♔h1 was an improvement, when Timman gives 13...c6 as unclear, although I believe that White is slightly better.

13...♘xd6 14 ♘f2 ♘4f5 15 ♘d5

There are many possible moves. 15 ♕f3 ♘d4 16 ♕d1 would be a draw, while 15 ♕g4 ♕h6! gives Black an edge according to Timman. 15 ♔h1 and 15 c4 were other ideas, but my general impression is that Black has full compensation for the pawn.

15...♔h8 16 ♘xb6 axb6 17 c3?

After this Black's attack crashes through. 17 ♗b3 was better, when Black may choose between 17...♘d4, with good compensation for the pawn, or the double-edged 17...♘h4 18 g3 ♖a5, playing directly for mate.

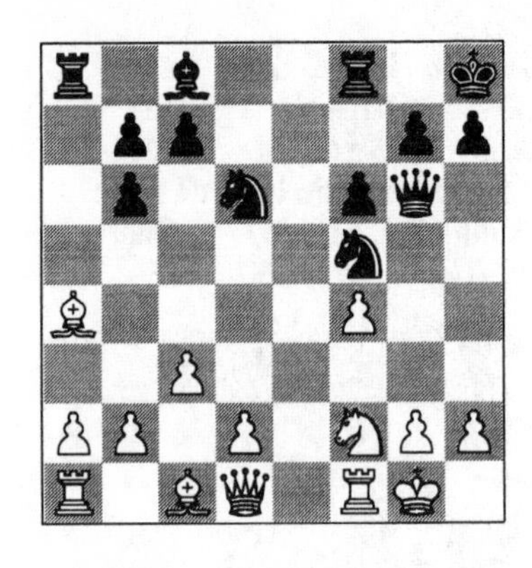

17...♖xa4! 18 ♕xa4 ♘h4 19 g3 ♘f3+ 20 ♔g2 ♘h4+ 21 ♔g1 ♘f3+ 22 ♔g2 ♗e6! 23 ♘h1

This looks horrible, but 23 ♔xf3 ♗d5+ 24 ♔e2 ♖e8+ 25 ♔d1 ♗f3 is mate, while 23 d3 ♕h5 24 ♕d1 ♗d5 25 ♘e4 ♕xh2+ 26 ♔xf3 f5 gives Black a decisive attack.

23...♗d5 24 ♖xf3 ♘f5!

Timman comments that 24...♕d3? 25 ♕d1 ♖e8 wins for Black after 26 ♘f2? ♖e2, but loses after 27 ♔f2!. This isn't quite right, because even 26 ♘f2 ♖e2 is a loss after 27 ♔f1!.

25 ♘f2

25 ♔f2 fails to 25...♕h5, so White's position collapses.

25...♘h4+ 26 ♔f1 ♘xf3 27 d3 ♘xh2+ 28 ♔e2 ♗c6 0-1

After 4 ♗b5 ♗b4 the main line runs 5 0-0 0-0 6 d3 d6 7 ♗g5 ♗xc3 8 bxc3 d6. This chapter analyses deviations from the main line. In game 32 we examine alternatives on or before White's 6th move. The two most important possibilities are 5 d3 by White and 5...d6 by Black. These do not necessarily transpose into the main line, since 5 d3 may be met by 5...♘d4 and 5...d6 by 6 ♘d5. There seems little reason to allow these variations since moving the d-pawn has no genuine advantages over immediate castling.

The only reason for an early ...d6 by Black would be to prevent the line 6 ♗xc6 dxc6, which we consider in game 33 (6 ♗xc6 bxc6 is in game 32). This may be followed either by 7 ♘xe5, or by the positional 7 d3. The 7 ♘xe5 line is especially innocuous, and often results in a quick draw. 7 d3 leads to positions which are similar both to the Ruy Lopez and to game 22 (Psakhis-Barua) from chapter 7. The difference is that in the Ruy Lopez Black's bishop is normally on e7, in chapter 7 the bishop was on c5 and here it is on b4. When the bishop is on b4 Black has the extra option of taking on c3, but other lines do not differ much from the two parallel situations. Readers should refer to chapter 7 and a book on the Ruy Lopez when studying this section.

In games 34 and 35 we examine deviations on Black's 6th move. Game 34 covers the two lines 6...♗xc3 7 bxc3 d5 and 6...♘d4. Game 35 has considerable importance, because although we have taken 6...d6 7 ♗g5 ♗xc3 8 bxc3 as the move-order for the main line, in practice a number of games follow the alternative path 6...♗xc3 7 bxc3 d6. The question arises as to whether White has nothing better than 8 ♗g5, or can he exploit the early exchange on c3? 8 ♖e1 is the main attempt to improve on 8 ♗g5, and this is covered in game 35.

Games 36 and 37 deal with the line 7 ♘e2. There are only two common replies, 7...♗g4 (game 36) and 7...♘e7 (game 37). The main line of game 37 probably represents Black's best play and should suffice for equality.

Game 32

M.Tseitlin-Haba
Ostrava 1991

1 e4 e5 2 ♘f3 ♘c6 3 ♘c3 ♘f6 4 ♗b5 ♗b4

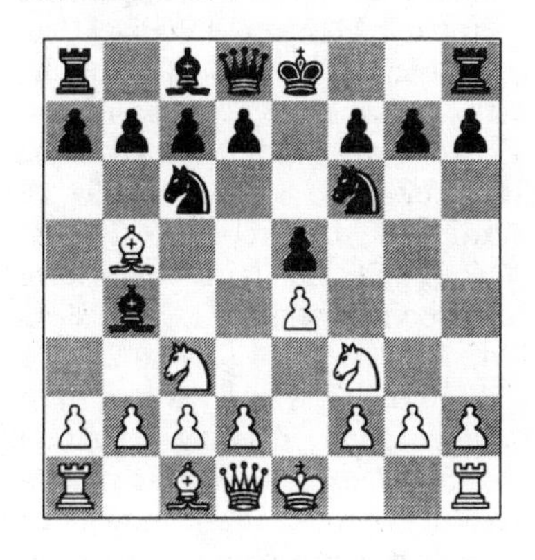

5 0-0

Or 5 d3 (this is probably inaccurate) 5...♘d4 (5...d6 is likely to transpose to normal lines) 6 ♗a4 b5 7 ♗b3 and now:

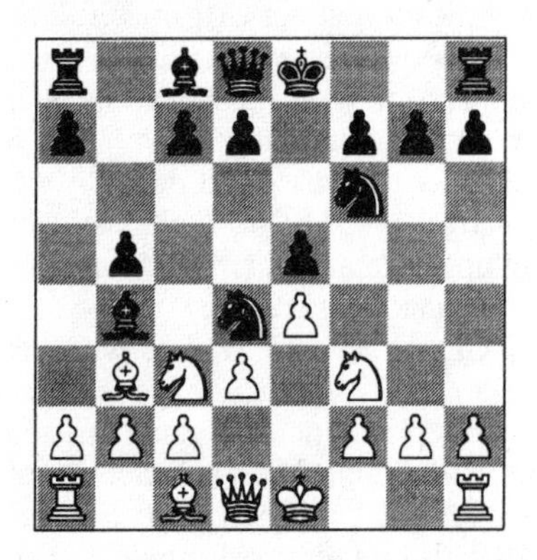

⇨ 7...d5! (threatening both 8...♘xf3+ 9 ♕xf3 d4 and 8...♗g4) 8 ♘xe5 ♘xb3 (Botvinnik recommends 8...♕e7, giving the lines 9 ♗f4 ♘xb3 10 cxb3 d4 and 9 f4 0-0 as good for Black; the second line is not completely clear after 9 f4 0-0 10 ♗e3, but there is little doubt that Black is at least equal) 9 cxb3 d4? (9...dxe4 is immediately equal) 10 ♘c6 dxc3 11 ♘xb4 c5 (Black had overlooked that 11...♕d4 is met by 12 bxc3 ♕xc3+ 13 ♗d2) 12 ♘c2 c4 13 bxc4 bxc4 14 e5 ♘g4 15 d4 cxb2 16 ♗xb2 ♕a5+ 17 ♕d2 ♕xd2+ 18 ♔xd2 ♘xf2 19 ♖hf1 ♘e4+ 20 ♔e3 ♗b7 21 ♖f4? (21 ♖ab1! would have been good for White) 21...c3 22 ♗a3 ♘d2 23 ♗c5 g5 24 ♖g4 h6 25 ♖c1 ♖c8 26 ♗xa7? (26 h4 would have offered good drawing chances) 26...f5! 27 exf6 ♔f7 (Black has a very dangerous attack now that White's bishop cannot move to e7 to block the open file) 28 ♗c5 ♔xf6 29 ♘b4 ♖he8+ 30 ♔d3 ♘e4 31 ♖f1+ ♔g6 32 ♖xe4 ♗xe4+ 33 ♔xc3 ♗xg2 34 ♖f2 ♗h3 35 ♘d3 ♗f5 36 ♘b4 ♗e4 37 ♔d2 h5 38 a3 h4 39 ♘a2 g4 40 ♘c3 ♗f3 41 ♗d6 ♖cd8 42 ♗c5 h3 43 ♘b5 ♗g2 0-1, Rochlin-Botvinnik, Leningrad 1930.

⇨ 7...d6 8 h3 (recommended by Botvinnik) 8...c6 9 0-0 ♘xb3 10 axb3 h6 11 d4 ♕e7 12 ♘e2! (a very awkward move; the threat is c3, and Black is forced to take desperate measures in order to rescue his bishop) 12...♕c7 13 c3 ♗a5 14 dxe5 dxe5 15 ♘xe5 ♕xe5 16 ♖xa5 ♕c7 17 ♖a1 ♘xe4 18 ♕d4 f5 (Black has avoided loss of material, but only at the cost of serious weaknesses on the black squares) 19 ♗f4 ♕d7 20 f3 ♘f6 21 ♖fe1 0-0 22 ♗e5 ♕f7 23 ♗xf6 ♕xf6 24 ♕xf6 ♖xf6 25 ♘d4 ♔f7 26 b4 f4 27 ♖e5 a6 28 ♖ae1 ♖a7 29 ♖e8 ♖c7 30 ♖1e5 ♖d6 31 h4 ♖d5 32 ♖e4 ♖h5 33 ♖h8 ♖xh4 34 ♖ee8 ♗b7 35 ♘e6 ♖d7 36 ♖hf8+ ♔g6 37 ♘xf4+ ♔g5 38 ♖e5+ 1-0, Kimelfeld-Estrin, USSR 1972.

⇨ 7...d6 8 h3 a5 (better than 8...c6) 9 a3 ♗xc3+ 10 bxc3 ♘xb3 11 cxb3 a4 (11...♗b7 12 c4 bxc4 13 bxc4 h6 14 ♗d2 0-0 15 g4!? was unclear in Kasparian-T.Petrosian, Armenian Ch. 1946) 12 c4 bxc4 13 bxc4 ♘d7 (Black adopts an aggressive plan based on ...f5, but this is not justified by the position; simply 13...0-0 is equal, because after ♗g5 Black can chase the bishop away by ...h6 and ...g5) 14 0-0 0-0 15 ♖b1 f5? (15...♘c5) 16 exf5 ♖xf5 17 ♗e3 (Black has problems meeting the threat of ♖b4) 17...♕e7 18 ♖b4 c5 19 ♖xa4 ♗a6 20 ♘d2 ♘b6 21 ♖a5 ♕c7 (the rook's position on a5 is a little strange, but Black can't take advantage of it) 22 ♘e4 ♖ff8 23 ♘g5 ♖fe8 24 ♕h5 g6 25 ♕h4 ♕e7 26 ♖b1 ♖eb8 27 ♕g3 ♕c7 28 f4 exf4 29 ♗xf4 ♘d7 30 ♖xb8+ ♘xb8 31 ♗xd6 ♕xa5 32 ♕f2 (and mates in a further six moves) 1-0, Petkovski-Djuric, Corfu Open 1991.

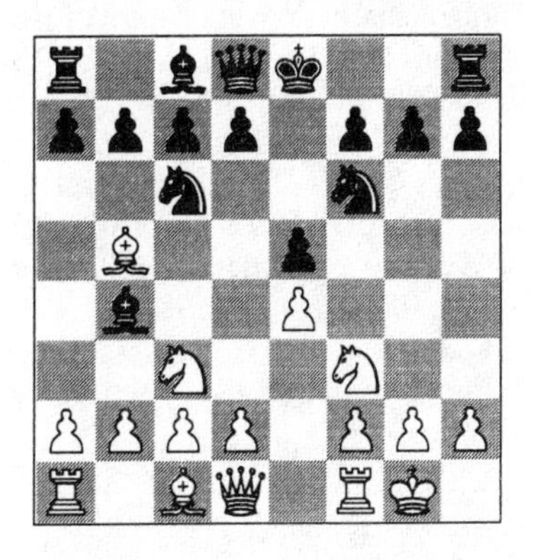

5...0-0

Or 5...d6 (certainly not 5...♘d4? 6 ♘xd4 exd4 7 e5 dxc3 8 bxc3 ♗e7 9 exf6 ♗xf6 10 ♗a3 with a crushing attack for White, Janowski-Taubenhaus, Ostend 1905) and now:

⇨ 6 ♘d5 (the best reply) 6...♗a5 7 d4 ♘d7 8 c3 0-0 9 b4 ♗b6 10 ♗e3?! (10 ♗g5 f6 11 ♗e3 may be stronger, but 10 a4!? is probably best of all, with advantage to White) 10...exd4 11 cxd4 ♘e7 12 ♘xb6 ♘xb6 (Black will play ...d5, when White's advantage is relatively slight) 13 ♗g5? f6 14 ♗h4 d5 15 e5 ♘g6 16 ♗g3 f5 (Black is at least equal, thanks to the horribly placed bishop on g3) 17 ♗d3 ♕e7 18 a3 a5 19 b5 ♘c4 20 ♕c1 ♗e6 21 ♘g5 f4 22 ♘xe6 ♕xe6 23 ♗xg6 fxg3 24 ♗d3 gxf2+ 25 ♔h1 ♖f7 26 ♖a2 ♖af8 27 ♖c2 ♕g4 (27...♕b6! is good for Black because after 28 ♗xc4 dxc4 29 ♖xc4 ♕xb5 White cannot take on c7) 28 ♗xc4 dxc4 29 ♖xc4 ♖f5 30 h3 ♕e4 31 ♖xc7 h6 32 ♕c4+ ♔h8 33 ♕c2 ♕xd4 34 e6 ♖e5 35 ♖f7 ♖e8 36 ♕xf2 ♕xf2 37 ♖1xf2 b6 38 ♖f8+ ♖xf8 39 ♖xf8+ ♔h7 40 ♖e8 ♖xb5 41 ♖b8 ♖e5 42 ♖xb6 ♔g6 43 ♖a6 ♔f6 44 ♔h2 h5 45 a4 h4 46 ♔g1 g5 47 ♔f2 ♖c5 ½-½, Podlesnik-Kupreichik, Vidmar Mem. 1989.

⇨ 6 ♘d5 ♗c5?! (now White is clearly better) 7 d4 exd4 8 ♘xd4 ♗xd4 9 ♕xd4 0-0 10 ♘xf6+ ♕xf6 11 ♕xf6 gxf6 12 ♗h6 (Black has a miserable ending) 12...♖e8 13 ♖fe1 a6 14 ♗f1 ♔h8 15 ♗d2 ♘e7 16 ♗c3 ♘g8 17 f4 ♔g7 18 ♖e3 ♔f8 19 ♗d3 ♗d7 20 ♖ae1 ♗b5 21 e5 (this looks premature) 21...♗xd3 22 ♖xd3 fxe5 23 fxe5 dxe5 24 ♖xe5 b6 25 ♖h5 h6 26 ♗d2 ♖e6 27 ♖d7 ♖c8 (27...♘f6 28 ♖xh6 ♘xd7 29 ♖h8+ ♔e7 30 ♖xa8 ♖e2 31 ♗c3 a5 is still better for White because of his passed h-pawn, but this gives Black fair drawing chances) 28 ♖f5 ♖e7 29 ♖xe7 ♔xe7 30 ♖e5+ ♔f6 31 ♗c3 ♔g6 32 ♖e3 ♖d8 33 ♖g3+ ♔f5 34 ♖g7 ♔e6 35 ♖h7 c5 (35...♖d1+ 36 ♔f2 ♖c1 looks better) 36 ♔f2 b5 37 ♔e2 b4 38 ♗d2 ♖d4 39 g3 ♖g4 40 ♗xh6 ♘f6 41 ♖h8 ♖c4 42 ♔d1 ♘g4 43 ♗f4 ♔f5 44 b3 ♖c3 45 ♗d2 ♖f3 46 ♖h5+ ♔e4 47 ♖h4 ♔f5 48 h3 ♘f6 49 ♖f4+ ♖xf4 50 ♗xf4 ♔e4 51 ♔e2 c4 52 ♗g5 ♘d5 53 bxc4 ♘c3+ 54 ♔d2 ♔f5 55 ♗f4 ♘xa2 56 c5 ♔e6 57 c6 ♘c3 58 ♔d3 ♘d5 59 ♔c4 ♘e7 60 ♔c5 a5 61 c7 ♔d7 62 ♔b6 ♘f5 63 ♔xa5 ♘d4 64 ♔xb4 ♘xc2+ 65 ♔c4 1-0, Tarrasch-Em.Lasker, World Ch. match, Munich 1908.

⇨ 6 d3 a6 (a weak move losing time; 6...0-0 is correct) 7 ♗xc6+ bxc6 8 ♘e2 ♗g4 9 ♘g3 0-0 10 c3 ♗c5 11 d4 exd4 12 cxd4 ♗b6 13 ♗e3 ♖e8 14 h3 (White is clearly better) 14...♗h5 15 ♘xh5 ♘xh5 16 e5 (this is not as strong as it looks, but 16 ♕c2 ♘f6 17 e5 ♘d5!? is also murky since 18 18 ♕xc6 ♘xe3 19 fxe3 dxe5 20 ♘xe5 runs into 20...♗xd4) 16...dxe5 17 ♘xe5 ♕d5! (a cunning defensive move) 18 ♕xh5 (18 ♖c1 is probably better, meeting the ingenious 18...♘g3!? by 19 ♖e1) 18...f6 19 ♖fd1 fxe5 20 dxe5 ♕xe5 21 ♕xe5 ♖xe5 22 ♖d3 (White retains a small advantage, but Black has good drawing chances) 22...♖ae8 23 ♖e1 ♖a5 24 a3 ♖d5 25 ♖c3 ♖b5 26 ♖e2 ♗d4 27 ♖cc2 c5 28 ♔f1 ♖b3 29 ♗c1 ♖xe2 (or 29...♖eb8 and while White is tied to the defence of b2 he will find it very hard to make progress) 30 ♔xe2 ♔f7 31 ♔d1 ♖d3+ 32 ♔e1 ♖b3 33 ♖e2 h6 (or 33...c4 immediately) 34 ♔d1 c4 (now the position is a clear draw) 35 ♖c2 c3 36 bxc3 ♖xc3 37 ♖e2 c5 38 ♖e4 1-0 (presumably a loss on time), Campora-Bex, Berne 1988.

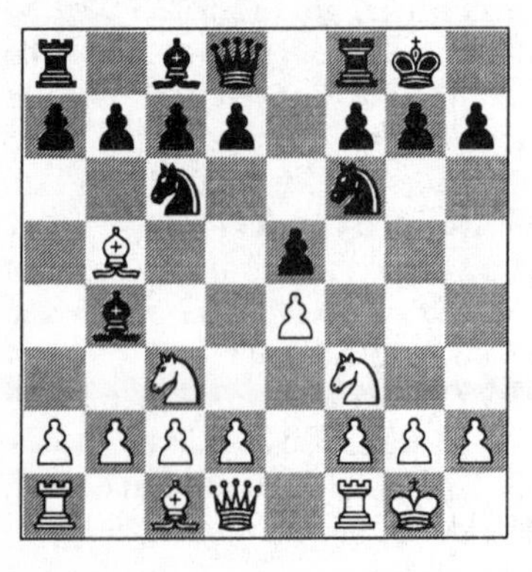

6 ♗xc6

⇨ 6 ♖e1 ♘d4 (6...d6 is also playable) 7 ♘xd4 exd4 8 e5 dxc3 9 dxc3 ♗c5 10 exf6 ♕xf6 11 ♗e3 (White has gained the tempo ♖e1 over the main line of game 25, but it is doubtful if this is enough to change the fundamentally drawish nature of the position) 11...d6 12 ♗d3 ♗xe3 13 ♖xe3 ♗d7 14 ♕h5 g6 15 ♕a5 b6 16 ♕a6 d5 17 ♖ae1 ♕d6 18 ♗f1 ♗f5 19 ♕a4 c5 20 ♖d1 ♖fd8 21 ♗d3 ♗xd3 22 ♖exd3 ♖e8 23 ♖3d2 ♖e5 24 ♕g4 ½-½, Van der Wiel-Van der Sterren, Wijk aan Zee 1988.

6...bxc6

For the safer 6...dxc6, see game 33.

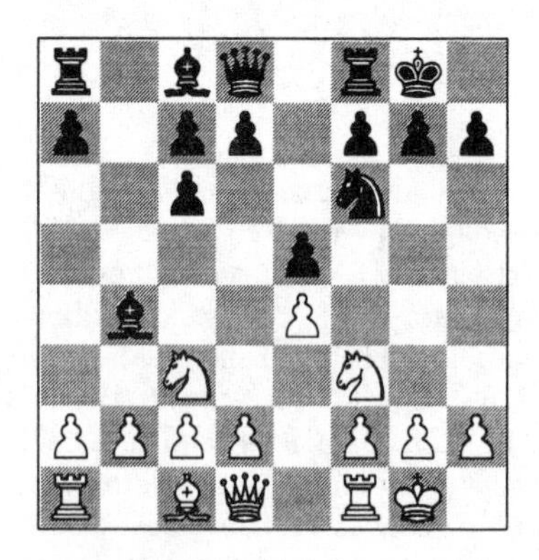

7 ♘xe5 ♕e8

⇨ 7...♗xc3 8 bxc3 ♘xe4 9 ♖e1 f5 10 f3 ♘d6 11 d3 ♘f7 12 ♘xf7 ♖xf7 (of course White is slightly better, but the open files and opposite coloured bishops mean that a draw is by far the most likely result) 13 c4 d6 14 ♗b2 ♖b8 15 ♗c3 ♗d7 16 ♕d2 c5 17 ♖e2 f4 18 ♖ae1 ♕g5 19 ♗a1 h6 20 ♕a5 ♗c6 21 ♔h1 ♔h7 22 ♗c3 ♕d8 23 d4 cxd4 24 ♗xd4 ♕d7 25

♖e6 ♔g8 26 ♕h5 ♖b1! (the end of White's winning hopes) 27 ♕g6 ♖xe1+ 28 ♖xe1 a5 29 h3 ♕f5 30 ♕xf5 ♖xf5 31 ♖e7 ♖f7 32 ♖xf7 ♔xf7 33 ♗c3 a4 34 ♗a5 d5 35 c5 ♔e6 36 ♗xc7 d4 37 ♗xf4 ♔d5 38 a3 ♔xc5 39 ♔g1 ♔c4 40 ♗d2 ♗e8 41 ♔f2 h5 42 ♔e2 ♗g6 43 ♔d1 ♗f5 44 ♗b4 d3 45 c3 ♗c8 46 ♔d2 g6 47 ♔e3 ♗d7 48 ♔d2 ♗c8 49 ♗e7 ♗d7 50 ♗g5 ♗c6 ½-½, Franzoni-Barus, Novi Sad Ol. 1990.

8 ♘d3 ♗xc3 9 dxc3 ♕xe4 10 ♖e1 ♕h4 11 ♕f3 ♗a6 12 ♘e5!

An improvement over 12 ♘c5, as played previously. However, it is not surprising that White has chances of an advantage; Black has lost time with his queen and his bishop is ineffectively posted on a6.

12...♖ae8 13 ♗f4 ♗c8?

Not a very attractive move. Tseitlin gives the variation 13...♖e6 (13...♕h5? 14 ♘xd7! wins a pawn) 14 h3 ♖fe8 15 ♖e3 ♘d5 16 ♗g5! ♕xg5 17 ♕xf7+ ♔h8 18 ♕xe6 ♖xe6 19 ♘f7+ ♔g8 20 ♘xg5 winning for White, but he overlooks the improvement 18...♕xg2+! 19 ♔xg2 ♘xe3+ 20 fxe3 ♖xe6 21 ♘xd7 ♖xe3 and Black is at least equal. In view of this 13...♖e6 is a distinctly better than the move played.

14 ♘d3 ♘d5

There is no other way to defend the c7 pawn.

15 ♗g3 ♕c4??

Black blunders away the exchange. Tseitlin analyses 15...♕a4 (15...♕d8 16 c4 is good for White) 16 b3 ♖xe1+ 17 ♖xe1 ♕xa2 18 c4 ♘f6 (18...♘b6 19 ♗xc7 ♕xc2 20 ♗d6 ♖d8 21 ♕e3 h6 22 ♕e7 wins for White) 19 ♗h4 ♕xc2 (19...♖e8 20 ♗xf6 ♖xe1+ 21 ♘xe1 gxf6 22 ♕xf6 is excellent for White) 20 ♗xf6 gxf6 21 ♕g4+ ♔h8 22 ♕d4 ♔g7 23 h3, intending ♖e3-g3, as very good for White. However, 23...d6 24 ♖e3 ♗f5 seems to offer defensive chances. Moreover, Black can improve on the game continuation by 15...♖xe1+ 16 ♖xe1 ♕c4 (so that 17 ♘e5 ♕xa2 18 ♘xf7?? loses to 18...♘e7!), when White may be slightly better but he has nothing clear-cut.

16 ♖xe8 ♖xe8 17 ♘e5 ♖xe5 18 ♗xe5 d6 19 ♗d4 ♘e7 20 b3 ♕e6 21 ♕e3 1-0

Game 33

Martorelli-Antunes
Reggio Emilia B 1986

1 e4 e5 2 ♘f3 ♘c6 3 ♘c3 ♘f6 4 ♗b5 ♗b4 5 0-0 0-0 6 ♗xc6 dxc6

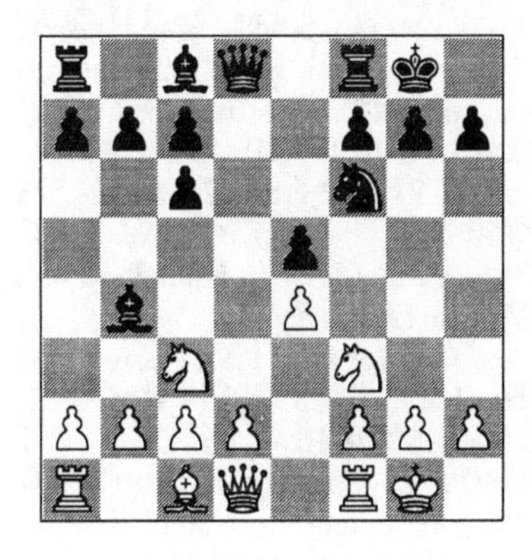

7 d3

Or 7 ♘xe5 (this line is exceptionally boring) 7...♖e8 (7...♗xc3 8 dxc3 ♘xe4 9 ♗f4 ♕f6 10 ♕f3 ♘d6 11 ♖fe1 ♗e6 12 ♘d3 ♖fe8 13 ♕g3 ♘f5 14 ♕g5 ♕xg5 15 ♗xg5 b6 16 ♗f4 ♖ac8 17 a4 f6 18 h3 c5 19 a5 g5 was completely equal in Istratescu-Stefansson, Manila Ol. 1992, although White lost in the end) 8 ♘d3 with two possibilities:

1) 8...♗xc3 9 dxc3 ♘xe4 (the safest continuation) and now:

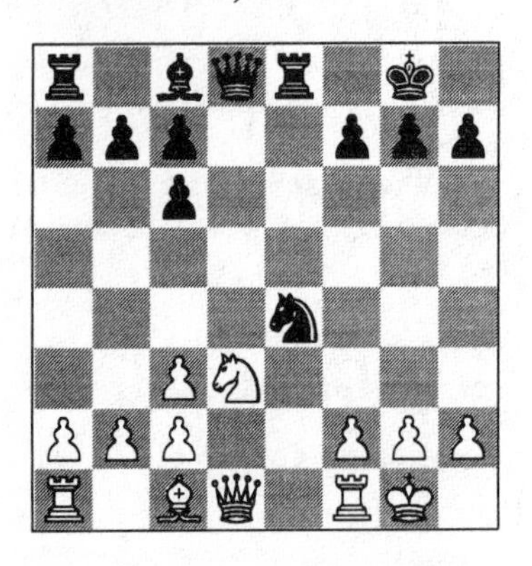

⇨ 10 ♕f3 ♘d6 11 ♗f4 ♕f6 12 ♖fe1 ♗f5 13 ♖xe8+ ♖xe8 14 ♖e1 ♖xe1+ 15 ♘xe1 (so-called "grandmaster" draws are certainly not a modern innovation) 15...♕e6 16 ♕e3 ♕xe3 17 ♗xe3 b6 18 f3 ♔f8 19 b3 ♔e7 20 ♔f2 f6 21 ♔e2 ♔d7 22 ♔d2 ♔e7 23 ♔e2 ♔d7 24 ♔d2 ♔e7 25 ♔e2 ♔d7 26 ♔d2 ♔e7 ½-½, Kmoch-König, Vienna 1922.

⇨ 10 ♗f4 ♘d6 11 ♖e1 ♖xe1+ 12 ♕xe1 ♗f5 13 b3 ♕f6 14 ♕e5 ♕xe5 15 ♗xe5 ♖e8 16 ♗xd6 cxd6 17 ♖e1 ♖xe1+ 18 ♘xe1 (it is curious that this equally tedious example is from the same tournament) 18...d5 19 ♔f1 ♔f8 20 ♔e2 ♔e7 21 ♔d2 ♔d6 22 ♘d3 g5 23 f3 h5 24 ♘b2 c5 25 c4 d4 26 ♘d3 b6 27 a3 f6 28 ♔e2 ♗d7 29 a4 ♗c6 30 ♔f2 a5 31 g3 ♔e6 32 ♔e2 ♔f5 33 ♘f2 h4 34 ♘d3 hxg3 35 hxg3 ♔e6 ½-½, Maroczy-Rubinstein, Vienna 1922.

⇨ 10 ♗f4 ♗f5 11 ♖e1 ♕d7 12 f3 ♘f6 13 ♕d2 ½-½, Tal-I.Sokolov, Barcelona 1992.

2) 8...♗a5 (a rather risky method of playing for the win)

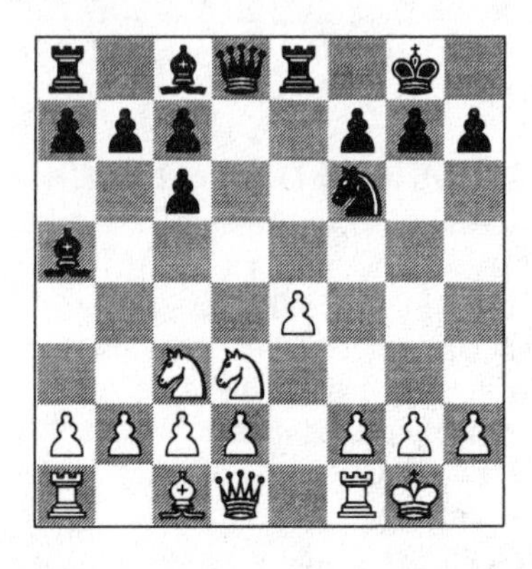

9 f3 ♘h5 10 ♘e2 f5 11 ♘f2 ♗b6 12 d4 fxe4 13 fxe4 c5 14 c3 cxd4 15 cxd4 ♗e6 16 ♕d3 ♕d7 (objectively Black doesn't have enough compensation for the pawn) 17 ♗e3 ♘f6 18 ♘f4 (if White wants to hold on to the pawn, then 18 ♘c3 is the safest method) 18...♗f7 19 ♖ae1 ♕a4 20 d5 ♗xe3 21 ♖xe3 ♕xa2 22 ♘d1?! (having returned the pawn to deflect Black's queen, it would have been more logical to play for the attack by 22 ♕d4! followed by ♖g3, with dangerous threats) 22...♖e5?! (a risky move, because the rook is not a good blockader; 22...♖ad8 is better) 23 ♘c3 ♕xb2 24 ♖b1 ♕a3 25 ♕d4 ♖ae8 26 ♖xb7?? (horrible; 26 ♘d3! ♖5e7 27 ♖xb7 looks good for White because the trick 27...♕a1+ 28 ♖b1

♖xe4 fails to 29 ♖xe4 ♖xe4 30 ♕c5!) 26...♕c1+ 27 ♔f2 ♘g4+ 28 ♔f3 ♘xh2+ 29 ♔g3 ♘f1+ 30 ♔f2 ♘xe3 31 ♕xe3 ♕c2+ 32 ♔g1 h6 33 ♖xc7 ♖xe4 34 ♘xe4 ♕xc7 35 ♕f3 ♕e5 36 ♘f2 ♕e1+ 37 ♔h2 ♖e3 0-1, Von Gottschall-Rubinstein, Hannover 1926.

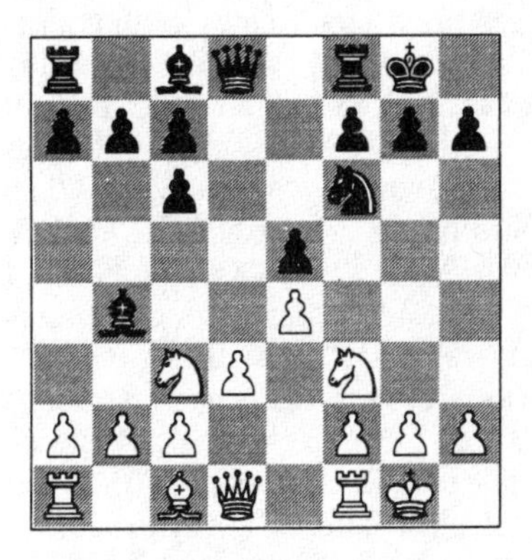

7...♘d7

It is not surprising that Black has a wide range of possibilities in this position. He can exchange on c3 to prevent White's typical manoeuvre ♘e2-g3, he can pin the knight with ...♗g4, or he can simply defend the e5 pawn. Here are some practical examples:

➪ 7...♗xc3 8 bxc3 ♗g4 9 h3 ♗xf3 10 ♕xf3 (this structure often arises after 7 d3; it is very slightly better for White because he has chances to becomes active with f4, coupled with c4 and ♗b2 to exert pressure on the long diagonal; the problem is that after the exchange of pawns on f4, Black's knight settles on e5 and White finds it very hard to make progress) 10...c5 (possibly designed to prevent d4, as played in Paulsen-Bier below) 11 c4 b6 12 ♗b2 ♘d7 13 ♕g3 f6 (Black is trying to wall up White's bishop) 14 f4 ♕e7 15 ♖f3 exf4 16 ♖xf4 ♘e5 (this is the problem mentioned above; the knight on e5 cannot be dislodged) 17 ♖af1 ♕d6 18 ♖f5? (after 18 ♖xf6 ♖xf6 19 ♖xf6 ♖xf6 20 ♗xe5 followed by ♗xc7 White has no advantage because he only obtains one passed pawn, which is easily blockaded on e6; the quiet 18 ♕f2 was better) 18...♘xc4 (Black makes off with a pawn and eventually the game) 19 e5 ♘xe5 20 ♗xe5 fxe5 21 ♕xe5 ♕xe5 22 ♖xe5 ♖xf1+ 23 ♔xf1 ♔f7 24 ♖h5 h6 25 ♔e2 ♖e8+ 26 ♔d2 ♔e6 27 ♖h4 ♖f8 28 ♖e4+ ♔d6 29 ♖g4 g5 30 g3 ♖f5 31 h4 b5 32 ♔c3 ♔e6 33 a4 c6 34 hxg5 hxg5 35 ♔b2 ♖d5 36 axb5 cxb5 37 c4 bxc4 38 ♖xc4 ♖xd3 39 ♖xc5 ♖xg3 40 ♖a5 ♔f6 41 ♔c2 ♖e3 42 ♖xa7 ♔f5 43 ♔d2 ♖e8 44 ♖f7+ ♔g4 45 ♖g7 ♔f4 46 ♖f7+ ♔g3 47 ♖g7 g4 48 ♖g6 ♔f3 49 ♖f6+ ♔g3 50 ♖g6 ♖e4 51 ♔d3 ♔f3 52 ♖g8 ♖f4 53 ♖g7 g3 0-1, Wittmann-Wijesuriya, Dubai Ol. 1986.

➪ 7...♗xc3 8 bxc3 ♗g4 9 h3 ♗xf3 10 ♕xf3 ♘d7 (Black doesn't try to stop d4) 11 d4 (an interesting but risky decision; the c4 square is severely weakened, but White avoids the type of blockade Black set up in the previous example) 11...♖e8 12 ♗b2 ♕h4 13 ♖ae1 (the correct rook, because White plans f4) 13...♖ad8 14 ♕e3 ♘b6 15 ♗c1 ♘c4 16 ♕d3 b5 17 f4 (both sides have got what they wanted; Black's knight is firmly rooted on c4, while White has played f4) 17...f6 18 ♔h2 ♕h5?!

(18...c5! looks fine for Black) 19 fxe5 ♘xe5? (and this is terrible; 19...fxe5 was compulsory) 20 ♕g3 (effectively finishing the game, because Black's queenside collapses) 20...♘d7 21 ♕xc7 ♕f7 22 ♕xc6 ♕xa2 23 ♕xb5 ♕xc2 24 ♕c4+ ♔h8 25 ♖e2 ♕b1 26 ♖fe1 ♕b8+ 27 ♔h1 ♖c8 28 ♕d3 ♕b3 29 ♗d2 ♖b8 30 ♕a6 ♖b7 31 ♕c6 h6 32 c4 ♖eb8 33 c5 ♕g3 34 ♗a5 ♘f8 35 ♕d6 ♕a3 36 ♗c7 ♖c8 37 c6 ♖b4 38 d5 ♕a4 39 ♗d8 ♘g6 40 c7 ♖c4 41 ♕e6 ♖a8 42 ♕f5 ♕e8 43 d6 ♖d4 44 ♖b2 ♖xd6 45 ♖b8 1-0, Paulsen-Bier, Leipzig 1879.

⇨ 7...♗xc3 8 bxc3 ♖e8 9 ♘d2 ♘d7 10 ♘c4 ♘b6?! (chasing White's knight to a better square, while Black's knight has no future on b6; 10...♘f8 was better) 11 ♘e3 ♕d6 12 ♕f3 ♕g6 13 ♔h1 h5? (very bad) 14 ♗d2 ♖f8 15 ♖ae1 ♗e6 16 c4 ♘d7 17 ♗c3 ♖ad8 18 ♕e2 f6 19 f4 exf4 20 ♖xf4 ♕g5 21 ♖ef1 ♘e5 22 ♘f5 ♖fe8 23 ♗xe5 fxe5 24 ♖4f3 h4 25 ♕f2 ♗xf5 26 ♖xf5 ♕h6 27 h3 (I can't see anything wrong with taking the pawn on a7, although the move played should also win) 27...b6 28 ♖f7 c5 29 ♖xc7 ♖f8 30 ♖f7 ♕d6 31 ♔h2 ♖de8 32 ♖xf8+ ♖xf8 33 ♕xf8+ ♕xf8 34 ♖xf8+ ♔xf8 35 g3 hxg3+ 36 ♔xg3 ♔f7 37 ♔g4 ♔f6 38 h4 g6 39 h5 gxh5+ 40 ♔xh5 ♔e6 41 a4 ♔f7 42 ♔g5 ♔e6 43 ♔g6 1-0, Har Zvi-M.Ginzburg, World Junior Ch., Duisburg 1992.

⇨ 7...♕e7 8 ♕e2 ♖e8 9 h3 g6 (the plan of ♕e2 and h3 is too slow to be dangerous for Black, but Capablanca gradually outplays his unknown opponent) 10 ♕e3 ♘h5 11 ♘e2 ♗c5 12 ♕h6 f6 13 g4 ♘g7 14 ♔g2 ♕f7 15 ♘h2 ♗f8 16 ♕e3 g5 17 ♘g3 ♘e6 18 ♕f3 c5 19 b3 ♗d7 20 h4 gxh4 21 ♘f5 ♘g5 22 ♕e2 ♗xf5 23 gxf5 ♔h8 24 ♕g4 ♕g7 25 ♔h1 ♕h6 26 ♖g1 (26 ♘f3 ♗e7 27 ♗xg5 fxg5 28 ♘xe5 would have regained the pawn, but 28...♕g7 followed by ...♗f6 offers some counterplay) 26...♗e7 27 f4 (the start of a faulty plan; 27 ♘f3 ♖g8 28 ♗xg5 fxg5 29 ♘xe5 ♕g7 30 ♘c4 ♗f6 31 ♖af1 was better, with f4 to come, when White still has the advantage) 27...exf4 28 ♗b2? (28 ♗xf4) 28...♖g8 29 ♕xf4 ♘h3! (White must have missed this move) 30 ♖xg8+ ♖xg8 31 ♕f1 (loses at once, but even 31 ♕f3 ♖g3 32 ♕e2 ♕h5 33 ♕d2 ♕g5! is winning for Black) 31...♕e3 0-1, Capablanca-Jaffe, New York 1913.

⇨ 7...♗g4 8 h3 ♗h5 9 ♕e2 ♘d7 10 ♘d1 ♖e8 11 ♘e3 f6 12 ♘f5 ♗f8 13 ♗e3 ♘c5 14 ♘g3 ♗f7 15 ♖fd1 (White has played too slowly and allowed Black to equalise; once Black's knight has reached e6, White's f4 plan is much less promising) 15...♕c8 16 ♗xc5 ♗xc5 17 d4 exd4 18 ♘xd4 ♗f8 19 ♕f3 c5 20 ♘b5 a6 21 ♘c3 ♕e6 22 ♘f5 ♗g6 23 a4 ♖ad8 24 ♕f4 ♗xf5 25 ♕xf5 ♕xf5 26 exf5 ♖d4 27 ♔f1 ♖e5 28 g4 g6 29 fxg6 hxg6 30 ♘e2 ♖xd1+ ½-½, Tarrasch-Rubinstein, Vienna 1922.

⇨ 7...♖e8 8 ♘e2 ♗g4 9 ♘g3 ♘h5 10 h3 ♘xg3 11 fxg3 ♗d7 12 ♕e2 ♗f8 13 ♗e3 b6 14 g4 h6 15 ♕f2 (White is slightly better and 15 g5 is promising) 15...f6 (now Black has some sort of blockade) 16 ♘h4 ♔h7 17 ♕g3 c5 18 ♖f2 ♗e6 19 b3 a5 20 a4 g6 21 ♘f3 ♗g7 22 ♖af1 ♕d7 23 g5!? hxg5 24 ♗xg5 ♖h8 (24...fxg5 25 ♘xg5+ ♔g8 26 ♕h4 ♗f8 27 ♖f7 wins) 25 ♗e3 ♕e7 26 ♘h4 ♗f7 27 ♗g5!? fxg5 28 ♖xf7 gxh4 29 ♕g4 ♕e8 (29...♕d8? 30 ♖d7 followed by ♖ff7) 30 ♖1f6 ♔g8 31 ♕xg6 ♖h7 32 g3 ♔h8?! (taking on g3 is unclear) 33 ♖e6 ♕g8 34 ♖xc7 ♖f8? (now Black should definitely have taken on g3) 35 g4 ♖f3 36 ♔g2? (36 ♖e8! ♖f8 37 ♖cc8 ♖h6 38 ♖xf8 ♗xf8 39 ♕f5 ♔g7 40 ♕xe5+ is very good for White) 36...♕f8 (forcing the draw) 37 ♖e8 ♖f2+ 38 ♔g1 ♖f1+ ½-½, Wittmann-Arlandi, Aosta Team 1988.

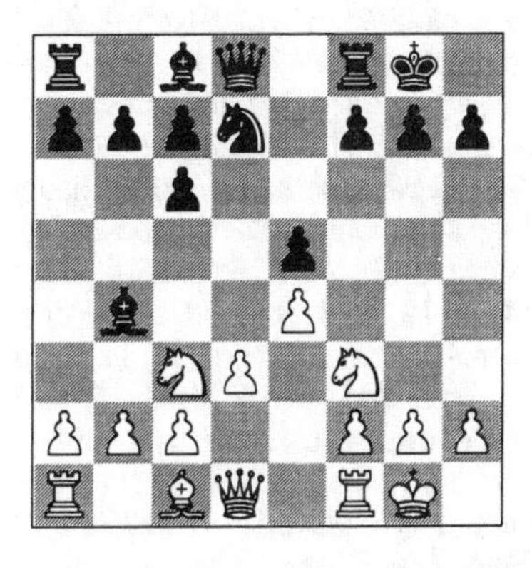

8 ♘g5

⇨ 8 ♘e2 ♗d6 9 ♘g3 ♘c5 10 ♗e3 ♖e8 11 ♘xe5!? ♗xe5 12 ♗xc5 ♗xb2 13 ♖b1 ♗d4 14 ♗xd4 ♕xd4 15 ♔h1 c5 16 f4 b6 17 f5 f6 18 ♖f4 ♗d7 19 ♕h5 (the position is very unclear; White has kingside attacking chances, but if he fails to break through he will suffer on the queenside) 19...♖e7 20 ♖h4 h6 21 ♕f3 ♗e8 22 ♘e2 ♕e5 23 ♕g4 ♔h7 24 ♖f1 ♗f7 25 ♖f3 (25 c3 and only then ♖f3 looks better) 25...♕a1+ 26 ♘g1 ♕c1 27 ♖g3 ♖g8 28 h3 ♕g5 (a safe move; in fact I don't see any refutation of 28...♕xc2, because 29 ♕f4 threatening ♖xg7+ may be met by 29...♗e8, but I certainly understand why Black didn't like to risk it) 29 ♕xg5 fxg5 30 ♖xg5 ♗xa2 (the outside a-pawn is a trump card) 31 ♘f3 ♖f8 32 e5 ♔g8 33 ♖xh6 ♖xf5 34 ♖g4 ♗d5 35 ♘h4 ♖f1+ 36 ♔h2 ♖xe5 37 ♘g6 gxh6 38 ♘xe5+ ♔h7 39 c4 ♖f5 40 ♘g6 ♖g5 41 ♖xg5 hxg5 42 ♘e5 ♗b7 43 ♘g4 a5 44 ♘e3 a4 45 ♘c2 ♗c8 46 g4 ♗d7 47 ♔g3 ♗e8 48 ♔f3 ♗g6 49 ♔e3 ♔g7 50 ♘a3 ♔f6 51 ♘b5 ♔e5 52 ♘a3 ♗e8 0-1, Lugo-G.Garcia, Capablanca Mem-B 1992.

The move 8 ♘g5 adopted in the main line is distinctly odd; White intends f4, but he never manages to play it!

8...♗d6 9 ♘e2 ♘c5 10 ♔h1 f6 11 ♘f3 ♘e6 (reaching a normal position, but with White having lost time) **12 ♖g1 c5 13 ♗e3 ♗d7 14 ♘d2 b5 15 f3 ♘d4** (it would have been better to develop the other pieces first) **16 g4 ♗e6 17 ♘g3 ♔h8 18 ♖g2 ♖f7 19 c3 ♘c6 20 ♕g1 ♗e7 21 ♘b3 c4 22 dxc4 ♗xc4 23 ♖d1 ♕e8 24 ♗c5 ♘d8 25 ♖gd2 g6 26 ♘a5** (now White has some advantage) **26...♗e6 27 ♗xe7 ♕xe7 28 b4 ♖f8 29 a3 a6 30 ♕e3 ♘f7 31 ♘c6 ♕e8 32 ♕c5 ♘d6 33 ♘f1??** (White overlooks the threat) **33...♘b7 34 ♕e3 ♕xc6** (Black is a piece up for nothing) **35 ♕h6 ♕e8 36 ♘e3 ♕e7 37 ♘d5 ♗xd5 38 ♖xd5 ♖ad8??** (after 38...♘d6 White can resign) **39 ♖d7 1-0??**

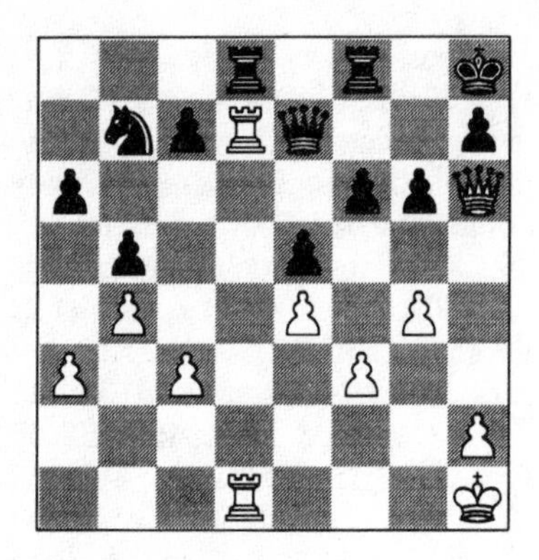

Black's resignation was a further serious error because he is winning in the final position! The reason is that after 39...♕f7! 40 ♖1d5 (40 ♖xf7 ♖xd1+ 41 ♔g2 ♖xf7 is hopeless) 40...♕g8! (not 40...♖xd7 41 ♖xd7 ♕g8 42 ♖xh7+ drawing) 41 ♖xc7 ♖f7 Black retains the piece.

Game 34

Perlis-Alekhine
Carlsbad 1911

1 e4 e5 2 ♘f3 ♘c6 3 ♘c3 ♘f6 4 ♗b5 ♗b4 5 0-0 0-0 6 d3 ♘d4

Or 6...♗xc3 (the immediate 6...d5 was good for White after 7 ♘xd5 ♘xd5 8 exd5 ♕xd5 9 ♗c4 ♕d6 10 c3 ♗c5 11 b4 ♗b6 12 a4 in Sterk-Marshall, Pistyan 1912; White finished efficiently by 12...a5 13 b5 ♘e7 14 ♘g5 ♕g6 15 ♕e2 ♗f5 16 g4 h6 17 gxf5 ♘xf5 18 ♔h1 hxg5 19 ♖g1 g4 20 ♗a3 ♘h6 21 ♗xf8 ♖xf8 22 ♖g2 ♖e8 23 f3 ♕g5 24 ♖e1 ♕e7 25 fxg4 ♕a3 26 g5 ♘f5 27 g6 ♖e7 28 ♕h5 ♘h6 29 ♕xh6 1-0) 7 bxc3 d5 (this line was once played by some of the world's leading players, so it should not be dismissed lightly) and now:

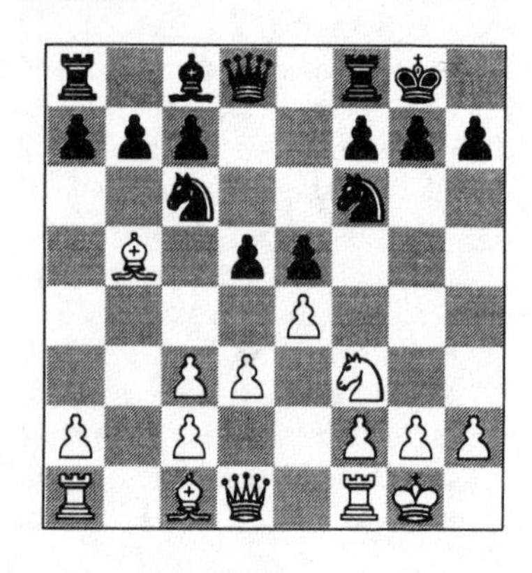

➩ 8 exd5 ♕xd5 (8...♘xd5 9 ♗xc6 bxc6 10 ♘xe5 ♘xc3 11 ♕d2 ♘d5 12 c4 is good for White) 9 c4 ♕d6 10 ♗xc6 bxc6 11 ♗b2 ♖e8 12 ♘d2 (12 ♖e1 ♗g4 is perhaps slightly better for White, but 12 ♕e1! is best of all because 12...♗g4 13 ♘xe5 ♘d7 14 f4 f6 15 ♕g3 is good for White, Korn-Frydman, corr. 1938) 12...♖b8 13 ♗c3 ♗f5 14 f3 ♖bd8 15 ♕e1 ♘d5 16 ♘e4 ♗xe4 17 fxe4 ♘f4 18 g3 ♘e6 19 ♕f2 f6 20 ♖fb1?! (White should have played 20 ♕xa7 ♖a8 21 ♕f2 ♖a4 22 a3, when 22...♖xa3 loses to 23 c5, while after 22...♖ea8 23 ♗b2 Black still has to justify his pawn offer) 20...a6 21 ♖b3 ♖b8 22 ♖ab1 ♖xb3 23 axb3 (White has some advantage, but it is very hard to exploit Black's pawn weaknesses) 23...c5 24 ♖a1 ♘g5 25 ♕e3 ♖f8 26 ♖a5 ♘e6 27 ♕f2 ♕c6 28 ♕e3 h6 29 ♕e1 ♘g5 30 ♕e3 ♘e6 31 ♖a1 ♘g5 32 ♖f1 ♖a8 33 ♖a1 ♘e6 34 ♕f2 ♖f8 35 ♖f1 ♕d6 36 ♕e3 ♕d7 37 ♕f2 ♖a8 38 ♖a1 ♕c6 39 ♗d2 ♖f8 40

♗e3 ♕d6 41 ♖a5 ♘d4 42 ♗xd4 cxd4 ½-½, Gunsberg-Marshall, St.Petersburg 1914.

➪ 8 exd5 ♕xd5 9 ♗c4 ♕a5 10 ♖b1 a6 11 ♖e1 b6 12 ♕e2 ♗g4 13 ♗b2? (13 ♗g5!? is better, when 13...e4 14 ♗xf6 exf3 15 ♕e4! is favourable for White, while 13...♕xc3 14 ♗xf6 gxf6 15 ♕e4 ♗d7 16 ♕h4 offers good play for the pawn) 13...♖fe8 14 ♕f1 ♗xf3 15 gxf3 ♘e7 (now Black is clearly better, but somehow Lasker wriggles out) 16 ♔h1 ♘g6 17 ♕h3 ♕c5 18 ♖e3 b5 19 ♗b3 ♘d5 20 ♗xd5 ♕xd5 21 ♖a1 ♖e6 22 a4 ♖ae8 23 ♕f5 ♖f6 24 ♕e4 ♕d8 25 axb5 axb5 26 d4 ♖fe6 27 c4 exd4 28 ♕xd4 ♕xd4 29 ♗xd4 ♖xe3 30 fxe3 bxc4 31 ♔g2 ♘f8 32 ♖a4 ♘e6 33 ♖xc4 ♘xd4 ½-½, Em.Lasker-Réti, Moscow 1925.

➪ 8 ♗xc6 bxc6 9 ♘xe5

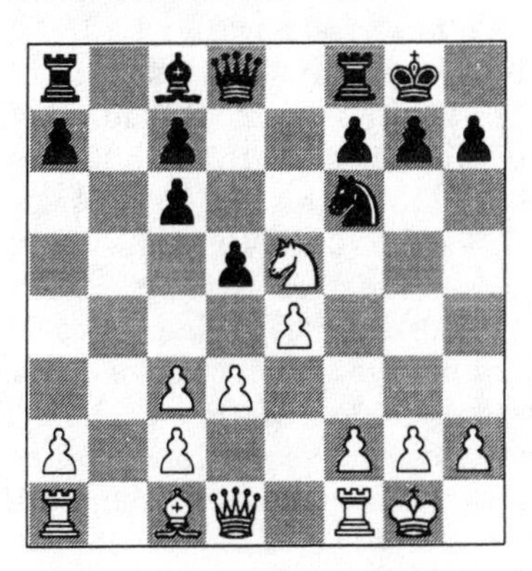

9...♕d6 10 ♗f4 ♖e8 11 ♕f3 (Keres gives 11 exd5 ♖xe5 12 d4 ♖e1 13 ♗xd6 ♖xd1 14 ♖fxd1 cxd6 15 dxc6 ♗e6 16 ♖ab1 ♖c8 17 ♖b7 with the better prospects for White) 11...dxe4 12 dxe4 ♖xe5 13 ♖fd1 ♗g4 14 ♕g3? (a blunder; 14 ♖xd6 ♗xf3 15 ♖xf6 gxf6 16 ♗xe5 fxe5 17 gxf3 ♖b8 is a draw) 14...♗xd1 15 ♗xe5 ♕d2! (winning a piece because of the mate threat on e1) 16 f3 ♘h5 17 ♕f2 ♕xf2+ 18 ♔xf2 ♗xc2 19 ♖c1 ♗a4 20 ♗xc7 ♖c8 21 ♖b1 ♗b5 22 ♖d1 ♔f8 23 ♗e5 ♔e7 24 a4 ♗c4 25 ♖d4 ♗e6 26 ♖b4 ♗d7 27 ♖b7 ♖a8 28 ♔e3 ♘f6 29 a5 ♔e8 30 ♗d4 a6 31 f4 c5 32 ♗xf6 gxf6 33 ♖b6 ♔e7 34 f5 ♗b5 35 g4 ♖d8 36 ♔f4 ♖d1 37 h4 h6 38 ♖b7+ ♔f8 39 ♖c7 c4 40 g5 hxg5+ 41 hxg5 ♖f1+ 42 ♔g4 ♖g1+ 43 ♔f4 fxg5+ 44 ♔e5 ♖e1 45 ♔f6 ♖xe4 46 ♖xf7+ ♔e8 47 ♖g7 g4 48 ♖g5 ♗c6 49 ♔g7 ♗d5 50 ♖g6 ♖e7+ 51 ♔h6 ♗e4 52 ♖xg4 ♗xf5 53 ♖xc4 ♖e5 54 ♔g5 ♗d3+ 55 ♔f4 ♖f5+ 56 ♔g4 ♖xa5 57 ♖d4 ♗b5 58 ♔f4 ♖a3 59 ♔e5 ♗d7 60 c4 ♔d8 61 ♖d2 ♔c7 62 ♔d4 a5 63 ♖d3 ♖a1 64 ♔c3 ♖c1+ 65 ♔b2 ♖h1 66 ♖d5 a4 67 ♖d2 ♗c6 68 ♔a2 ♔b6 69 ♖b2+ ♔c5 70 ♖b1 ♖h3 71 ♖g1 ♔xc4 72 ♖c1+ ♔b5 73 ♖b1+ ♔c5 74 ♖c1+ ♔d6 75 ♖d1+ ♗d5+ 76 ♔b2 a3+ 77 ♔a1 ♔c5 78 ♖c1+ ♗c4 79 ♖g1 ♖h2 80 ♖g5+ ♔b4 81 ♖g1 ♖a2+ 82 ♔b1 ♖d2 0-1, Capablanca-Tarrasch, St.Petersburg 1914.

➪ 8 ♗xc6 bxc6 9 ♘xe5 dxe4 10 dxe4 ♕e7 (very risky; objectively 10...♕xd1 11 ♖xd1 ♘xe4 was the right course, but Marshall was probably playing for a win) 11 ♗f4 ♘xe4 12 ♕d4 ♗f5 13 ♖fe1 c5 14 ♕c4 ♘d6 15 ♕xc5 ♕f6 16 ♗g3? (White has a clear advantage and after 16 ♘c6 Black would be in trouble because 16...♗xc2 loses his queen to 17 ♗g5) 16...♖fe8 17 ♕c6 ♘e4 18 ♕xf6 (White has thrown away most of his advantage but it is incredible that he succeeds in losing) 18...gxf6 19 ♘d3 ♘xc3 20 ♗xc7 ♘e2+ 21 ♔f1 ♘d4 22 ♖xe8+ ♖xe8 23 ♘b4 (23 ♖d1 ♘xc2 24 ♘c5 is a draw) 23...♖c8 24 ♘d5 ♔g7 25 c3?? (25 ♖d1 still draws) 25...♗d3+ 26 ♔g1 ♘e2+ 27 ♔h1 ♗c4 (a typical Marshall swindle) 28 ♗b6 ♗xd5 29 ♗xa7 ♖xc3 30 a4 ♘f4 31 f3 ♖c2 32 ♖g1 ♔f8 33 ♖d1 ♗c6 34 ♗d4 ♔g7 35 a5 ♘xg2 0-1, Bohatirchuk-Marshall, Moscow 1925.

⇨ 8 ♗xc6 bxc6 9 ♘xe5 ♗xc3 10 bxc3 dxe4 10 ♗a3 (this gives White some advantage) 10...♖e8 11 ♘xc6 ♕d7 12 ♘d4 ♘d5 13 ♕d2 ♗b7 (White has an extra pawn, but the opposite-coloured bishops and Black's active pieces make it hard to convert into a win) 14 ♖e1 ♕g4 15 dxe4 ♖xe4 16 f3 ♕f4 17 ♕f2 (17 ♕xf4 is more promising) 17...♖xe1+ 18 ♖xe1 ♘xc3 19 ♗c1 ♕d6 20 ♘f5 ♕f6? (20...♕b4) 21 ♕xa7! ♕b6+ 22 ♕xb6 cxb6 23 ♗b2 ♘xa2 24 ♗xg7 (White is winning because he has an extra pawn and threats against Black's king; it takes several mistakes for White to ruin his position) 24...♘b4 25 c3? (a weak move, which blocks the long diagonal and so prevents White's rook leaving the first rank; after 25 c4 ♘d3 26 ♖e3 ♘c5 27 ♗d4 Black is lost) 25...♘d3 26 ♖d1 ♖a5! 27 g4 (27 ♘e3 would have offered good winning chances) 27...♗c8 28 ♗h6 (28 ♘d6 was also very promising) 28...♗xf5 29 gxf5 ♖d5 30 ♖a1? (White misses his last chance with 30 ♔f1!, when Black is still in trouble) 30...♖a5?! 31 ♖d1 ♖d5 32 ♖a1? f6! (now Black should draw) 33 ♖a7 ♘e5 34 ♖g7+ ♔h8 35 ♖e7 ♔g8 36 ♔f2 ♖d7 37 ♖e6 ♔f7 38 ♖xb6 ♖d3 39 ♖b7+ ♔e8 40 ♗e3 ♖xc3 41 ♖xh7 ♖c2+ 42 ♔g3 ♖c3 43 ♔f2 ♖c2+ 44 ♔g3 ♖c3 45 ♔f2 ♖c2+ ½-½, Cohn-Marshall, Carlsbad 1911.

7 ♘xd4 exd4 8 ♘e2

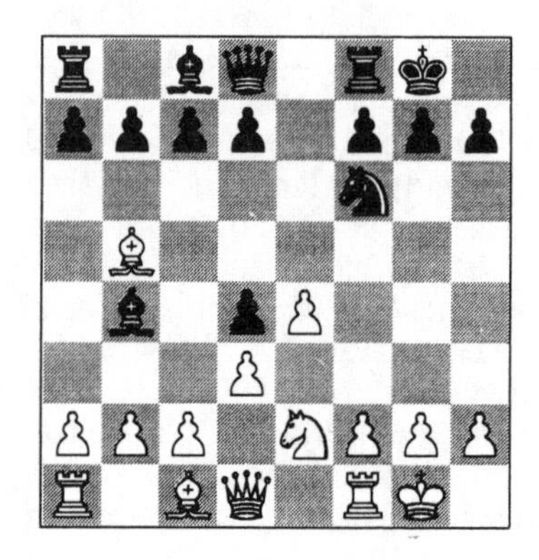

8...c6

Or 8...d5 and now:

⇨ 9 exd5 ♕xd5 10 ♗c4 ♕d8 11 h3 ♖e8 12 ♗d2 ♗xd2 13 ♕xd2 ♗e6 (with equality) 14 ♗b3 ♕d6 15 ♖fe1 ♖e7?! (15...c5 is safer) 16 ♕f4! ♖d8 17 ♕xd6 ♖xd6 18 ♘f4 (now White has an edge) 18...♔f8 19 ♘xe6+ fxe6 20 ♖e2 ♘d7 21 ♖ae1 ♘c5 22 ♗c4 b5? (a panicky move which leads to the loss of a pawn; 22...♔f7 was a better defence) 23 ♗xb5 ♖b6 24 a4 a6 25 b4! (with a winning position for White) 25...♘b7 26 ♗c4 ♖xb4 27 ♖xe6 ♖xe6 28 ♖xe6 ♘c5 29 ♖c6 ♘xa4 30 ♖xc7 a5 31 ♖f7+ ♔e8 32 ♖xg7 ♘b6 33 ♖xh7 a4 34 ♖a7 ♖b2 35 ♗e6 ♖xc2 36 f4 ♖d2 37 f5 ♖xd3 38 ♖b7 ♖d1+ 39 ♔f2 ♖b1 40 f6 ♖b2+ 41 ♔f3 ♘c4 42 ♖e7+ 1-0, Maroczy-Marshall, Carlsbad 1929.

⇨ 9 e5 ♘g4 10 c3 (this gives White a clear advantage, much as in the main line) 10...dxc3 11 bxc3 ♗a5 12 d4 ♕h4 13 ♗f4 ♘h6 14 ♕d2 f6 15 ♗d3 ♘f5 16 exf6 ♕xf6 17 ♗e5 ♕f7 18 f4 ♘d6 19 f5! ♘c4 20 ♗xc4 dxc4 21 ♘g3 c5 22 f6 g6 23 d5 ♖d8 24 d6 ♖e8 25 ♕f4 ♗d7 26 ♖ae1 ♗c6 27 ♕h6 ♖ad8 28 ♘f5! gxf5 29 ♖xf5 ♔h8 30 ♖g5 ♖g8 31 ♖g7 ♖xg7 32 fxg7+ ♔g8 33 ♖f1 ♕xf1+ 34 ♔xf1 ♖e8 35 ♕f4 b5 36 g4 ♗d7 37 g5 ♗e6 38 ♗f6 ♗d7 39 ♗e7 ♔xg7 40 ♕f6+ ♔g8 41 g6 ♗h3+ 42 ♔f2 1-0, Campora-Acosta, Argentinian Ch. 1987.

9 ♗a4 d5 10 e5 ♘g4 11 c3 dxc3 12 bxc3 ♗a5 13 d4 ♕h4 14 h3 (14 ♗f4 was also possible, as in Campora-Acosta above) **14...♘h6 15 ♗c2 ♗f5 16 ♖b1 b5** (16...♖ab8 is bad after 17 ♗a3 followed by ♗d6) **17 ♗xf5 ♘xf5 18 ♕d3 ♕e4** (the ending is worse for Black, but if the knight moves then White can start a kingside pawn advance) **19 ♕xe4 dxe4 20 f3 exf3 21 ♖xf3 ♘e7 22 ♗a3 ♖fe8** (after 22...♖ae8 23 ♘g3 Black can hardly free himself because 23...f6 is met by 24 ♖bf1) **23 ♖bf1 f6** (23...♘d5 24 ♖xf7 ♘xc3 25 ♘xc3 ♗xc3 26 ♗c5 is also very good for White, for example 26...♖ad8 27 e6! ♗xd4+ 28 ♗xd4 ♖xd4 29 e7 and wins) **24 exf6 gxf6 25 ♘f4** (not 25 ♖xf6 ♘d5, but now 26 ♘h5 is threatened) **25...♘d5 26 ♘xd5 cxd5 27 ♗c5 ♖ac8 28 ♖xf6 ♗xc3 29 ♖6f5 ♖e2 30 ♖g5+ ♔h8 31 ♖xd5 ♖xa2 32 ♗d6 ♖a1** (Black is forced to head for the exchange of rooks or else he will be mated) **33 ♗e5+ ♔g8 34 ♖xa1 ♗xa1 35 ♖xb5** (White's extra pawn and more active pieces make the technical task relatively easy) **35...♖c4 36 ♖d5 a5 37 ♔f2 a4 38 ♔e3 a3 39 ♖a5 ♗b2 40 ♔e4 ♖c2 41 g4 ♖f2 42 h4 ♔f7 43 h5 h6 44 ♔d5 ♗c1 45 ♖a7+ ♔g8 46 ♔e6 ♗b2 47 ♖g7+ ♔f8 48 ♖h7 ♔e8 49 ♖a7 1-0**

Game 35

Janowski-Vidmar
Carlsbad 1907

1 e4 e5 2 ♘f3 ♘f6 3 ♘c3 ♘c6 4 ♗b5 ♗b4 5 0-0 0-0 6 d3 ♗xc3 7 bxc3 d6 8 ♖e1

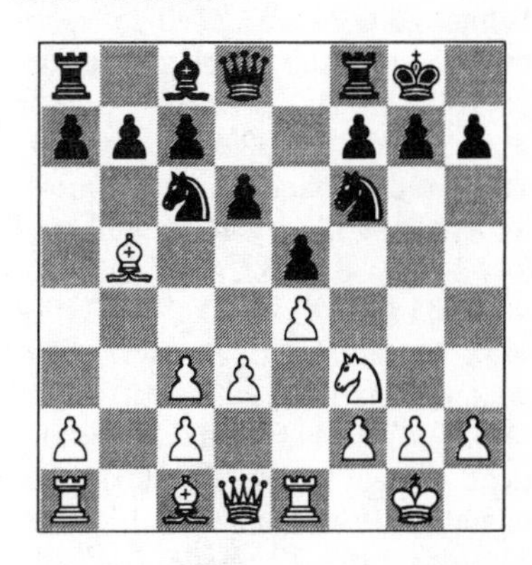

We are devoting some time to 8 ♖e1, even though there are no recent games. The reason is that this more or less forgotten move is a logical attempt to exploit Black's early exchange on c3 by missing out ♗g5. In the Metger unpin, for example, the bishop usually returns to c1 after ...♘d8-e6, so unless Black can come up with a radically different plan White will save time. Theory gives

8...♘e7 as the best reply, which is probably correct, but even this doesn't guarantee equality.

8...♕e7

⇨ 8...♘e7 9 d4 ♗d7 10 ♖b1 c6 11 ♗f1 ♕c7 12 ♗g5 ♘g6 13 ♕d2 (even the simple 13 ♗xf6 gxf6 14 ♕d2 should be slightly better for White) 13 ♕d2 ♘h5 14 ♘h4 ♖ae8 (*ECO* assesses this position as equal, but I believe that White has an edge) 15 ♘xg6 hxg6 16 ♖ed1 ♗c8 17 ♗e3 ♖d8 18 ♗d3 b6 19 f4 exf4 20 ♗xf4 ♘xf4 21 ♕xf4 ♕d7 22 ♖f1 (I prefer 22 c4) 22...♕g4 23 ♕e3 ♖de8 24 ♖f4 ♕e6 25 ♖bf1 d5 (25...♕xa2 26 c4 offers some compensation, but there is certainly nothing clear for White) 26 ♕g3 ♕e7 27 e5 g5? (seriously weakening Black's kingside) 28 ♖4f2 c5 29 ♗f5 cxd4 30 cxd4 ♗a6 31 ♕h3 g6 32 ♗d3 ♗xd3 33 ♕xd3 ♕d7 (Black is in big trouble) 34 ♖f6 ♕g4 35 h3 ♕e4 36 ♕d2 ♕h4 37 c3 ♔g7 38 ♕e3 ♖e7 39 ♖d6 ♖c7 40 ♖xd5 ♖fc8 41 e6 ♖xc3 42 ♖xf7+ ♔g8 43 ♕xc3 1-0, Janowski-Showalter, Paris 1900.

⇨ 8...♘e7 9 d4 c6 10 dxe5 (this tactical sequence gives White no advantage; 10 ♗f1 is better) 10...dxe5 11 ♗a3 cxb5 12 ♕xd8 ♖xd8 13 ♗xe7 ♖e8 14 ♗d6 ♘d7 (once Black has played ...f6, freeing the knight, he will be able to continue his development) 15 ♖ed1 f6 16 ♖ab1 a6 17 ♘d2 ♘b6 18 c4 ♘a4! 19 ♖e1 ♖d8 20 c5 ♘xc5 21 ♗xc5 ♖xd2 22 ♖b2 ♗e6 23 ♗e3 ♖d7 (the position is probably lost for White and Capablanca needs all his endgame skill to escape) 24 f3 ♖c8 25 ♖c1 ♖c3 26 ♔f2 ♖dc7 27 ♗d2 ♖a3 28 ♖a1 ♖c4 29 ♗b4 ♖a4 30 ♗d2 f5? (Black should only play a move like this if he cannot make further progress on the queenside, but the obvious plan of ...b4 followed by ...a5 and ...♖a3 was available, pinning down the weaknesses on a2 and c2) 31 exf5 ♗xf5 32 c3 e4 33 fxe4 ♗xe4 34 a3 ♗c6 35 ♖b4 ♖c5 36 ♖xa4 bxa4 37 ♖b1 ♖f5+ 38 ♔g1 ♖d5 39 ♖b2 ♖d3 40 ♔f2 ♗d5? (Black makes no serious attempt to win, even though the position is still very favourable for him) 41 ♗e1 ♔f7 42 ♖d2 ♖xd2+ 43 ♗xd2 ♔e6 44 g3 ♗a2 45 ♗f4 ♔d5 46 ♔e3 ♔c4 47 ♔d2 ♔b3 48 ♗d6 ♗b1 49 h4 ♗f5 50 ♗f8 b5 51 ♗d6 a5 52 ♗f8 g6 53 ♗e7 b4 54 cxb4 ♔xa3 55 bxa5+ ♔b3 56 a6 ♔c4 ½-½, Capablanca-Marshall, match, USA 1909.

⇨ 8...♗d7 9 d4 ♘xd4 (this liquidation leaves White with a central superiority) 10 ♘xd4 exd4 11 ♗xd7 ♕xd7 12 cxd4 ♖fe8 13 f3 d5 14 e5 ♕e6 15 ♖b1 b6 16 ♖f1 ♘d7 17 f4 f5 18 ♕f3 (theoretically White has a bad bishop, but on the a3-f8 diagonal it is far from bad, preventing Black's rooks reaching the f-file and thereby supporting an eventual g4) 18...a6 (the threat was 19 c4 c6 20 cxd5 cxd5 21 ♖b5) 19 ♗a3 b5 (preventing c4, but dooming Black to eternal passivity) 20 ♔h1 ♔h8 21 ♖g1 ♖g8 22 ♖bf1 a5 23 g4 g6 24 c3 ♖ab8 25 ♖g2 b4 (panic, but otherwise Black can only wait for the axe to fall) 26 cxb4 axb4 27 gxf5 gxf5 (or 27...♕xf5 28 ♗c1, followed by ♖g5 and f5) 28 ♖xg8+ ♕xg8 29 ♖g1 ♕f7 30 ♗c1 ♖b6 31 ♗d2 ♖a6 32 ♗xb4 ♖xa2 33 ♕g3 (threat e6) 33...♘f8 34

♗e7 ♘g6 35 ♗f6+ ♔g8 36 h4 ♔f8 37 ♕b3 ♖a8 38 ♕b4+ 1-0, Tarrasch-Schlechter, Vienna 1898.

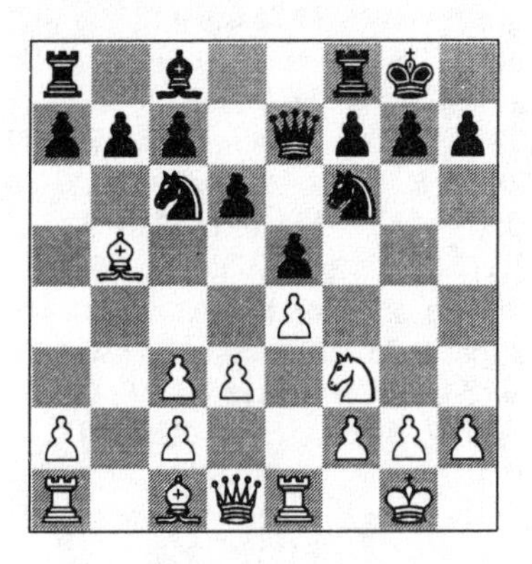

9 d4

⇨ 9 ♕e2 ♘d8 (if Black plays the Metger unpin when the bishop is not on g5 then White simply gains time over normal lines) 10 d4 c5 11 ♗d3 ♔h8 12 h3 ♘g8 13 ♗b2 (a very odd move, because b2 is obviously not the right square for the bishop; 13 a4 is more logical) 13...♘e6 14 g3 f6 15 ♔g2 ♗d7 16 d5 ♘g5 17 ♘xg5 fxg5 18 ♗c1 ♖f7 19 ♗e3 ♖af8 (Black is at least equal) 20 ♖h1 ♕d8 21 c4 h6 22 ♕d2 ♘f6 23 ♖af1 ♘h5 24 f3 ♖f6 (aiming for ...♖g6 and ...♘f4+) 25 h4? (Black has some pressure, but if White is careful he should be able to prevent a breakthrough; Alekhine recommended 25 ♕e1) 25...gxh4 26 ♖xh4 ♘f4+? (a complete blunder; 26...♘xg3! is very good for Black after 27 ♗xh6 ♘xf1 28 ♗g5+ ♔g8 29 ♗xf1 ♖g6 30 ♖g4 ♗xg4! 31 ♗xd8 ♗xf3+ 32 ♔h2 ♖xd8 or 27 ♔xg3 ♖g6+ 28 ♖g4 ♖xf3+ 29 ♖xf3 ♗xg4 30 ♖f1 ♗d7+! 31 ♔f3 ♕h4) 27 ♗xf4 exf4 28 ♖xf4 (White is a clear pawn up) 28...g5 29 ♖xf6 ♕xf6 30 ♕d1 ♔g8 31 f4 gxf4 32 ♖xf4 ♕g7 33 ♖xf8+ (Alekhine correctly pointed out that 33 ♕f3 is very good for White; it is surprising that White doesn't even try to win this position) 33...♔xf8 34 ♕f3+ ♔e7 35 ♕f4 ♕g5 36 ♗e2 ♗a4 37 ♗d3 ♕h5 38 ♕h4+ ♕xh4 39 gxh4 ♔f6 40 ♔f3 ♔e5 41 ♔e3 ♗d7 42 c3 ♗g4 43 ♗c2 ♗h3 44 a3 ♗f1 45 ♗b3 a6 46 ♗a2 ♗h3 47 ♗b1 ♗g4 48 ♗c2 ♗h5 49 ♗a4 ♗g6 50 ♗c2 ♗e8 51 ♗d1 ♗d7 52 ♗c2 b6 53 ♔f3 ♗h3 54 ♗d3 ♗c8 55 ♗b1 ♗d7 56 ♗c2 a5 57 ♗d1 ♗e8 58 ♔e3 ♗f7 59 ♗e2 ♗g8 60 ♗f1 ♗h7 61 ♗g2 ♗g6 62 ♗f3 ♗f7 63 ♗e2 ♗e8 64 ♗d1 ♗d7 65 ♔f3 ♗c8 66 ♗e2 ♗a6 67 ♔e3 ½-½, Tylor-Vidmar, Nottingham 1936.

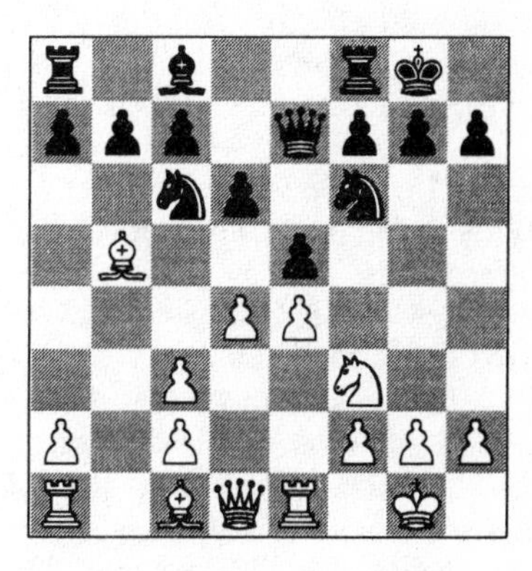

9...♗g4

⇨ 9...♘d8 (27 years earlier Vidmar adopted the same dubious idea) 10 ♗f1 c5 11 g3 ♕c7 12 ♗g2 ♖e8 13 d5 (it can't be bad to imprison the knight on d8, but White could have considered a preparatory move as Black isn't threatening anything)

13...♘d7 14 ♘h4 ♘f8 15 f4?! (White commits himself very early; 15 c4 is probably better because ...♘g6 can always be met by ♘f5) 15...exf4 16 gxf4 ♕e7 17 ♘f3 ♗g4 18 e5 ♗xf3 19 ♗xf3 ♘d7 20 e6 (20 ♗g4! is good for White) 20...♕h4 21 ♗d2 fxe6 22 dxe6 ♘f6 23 e7 (now the position is very unclear) 23...♘c6 24 ♗xc6 bxc6 25 ♕e2 ♕h3 26 ♕e6+ ♕xe6 27 ♖xe6 ♔f7 28 ♖ae1 ♖ac8 29 ♖xd6 ♖xe7 30 c4 ♘e4 31 ♖d3 ♘xd2 (31...♖ce8 is better for Black) 32 ♖xe7+ ♔xe7 33 ♖xd2 (after 33...♖b8 Black still has an edge) ½-½, Forgacs-Vidmar, St.Petersburg 1909.

10 h3 ♗h5 11 g4 ♗g6 12 d5 ♘b8

The best square, because after 12...♘d8 the knight has no future. From b8 it can be activated by ...♘d7 and ...♘c5.

13 ♘h4 ♗xe4

Black accepts the tactical challenge. 13...♘bd7 14 ♘f5 ♗xf5 15 gxf5 (15 exf5? ♘b6) is better for White. The next few moves are forced.

14 g5 ♘xd5 15 ♖xe4 ♘xc3 16 ♕d3 ♘xe4 17 ♕xe4

A hard position to assess. Black, with ♖+3♙ v 2♗, is ahead on material, but there are no open files for Black's rooks and White has attacking chances on the kingside. The usual cop-out "unclear" seems justified.

17...c6 18 ♘f5 ♕e6 19 ♗d3 g6 20 ♘h6+ ♔g7 21 ♕h4 ♘d7 22 ♘g4 f5?! (perhaps 22...♔g8 was better, for example 23 ♘f6+ ♘xf6 24 gxf6 d5 25 ♗g5 h5 is unclear) **23 gxf6+ ♘xf6 24 ♕h6+ ♔f7?!** (24...♔h8 25 ♗xg6 ♖g8 offered better defensive chances) **25 ♗g5!** (suddenly White has a crushing attack) **25...♘xg4 26 ♕xh7+ ♔e8 27 ♗xg6+** (27 ♕xb7! would have been lethal, for example 27...e4 28 ♕xc6+ ♔f7 29 ♗c4, or 27...♖c8 28 ♗xg6+ mating) **27...♖f7 28 ♕g8+ ♔d7 29 ♕xf7+ ♕xf7 30 ♗xf7 ♘xf2 31 ♔xf2 ♖f8 32 h4 ♖xf7+ 33 ♔g3** (White should still win because the h-pawn is just too strong) **33...♔e6 34 ♖h1 ♖f5 35 ♗e3 e4 36 ♗f4 ♖c5 37 h5 ♔f5 38 ♗d2 ♖e5 39 h6 e3 40 ♗c3 1-0**

Game 36

Juarez-De La Vega
Buenos Aires 1985

1 e4 e5 2 ♘f3 ♘c6 3 ♘c3 ♘f6 4 ♗b5 ♗b4 5 0-0 0-0 6 d3 d6 7 ♘e2

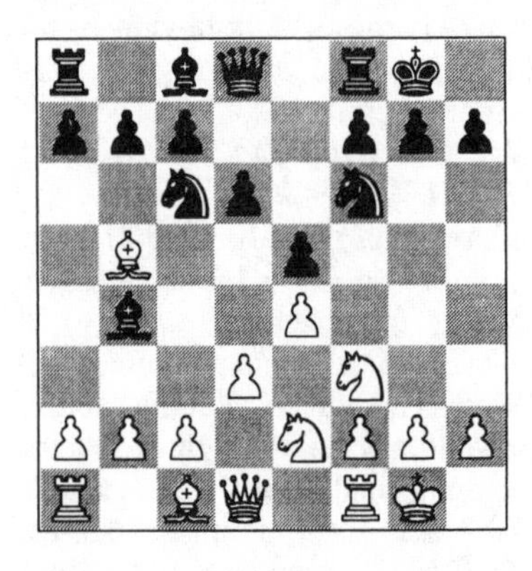

This is another slow White system. The knight is heading for g3, rather like the manoeuvre ♘d2-f1-g3 in the Ruy Lopez. From g3 the knight will defend e4 and thereby support a central push with c3 and d4.

There are two possible replies. Black can either respond symmetrically with 7...♘e7 (game 37), or he can play ...♗g4, so that ♘g3 can be answered by ...♘h5 exchanging the knight.

7...♗g4 8 ♗xc6

Or 8 c3 (this is very similar to the main line, except that White does not exchange on c6; readers should compare the following examples with the main line games, because transposition can easily occur) 8...♗c5 9 ♘g3 ♘h5 10 ♘f5 with a branch:

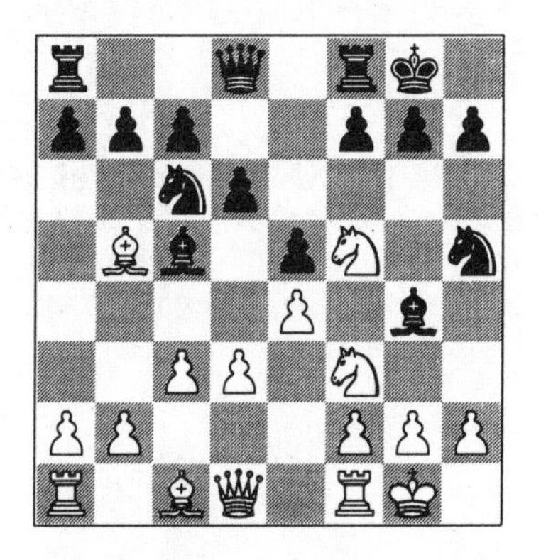

1) 10...♕f6 (Black players should be aware that this move involves a piece sacrifice) and now:

⇨ 11 d4 exd4 12 cxd4 ♗b6 13 h3 (White initiates a sharp tactical struggle, but it eventually proves favourable for Black) 13...♗xf5 14 ♗xc6 (the idea is to meet 14...bxc6 by 15 ♗g5 ♕g6 16 exf5 ♕xf5 17 g4) 14...♗xh3 15 ♗xb7 ♖ab8 16 e5 (16 ♗c6 ♗g4 is good for Black) 16...dxe5 17 dxe5 ♕f5 18 ♘g5 ♗g4 (18...♘g3! gives Black a bigger advantage than in the game) 19 ♗f3 ♗xf3 20 ♕xf3 ♕xe5! (this leads to an endgame plus for Black) 21 ♕xh5 h6 22 ♕h4 hxg5 23 ♕xg5 ♕xg5 24 ♗xg5 ♗d4 25 ♖ac1 ♖xb2 26 ♖xc7 ♗b6 (26...♖xa2 is objectively better) 27 ♖e7 ♗d8 28 ♗c1 ♖xf2 29 ♔xf2 ♗xe7 30 ♗e3 (now White has fair drawing chances) 30...a5 31 a4? (White voluntarily weakens the a-pawn) 31...♖c8 32 ♖d1 ♗b4 33 ♗d2?? ♖c2 34 ♔e3 ♗xd2+ 35 ♖xd2 ♖xd2 36 ♔xd2 f5 37 ♔d3 g5 38 ♔c4 f4 0-1, Podlesnik-Todorovic, Yugoslavian Ch. Semi-Final 1990.

⇨ 11 h3 ♗xf5 (taking on f3 is positionally good for White, so Black is more or less forced to sacrifice a piece) 12 ♗g5 ♕e6 13 exf5 ♕xf5 14 g4 ♕c8 15 gxh5 ♕xh3 16 ♗e3 ♗xe3 17 fxe3 ♕xh5 (Black can take the e-pawn instead by 17...♕g3+ 18 ♔h1 ♕h3+ 19 ♘h2 ♕xe3, but it looks better to take the pawn which menaces Black's kingside) 18 ♖f2 (this position is not so easy to assess; White should be better, but it is hard to judge the scale of his advantage) 18...♘e7 19 ♖h2 ♕g6+ 20 ♔f2 d5! (Black must disturb White quickly, or else the a1 rook will cross to the kingside, supporting the attack) 21 ♘xe5 ♕f5+ 22 ♘f3 d4 23 ♕a4 (returning the piece; 23 ♗c4 was possible) 23...c6 24 ♕xd4 ♕xb5 25 c4 ♕f5 26 ♕h4 ♕xd3 (a key moment; Black decides to re-sacrifice the piece, but this is hopeless and he should have tried 26...f6 27 e4 ♕c5+, even though White has a very strong attack after either 28 ♔e2 or 28 d4) 27 ♕xe7 ♖fe8 28 ♕c5 (this position is winning for White; Nimzowitsch almost makes a mess of it, but he gets there in the end) 28...♖e6 29

♖e1 ♖ae8 30 ♕d4 ♕f5 31 ♖h4 ♖g6 32 ♖f4 ♕h3 33 ♖g1 ♖xg1 34 ♘xg1 ♕h2+ 35 ♔f1 ♕c2 36 ♘e2 h6 37 ♔f2 ♖f8 38 a3 f5 39 ♕e5 ♔h7 40 b4 ♖f6 41 c5 b6 42 e4 fxe4 43 ♖xf6 gxf6 44 ♕xf6 bxc5 45 ♕f7+ ♔h8 46 ♕e8+ ♔h7 47 ♕d7+ ♔h8 48 ♕c8+ ♔g7 49 ♕b7+ ♔f8 50 ♕b8+ ♔e7 51 ♕xa7+ ♔d6 52 ♕g7 h5 53 ♕f6+ ♔d7 54 ♕g7+ ♔d6 55 ♕f6+ ♔d7 56 ♕g7+ ♔d6 57 ♕g3+ ♔d7 58 ♕h3+ ♔d6 59 ♕h2+ ♔d7 60 ♕xh5 cxb4 61 axb4 ♔c7 62 ♕c5 ♕d3 63 ♘d4 ♕d2+ 64 ♔g3 ♕e1+ 65 ♔g4 ♕g1+ 66 ♔f5 ♕f1+ 67 ♔e5 ♕a6 68 b5 ♕b6 69 ♕xc6+ ♕xc6 70 bxc6 e3 71 ♔d5 ♔d8 72 ♔d6 ♔c8 73 c7 1-0, Nimzowitsch-Cohn, Ostend B 1907.

2) 10...♗b6 (more reliable than 10...♕f6) 11 ♘e3 (11 ♔h1 is possible) 11...♗xe3 12 ♗xe3 ♕f6 and now:

➪ 13 d4 ♘e7 14 ♗e2 ♘f4 15 ♗xf4 ♕xf4 16 ♘e1 ½-½, Podlesnik-Sorokin, Sochi B 1989.

➪ 13 ♔h1 (not very dynamic) 13...a6 14 ♗a4 ♘f4 15 ♗xf4 ♕xf4 16 ♕e2 f5 (already Black has taken over the initiative) 17 ♗d1 ♕h6 18 ♕e3 f4 19 ♕d2 ♖f6 20 d4 ♔h8 21 ♕d3 ♖af8 22 ♘d2 ♗c8 23 d5 ♘d8 (if only I could get such positions from the King's Indian...) 24 ♕f3 g5 25 g4 fxg3 26 ♕xg3 g4 27 ♘c4 ♖f4 28 ♘e3 ♕g6 29 ♘g2 ♕xe4 30 f3 ♖4f6 31 ♖f2 ♕xd5 32 ♘e3 ♕c6 33 ♘xg4 ♖xf3 0-1, Euwe-Bogoljubow, Bad Pistyan 1922. White played horribly in this example, but the evidence suggests that 10....♗b6 is a solid equalising move.

3) 10...♗xf5 11 exf5 ♘f6 (this continuation is good for White) 12 d4 exd4 13 cxd4 ♗b6 14 h3 ♘e4 15 ♕c2 ♖e8 16 ♗xc6 bxc6 17 ♖e1 ♘f6 18 ♗g5 (Black has no reasonable escape from this pin; moreover, c6 is under attack and 18...♖xe1+ 19 ♖xe1 c5 20 d5 is clearly better for White) 18...♕d7 19 ♗xf6 gxf6 20 g4 ♖xe1+ 21 ♖xe1 ♖e8 22 ♖e4 d5 23 ♖xe8+ ♕xe8 24 ♔g2 a5 25 ♕c3 ♔g7 26 a4 (fixing the a-pawn on a black square) 26...♕d7 27 ♘d2 c5 (desperation, but otherwise ♘b3 will win a pawn) 28 dxc5 d4 29 c6 ♕d6 30 ♕c4 ♕f4 31 ♕d3 ♕d6 32 ♕f3 ♕b4 33 ♘e4 (so that 33...♕xb2 34 g5 fxg5 35 f6+ ♔g6 36 ♕d3! ♔h6 37 ♘g3! gives White a decisive attack) 33...h6 34 b3 ♕e1 35 ♕d3 ♕c1 36 ♕c4 ♕e1 37 ♕d5 (threat ♘g3-h5) 37...h5 38 g5 ♕e2 39 ♘g3 ♕d1 40 ♕d8 fxg5 41 ♕xg5+ 1-0, Nimzowitsch-Schories, Ostend 1907.

8...bxc6 9 ♘g3 ♘h5

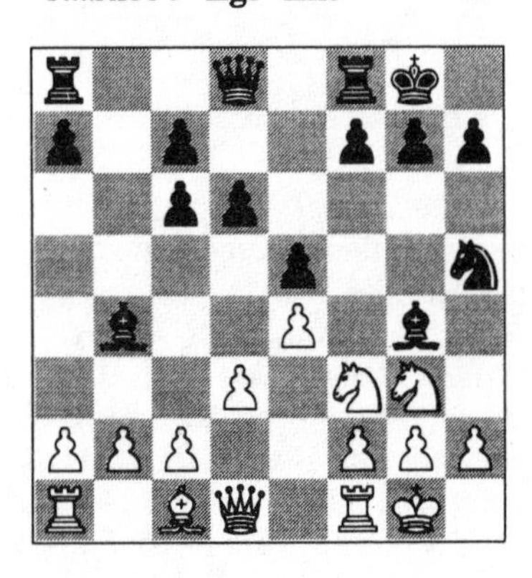

10 h3

Or 10 c3 ♗c5 11 ♘f5 and now:

➪ 11...♕f6 (this is effectively a piece sacrifice) 12 h3 ♗xf5 13 ♗g5 ♕e6 14 exf5 ♕xf5 15 g4 ♕e6 16 gxh5 ♕xh3 (the position is identical to Nimzowitsch-Cohn above, except for the exchange on c6, a difference which slightly favours Black) 17 h6? (too slow because Black can ignore the possibility of hxg7; 17 ♗e3 is better, with an unclear position) 17...e4 18 dxe4 ♖fe8 19 ♘d4 ♖xe4 (Black has a winning attack) 20 f3 ♕g3+ 21 ♔h1 ♖e5 22 f4 ♕h3+ 23 ♔g1 ♖e3 24 ♗h4 ♕xh4 25 ♖f2 ♖h3 0-1, Berg-D.Bronstein, Tastrup 1990.

➩ 11...♗b6 12 ♔h1 ♕f6? (very casual; now White can win the piece under much more favourable circumstances) 13 h3 ♗xf5 14 ♗g5 ♕e6 15 exf5 ♕xf5 16 g4 ♕g6 (16...♕e6 17 gxh5 ♕xh3+ 18 ♘h2 wins) 17 gxh5 ♕xh5 18 ♔h2 f5 19 ♗e3 (Black has only two pawns for the piece and few attacking chances) 19...e4 20 ♘g1 ♕h4 21 dxe4 fxe4 22 ♕g4 ♕e7 23 ♘e2 d5 24 ♖g1 ♖f6 25 ♘f4 ♖af8 26 ♖g3 g6 27 h4 ♕e5 28 ♘h3 ♖f3 29 ♖ag1 ♗xe3 30 fxe3 ♖xe3 31 h5 ♖ff3 32 hxg6 ♖xg3 33 gxh7+ ♔xh7 34 ♖xg3 ♖xg3 35 ♕xg3 ♕xg3+ 36 ♔xg3 ♔g6 37 ♔f4 ♔f6 38 c4 ♔e6 39 c5 ♔d7 40 ♘g1 ♔c8 41 ♘e2 ♔b7 42 ♘d4 ♔a6 43 b4 ♔b7 44 a4 1-0, Maroczy-Schlechter, Barmen 1905.

10...♘xg3 11 fxg3 ♗c5+ 12 ♔h2 ♗d7

I prefer 12...♗xf3, when White's advantage is microscopic.

13 ♘h4 d5 14 ♕e2 ♖e8 15 ♘f5 ♗f8 16 ♗d2 f6 17 g4

Black's problem is that he has no source of counterplay, while White can slowly generate a kingside attack.

17...♗e6 18 b3 ♕d7 19 ♖f3 ♖ad8 20 ♗e3 c5 21 ♖af1 c4 (Black is finally making progress, but White's assault is already dangerous) 22 **g5 cxd3 23 cxd3 dxe4 24 dxe4 fxg5 25 ♗xg5 ♖a8 26 ♖g3 ♔h8 27 ♖d1 ♕f7 28 ♖f1 ♕d7 29 ♕h5 ♗f7 30 ♕h4** (threatening 31 ♗f6) **30...♗e6 31 ♖ff3 a5 32 ♖d3**

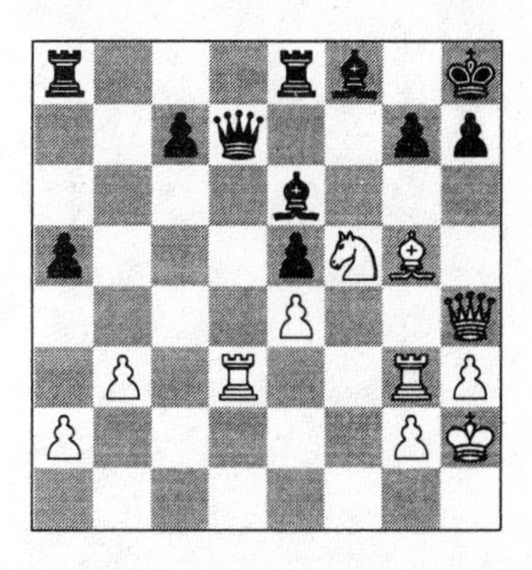

32...♕c6 (or 32...♕f7 33 ♘h6 ♕g6 and now not 34 ♗f6??, as given in *New in Chess*, which loses to 34...♕xf6, but 34 ♗d8! winning Black's queen) **33 ♕h6** (a neat move, but White could have won more convincingly 33 ♘xg7! ♗xg7 34 ♗f6 ♖e7 35 ♖xg7 ♖xg7 36 ♕h6 ♖g8 37 ♗xg7+ ♖xg7 38 ♖d8+) **33...♗d7** (Black must meet the threat of 34 ♗f6) **34 ♖d6! ♕xd6** (the only move because 34...cxd6 fails to 35 ♗f6 ♖e7 36 ♘xe7 and mate in three more moves) **35 ♘xd6 cxd6** (35...gxh6 36 ♗f6+ ♗g7 37 ♗xg7+ ♔h8 38 ♗xh6+ mates) **36 ♗f6 ♖e6?** (36...♖e7 is the only move, but White still wins by 37 ♗xe7 gxh6 38 ♗f6+ ♗g7 39 ♖xg7 netting a piece) **37 ♗xg7+ 1-0**

Game 37

Sveshnikov-Yusupov
USSR Ch. 1979

1 e4 e5 2 ♘f3 ♘c6 3 ♘c3 ♘f6 4 ♗b5 ♗b4 5 0-0 0-0 6 d3 d6 7 ♘e2 ♘e7 8 c3

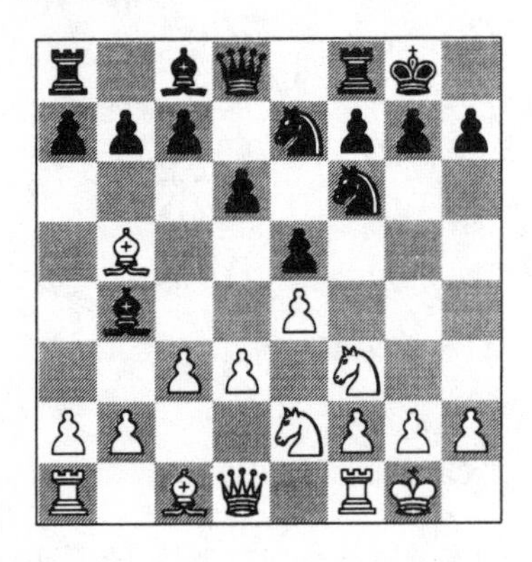

8...♗a5

⇨ 8...♗c5 9 d4 exd4 10 cxd4 ♗b6 11 ♘g3 ♘g6 12 ♗d3 ♖e8 13 h3 (White's extra central pawn gives him some advantage) 13...♗d7 14 ♗e3 c5 15 ♖c1 cxd4 16 ♗xd4 ♗xd4 17 ♘xd4 d5 18 exd5 ♘xd5 19 ♗e4 ♘df4 20 ♗xb7 ♖b8 21 ♘c6 ♗xc6 22 ♗xc6 (White is a pawn up for nothing) 22...♖f8 23 ♕xd8? (it isn't necessary to activate Black's f8 rook; simply 23 b3 should win) 23...♖fxd8 24 ♖c2 ♘d3 25 ♖d1 ♘b4 26 ♖xd8+ ♖xd8 27 ♖c4 ♖d1+ 28 ♔h2 ♘xc6 29 ♖xc6 ♖d2 30 ♔g1 (30 ♘f5 was no better, for example 30...h6 31 ♖c8+ ♔h7 32 ♖c7 ♖xf2 33 ♖xf7 ♘h4) 30...♖xb2 31 ♖a6 ♖b1+ 32 ♔h2 ♖b7 33 ♘e4 h5 34 a4 h4 35 ♘d6 ♖b2 36 ♔g1 ♖b1+ 37 ♔h2 ♖b2 38 ♖xa7 ♖xf2 39 a5 ♘f4 40 ♖xf7 ♖xg2+ 41 ♔h1 ♖f2 42 a6 ♖f1+ 43 ♔h2 ♖f2+ 44 ♔g1 ♘xh3+ 45 ♔h1 ♖a2 46 a7 ♘g5 47 ♖f4 ½-½, Maroczy-Kupchik, Lake Hopatcong 1926.

9 ♘g3 c6

⇨ 9...♘g6 10 d4 a6 11 ♗a4 b5 12 ♗c2 ♗b7 13 a4 h6 14 h3 b4 15 ♗d2 bxc3 16 bxc3 ♖e8 17 ♖e1 ♖b8 ½-½, Gulko-Sosonko, Thessaloniki Ol. 1988.

10 ♗a4

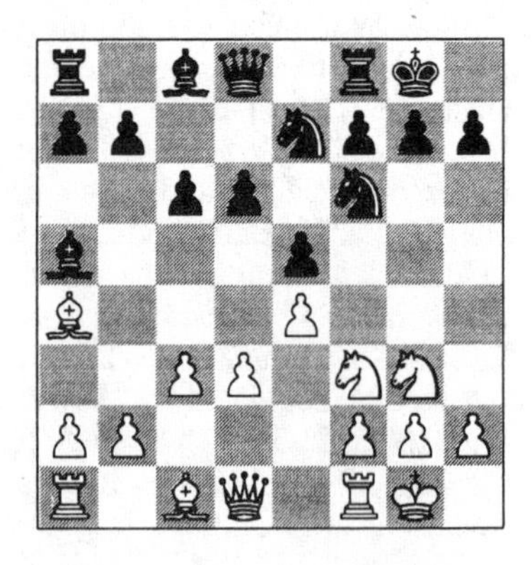

10...♘g6

⇨ 10...♗b6 11 d4 exd4 12 cxd4 d5 13 e5 ♘e4 14 ♗c2 ♘xg3 15 fxg3 (very ambitious; 15 hxg3 would be a little better for White) 15...♗f5 16 ♗xf5 ♘xf5 17 ♕d3 ♕d7 18 g4 ♘e7 19 ♘g5 ♘g6 20 h3 (White's attack has got nowhere and now Black moves over to the counterattack) 20...♖ae8 21 ♗e3 f6 22 exf6 gxf6 23 ♘f3 ♖e4 24 ♘d2 ♖e6 25 g3 ♖fe8 26 ♖f3 ♕e7 27 ♘f1 ♖e4 28 ♖c1 ♘f8! (heading for e6 and d4) 29 ♔g2 ♘e6 30 ♘d2 ♘xd4 31 ♘xe4 ♘xf3 32 ♗xb6 axb6 33 ♕xf3 ♕xe4 34 ♕xe4

♖xe4 35 ♔f3 ♔f7 36 ♖c3 b5 37 ♔f2 ♖c4 0-1, Podlesnik-Djuric, Yugoslavian Ch. 1988.

11 d4 ♖e8

➩ 11...exd4 12 ♘xd4 (12 cxd4 is more natural) 12...♖e8 13 ♖e1 ♗b6 14 ♗c2 ♗d7 15 ♘h5? (15 h3 gives White an edge) 15...♘g4 16 ♘g3 (16 h3 ♕h4! is dangerous) 16...♕f6 17 ♗e3 ♘6e5 18 h3 ♘xe3 (now Black is a little better) 19 ♖xe3 g6 20 ♕f1 ♗e6 21 b3 ♖ad8 22 ♖d1 ♗c8 23 f4 ♘d7 24 ♔h1 ♕h4 25 ♖de1 ♘f6 26 ♔g1 ♘d7 27 ♔h2 ♕f6 28 ♖d1 ♘f8 29 ♘ge2 ♘e6 30 g4 (30...h6 allows Black to retain his edge) 30...♗c7 ½-½, Marco-Schlechter, Vienna 1898.

➩ 11...♗b6 12 ♗e3 h6 13 ♗c2 ♖e8 14 ♖e1 ♘g4 15 ♗c1 ♗e6 16 h3 ♘f6 17 ♘f5 (after 17 ♗e3 White has his usual slight plus) 17...♗c7 18 dxe5 dxe5 19 ♗e3 ♕xd1 20 ♖axd1 ♖ed8 ½-½, Znosko-Borovsky-Teichmann, St.Petersburg 1909.

12 ♗b3

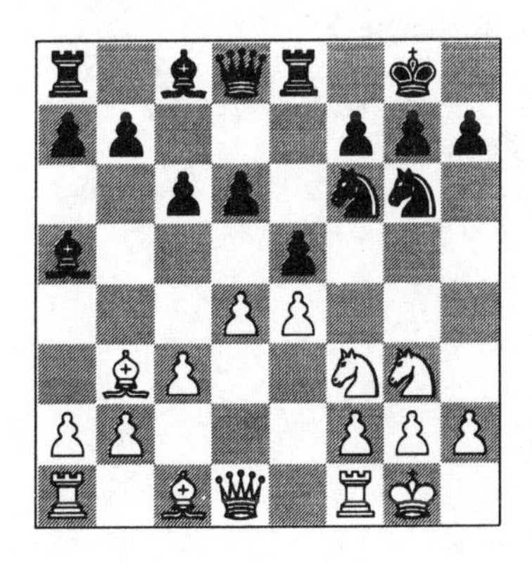

12...h6

➩ 12...exd4 13 cxd4 (threat ♘g5) 13...♗e6 (13...♘xe4 14 ♘xe4 ♖xe4 15 ♘g5 ♖e7 16 ♕h5 is very good for White) 14 ♘g5 ♗xb3 15 ♕xb3 ♕d7 16 f3 (White has secured his centre and has the advantage) 16...h6 17 ♘h3 ♖e6 18 ♘f4 ♘xf4 19 ♗xf4 ♗b6 20 ♖ad1 ♖ae8 21 ♔h1 d5 22 e5 ♘h7 23 ♘f5 f6 24 g4 (White's initiative appears very dangerous, but in the subsequent play there was nothing clear for him; this game was an excellent defensive performance by Euwe) 24...fxe5 25 ♗xe5 ♘f6 26 ♕d3 ♔h8 27 ♖g1 (Euwe gave the line 27 g5 hxg5 28 ♖g1 ♖xe5 29 dxe5 ♗xg1 30 exf6 ♗b6 31 fxg7+ ♔g8 as unclear; in fact it is probably good for Black) 27...♗c7 28 f4 ♕f7 29 ♖df1 (29 ♘xg7 gives White no advantage after 29...♖xe5 30 fxe5 ♘e4) 29...♗xe5 30 fxe5 ♘e4 31 g5 (31 ♘d6 ♕g6 32 ♘xe4 ♕xe4+ 33 ♕xe4 dxe4 34 ♖e1 c5 leads to a draw and White should have been satisfied with this result) 31...hxg5 32 ♘d6 ♘f2+ 33 ♔g2 ♘xd3 34 ♘xf7+ ♔g8 35 ♘xg5 ♖g6 36 h4 c5 (suddenly it is White who has to be careful) 37 dxc5 ♖xe5 38 ♔h3 ♘xc5 39 ♖c1 ♖c6 40 ♖ge1 ♘e4 41 ♖xc6 bxc6 42 ♖c1? (Euwe gave 42 ♘xe4 ♖xe4 43 ♖xe4 dxe4 44 ♔g4 ♔h7 45 ♔f4 ♔g6 46 ♔xe4 ♔h5 47 ♔f5 as a draw, which is correct if one adds that 47...c5 must be met by 48 b3!, when Black runs out of tempo moves on the queenside) 42...♘xg5+ 43 hxg5 ♖e6 44 ♔g4 ♔f7 45 ♖c3 a5 46 ♔f3 ♔g6 47 ♖a3 ♔xg5 48 ♖xa5 ♔f5 49 a4 g5 50 ♖a8 ♖e4 51 ♖f8+ ♔e5 52 ♖e8+ ♔d4 53 ♖b8 c5 54 b4 c4 55 a5 ♖e3+ 56 ♔f2 ♖a3 57 ♖g8 c3 58 ♖xg5 ♖a2+ 59 ♔f3 c2 60 ♖g1 0-1, Alekhine-Euwe, Amsterdam 1936.

13 h3

13 ♖e1 is met by the awkward 13...♗g4.

13...♗e6

⇨ 13...exd4 (not 13...♘xe4 14 ♘xe4 ♖xe4 15 ♗xf7+) 14 ♘xd4 d5 (a very safe way for Black to play) 15 exd5 ♘xd5 16 ♘df5 ♕f6 17 ♕f3 ♘e5 18 ♕h5 ♘d3 19 ♗xd5 cxd5 20 ♘d4 ♗b6 21 ♕xd5 ♖d8 22 ♕e4 ♗xd4 23 cxd4 ♕xd4 24 ♕xd4 ♖xd4 25 ♗e3 ♖d5 26 ♖fd1 ½-½, Kuzmin-Kharitonov, Moscow 1991.

14 ♖e1 ♗b6 15 ♗e3 ♕c7 16 ♕d2 exd4 17 ♗xh6

Accepting the challenge. 17 ♗xd4 was safe, but offers few chances of an advantage after 17...♗xd4 18 ♕xd4 ♘e5.

17...dxc3 18 bxc3 d5!

An excellent defensive move, counterattacking the knight on g3. On the other hand after 18...gxh6 19 ♕xh6 Black has severe problems because ♘f5 is a threat and 19...♕d7 20 e5 dxe5 21 ♘xe5 ♘xe5 22 ♖xe5 ♘h7 23 ♘h5 wins for White.

19 e5

Yusupov assess 19 exd5 ♗xd5 20 ♘f5 as unclear, but after 20...♖xe1+ 21 ♖xe1 ♘e4 White is in trouble.

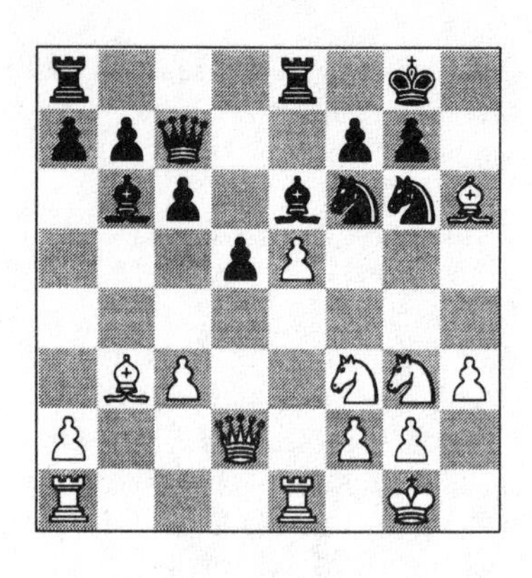

19...♘e4 20 ♖xe4?

20 ♘xe4 dxe4 21 ♖xe4 ♖ad8 22 ♕c1 (22 ♕g5 ♗xb3 23 axb3 ♖e6 followed by ...gxh6 is good for Black) 22...♗xb3 23 axb3 gxh6 24 ♕xh6 is best, with a completely unclear position.

20...dxe4 21 ♘xe4

Not 21 ♗xg7? e3 and wins.

21...♗xb3 22 axb3 ♘xe5!

The end of White's attack.

23 ♗xg7

Or 23 ♕g5 ♘xf3+ 24 gxf3 ♕e5 defending g7.

23...♘xf3+ 24 gxf3 ♖xe4 25 ♕h6

25 ♕g5 ♕f4 26 ♕g2 ♔h7 27 fxe4 ♖g8 wins.

25...♕g3+ 26 ♔h1 ♕xf3+ 0-1

In this chapter we cover all the lines arising after 4 ♗b5 ♗b4 5 0-0 0-0 6 d3 d6 7 ♗g5 except the Metger Unpin. The division of material is more complex than usual because there are a number of transpositional possibilities. Game 38 deals with 7...♘e7 and 7...♗e6, lines which were once popular but are rarely seen today. Game 39 covers the similar variation 7...♗xc3 8 bxc3 ♘e7, which has been played from time to time over the past 100 years, but has retained its poor theoretical reputation. The game Chandler-Agdestein is critical for the assessment of this line. Transpositions can easily occur between game 38 and game 39, so readers should study them together.

In game 40 we deal with the remaining systems in which Black does not play an immediate ...♕e7. The most important of these is 8...♗d7, which is a solid but slightly passive continuation. White has good chances to retain a very slight advantage, but cannot hope for anything more. Game 40 also includes various lines in which Black plays ...h6, but doesn't continue with a quick ...♕e7.

The rest of the chapter covers lines starting with 8...♕e7. In a number of games White has played 9 ♗xc6, possibly with the idea of reaching a draw. The examples in game 41 show that this is not a safe route to the half-point and indeed Black has a very good score in this line.

In game 42 we deal with some miscellaneous alternatives for both sides. The first of these is 8...♕e7 9 d4, whereby White attempts to save time by missing out ♖e1. Play can become very sharp since White may be forced to sacrifice a piece on g5 in order to avoid losing his e4 pawn after ...h6 and ...g5. No refutation is known and this line deserves further investigation. The second unusual line is 8...♕e7 9 ♘d2, but it is hard to believe that this is promising for White. The final unusual line involves an early ...h6 by Black. Normally Black would prefer to keep the bishop on g5, so that the manoeuvre ...♘d8-e6 gains a tempo, but in this case White normally retreats his bishop to c1. The idea behind an early ...h6 is that White's bishop is committed to h4, so that after ...♘d8-e6 White cannot go back to c1. It is hard to say whether the inferior placing of the bishop on h4 is worth the tempo Black expends on playing ...h6.

Game 43 covers the line 8...♕e7 9 ♖e1 ♘d8 10 d4 ♗g4, which was once quite popular but is seldom played today, possibly because the game Spassky-Gligoric put people off the line. However, this obscurity is unjustified and 10...♗g4 deserves more attention than it is currently receiving.

Game 38

Tarrasch-Janowski
Ostend 1907

1 e4 e5 2 ♘f3 ♘c6 3 ♘c3 ♘f6 4 ♗b5 ♗b4 5 0-0 0-0 6 d3 d6 7 ♗g5

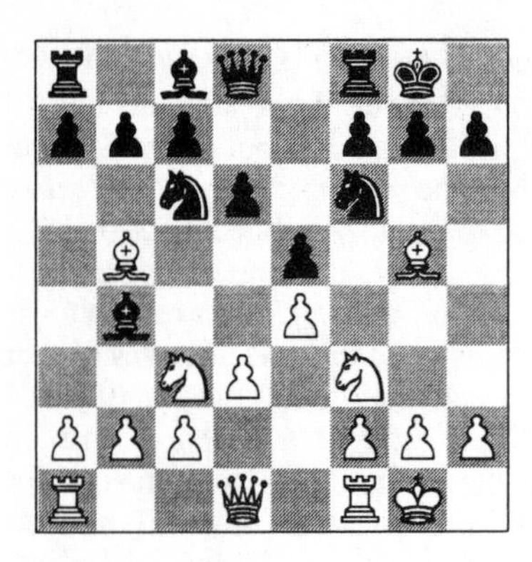

7...♘e7

Or 7...♗e6 and now:

⇨ 8 d4 exd4 9 ♘xd4 h6 (9...♘xd4 10 ♕xd4 ♗c5 11 ♕d3 c6 12 ♗a4 ♕b6 13 ♗b3 ♕a5 14 ♗xf6 gxf6 15 ♖ad1 ♗xb3 16 axb3 ♖ae8 17 ♘e2 ♔h8 18 c3 ♕d8 19 ♘g3 ♖e6 20 b4 ♗b6 21 ♘f5 was good for White in Janowski-Chajes, Havana 1913) 10 ♗h4 ♘e5 11 f4 ♗c5 12 ♗xf6? (accepting the offer is a mistake; 12 ♔h1 would have been slightly better for White) 12...♕xf6 13 fxe5 ♕xe5 14 ♘ce2 ♗g4 15 ♖f3 ♗xf3 16 gxf3 f5 (material is roughly equal, but White is in an awkward pin and his king is exposed) 17 ♕d3 c6 18 ♗c4+ ♔h8 19 ♔h1 b5 20 ♗b3 fxe4 21 ♕xe4 ♕xe4 22 fxe4 ♖ae8 23 ♘xc6 ♖xe4 24 ♘g3 ♖ee8 25 ♖d1 ♖f2 26 ♘d4?? (Black was better, but this is a dreadful blunder) 26...♗xd4 0-1, Tarrasch-Em. Lasker, World Ch. match, Munich 1908.

⇨ 8 ♘d5 ♗xd5 9 exd5 ♘e7 10 c4 ♘g6 11 ♗a4 h6 12 ♗e3 ♗a5 13 h3 ♗b6 14 d4 exd4 15 ♘xd4 ♗xd4 16 ♕xd4 ♕e7 17 ♖fe1 and the two bishops give White some advantage, Janowski-Caro, Vienna 1898.

⇨ 8 ♘e2 ♗a5 (or 8...♘e7 9 c3 ♗a5 10 ♘g3 c6 11 ♗a4 ♘e8 12 d4 with a slight plus for White, Duras-Kupchik, New York 1913) 9 ♘g3 ♘b8 10 d4 c6 11 ♗d3 ♘bd7 12 h3 again with some advantage for White, Znosko-Borovsky-Von Scheve, Ostend B 1907.

The conclusion is that 7...♗e6 is insufficient for equality.

8 ♘h4

Various other moves have been played, but here we concentrate on 8 ♘h4, which is the critical reply.

8...c6 9 ♗c4

⇨ 9 ♗a4 (definitely less dangerous than ♗c4) 9...♘e8 10 ♗b3 (White has lost time) 10...♔h8 11 f4 f6 12 fxe5 dxe5 13 ♗e3 ♘c7 14 ♕f3 ♘e6 15 ♘e2 ♗c5 16 ♔h1 ♗xe3 17 ♕xe3 a5 18 a4 b6 19 ♗c4 ♘c5 20 d4 exd4 21 ♘xd4 ♗d7 22 e5 fxe5 23 ♕xe5 ♘g8 24 ♘hf3 ½-½, Bagirov-Korchnoi, USSR Ch. 1963.

⇨ 9 ♗xf6 gxf6 10 ♗a4 f5 11 ♕h5 ♗xc3 12 bxc3 fxe4 13 dxe4 f5? (opening up the kingside is too risky) 14 ♗b3+ d5 15 f4! fxe4 16 f5 ♖f6 17 ♖ae1 ♔h8 18 g4 ♗d7 19 ♘g6+! (White has a decisive attack) 19...♘xg6 20 fxg6 ♖xg6 21 ♖f7 ♕b6+ 22 ♔h1 ♖g7 23 ♕xe5 ♖ag8 24 ♖ef1 ♕b5 25 ♖1f2 ♕c5 26 ♖xg7 1-0, Perlis-Salwe, St.Petersburg 1909.

9...♗g4

The alternatives are:

⇨ 9...♗e6 10 ♗xf6 gxf6 11 ♗xe6 fxe6 12 ♕g4+ ♔f7 13 f4 ♘g6 14 f5 exf5 15 ♘xf5 was very good for White in Schlechter-Janowski, Ostend 1907; this is similar to the main line game.

⇨ 9...♔h8 10 f4 exf4 11 ♗xf6 gxf6 12 ♖xf4 ♘g6 13 ♘xg6+ fxg6 was roughly equal in the game Tylor-Em.Lasker, Nottingham 1936. Alekhine suggested 11 ♖xf4 ♘g6 12 ♘xg6+ fxg6 13 ♕f3 as an improvement, but after 13...♗c5+ 14 ♔h1 b5 15 ♗b3 ♗d4, threatening 16...♗e5 and 16...b4, I see no advantage for White. Perhaps 10 ♔h1 is better.

⇨ 9...♘g6 10 ♘xg6 hxg6 11 f4 ♗c5+ (11...♕b6+ 12 ♔h1 ♘g4 13 ♕e1 ♘e3 14 f5! is very dangerous for Black) 12 ♔h1 ♗e3 13 ♕f3 ♗xf4 14 ♗xf4 exf4 15 ♕xf4 ♕e7 16 ♕g3 with a small advantage for White, Bachmann-Marron, Stockholm 1930.

The other main possibility is 9...d5, a line which deserves further investigation by Black players. After 10 ♗b3 (not 10 ♗xf6?! gxf6 11 ♗b3 ♕d6 12 ♕f3 ♔h8 13 exd5 ♗xc3 14 bxc3 cxd5 15 c4 d4 16 c5 ♕c6 17 ♕h5 ♘g6 with advantage to Black, Tarrasch-Yates, Carlsbad 1923) 10...♕d6 White may try:

⇨ 11 h3 (in game 39 we reach the same position, except that Black has already exchanged on c3; in that case f4 is the accepted move, but it has never been played here, even though I cannot see anything clearly wrong with it, for example 11 f4 ♗g4 may be met by 12 fxe5 when 12...♕xe5 13 ♗xf6 and 12...♕c5+ 13 d4 are good for White) 11...h6 12 ♗xf6 ♕xf6 13 ♕h5 ♗xc3 14 bxc3, Tarrasch-Yates, Hastings 1922, and now Yates lost a pawn by 14...♔h7 15 ♘f3 ♘g6? 16 exd5 cxd5 17 ♗xd5. However, 14...dxe4 15 dxe4 ♗e6 is fine for Black.

⇨ 11 ♕e2 h6 12 ♗d2 g5 13 ♘f3 ♘g6 14 exd5 ♗xc3 15 ♗xc3 ♖e8 16 ♖fe1 ♗g4 17 ♕e3 (17 dxc6 ♕xc6 18 ♕e3 is critical) 17...♘xd5 18 ♗xd5 ♕xd5 19 ♘d2 ♗e6 20 ♕g3 f6 21 ♘e4 ♔g7 22 ♖e2 c5 and now Black is slightly better, Bohatirchuk-Yates, Moscow 1925.

10 f3 ♗e6 11 ♗xf6 gxf6 12 ♗xe6 fxe6

The position is the same as in Schlechter-Janowski above, except that White's pawn is on f3 instead of f4. This prevents ♕g4+, but doesn't alter the fundamental structure of the position, which is bad for Black.

13 f4 ♘g6 14 ♘xg6 hxg6 15 ♕g4 ♕e8 16 f5 exf5 17 exf5 ♗xc3 18 bxc3 ♔g7 19 ♖f3 ♖h8 (19...g5 is met by 20 h4, but now ...g5 is a threat) **20 fxg6 ♕e7** (20...♕xg6 loses to 21 ♕d7+, so Black has lost not only a pawn, but also the main defence for his king; the rest is slaughter) **21 h4 d5 22 ♖af1 ♖af8 23 h5 ♖h6 24 ♖1f2 ♖hh8 25 ♕f5 ♕d6 26 g4 ♕e7 27 g5 fxg5 28 ♕xf8+ ♖xf8 29 ♖xf8 ♕xf8 30 h6+ 1-0**

Game 39

Nunn-Tatai
Manila Ol. 1992

1 e4 e5 2 ♘f3 ♘c6 3 ♘c3 ♘f6 4 ♗b5 ♗b4 5 0-0 0-0 6 d3 d6 7 ♗g5 ♗xc3 8 bxc3 ♘e7

In my opinion, this line is worse for Black than game 38. In many lines the exchange on c3 frees White's hand and reduces Black's control of the dark squares. Once again we only investigate the key line with 9 ♘h4.

9 ♘h4

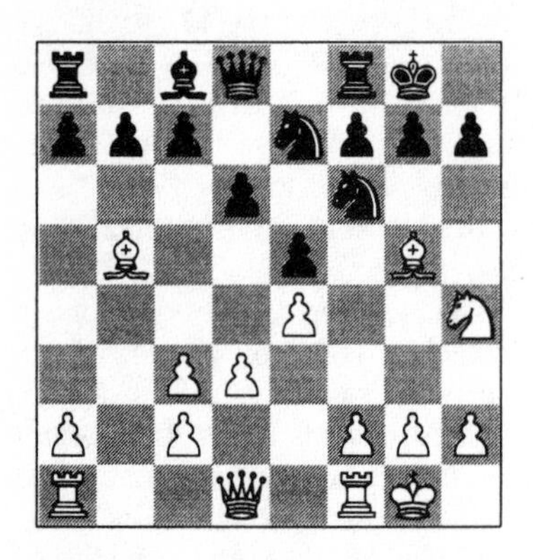

9...c6

➪ 9...♘e8 (this line is critical) 10 ♗c4 (*ECO* suggests 10 f4 f6 11 fxe5 fxg5 12 ♖xf8+ ♔xf8 13 ♕f3+ followed by ♖f1, but 11...dxe5 is much stronger, when it is doubtful if White has any advantage) 10...♗e6 11 ♗xe6 (11 ♘f5 ♗xf5 12 exf5 ♕d7 13 g4 c6 14 d4! was better for White in Tarrasch-Vidmar, San Sebastian 1911, but 12...♔h8 followed by ...f6 and ...d5 was better) 11...fxe6 12 ♕g4 ♕d7 13 f4 exf4 14 ♖xf4 ♖xf4 15 ♕xf4 ♘f6 16 ♗xf6 ♖f8 17 ♕e3 ♖xf6 18 ♕xa7 (curiously, this is identical to Marshall-Capablanca below, except that Black's pawn is on c7 and not c6; this difference favours Black because the move ...b6 is available to cut off the retreat of White's queen, while in some lines ...♕b5 is possible) 18...b6?! (Chandler analyses 18...♕b5 19 ♕b8+ ♖f8 20 ♕xc7 ♕b2 21 ♖f1 ♖xf1+ 22 ♔xf1 ♕c1+ 23 ♔f2 ♕xc2+ 24 ♔g3 ♕xd3+ 25 ♘f3 as slightly better for White; this line is Black's best continuation and offers good drawing chances) 19 ♖f1 ♖xf1+ 20 ♔xf1 g5 21 ♘f3 g4 22 ♘d4 ♘g6?! (22...e5 23 ♘e2 ♘g6 24 g3 ♘f8 heading for e6, g5 and f3 is a better chance) 23 ♕b8+ ♘f8 24 ♔e1 (now White should win) 24...♕f7 25 ♕d8 ♕f4 26 ♘e2 ♕xh2 27 ♕g5+ ♔f7 28 ♕xg4 ♕h1+ 29 ♔d2 ♕a1 30 ♕h5+ ♔g7 31 ♕g5+ ♘g6 32 ♘c1 ♕b1 33 ♕d8 ♕b5 34 ♕xc7+ ♔h6 35 ♕d8 ♕c5 36 ♘e2 ♕f2 37 ♕xd6 ♕xg2 38 ♕xe6 ♔g7 39 ♕xb6 h5 40 ♕g1 ♕f3 41 ♕a7+ ♔g8 42 ♕e3 ♕f6 43 ♕h6 h4 44 a4 ♕e6 45 a5 1-0, Chandler-Agdestein, Hastings 1991/2.

➪ 9...♘g6 10 ♘xg6 fxg6 (10...hxg6 11 f4 c6 12 ♗c4 ♕b6+ 13 ♔h1 is also good for White) 11 ♗c4+ ♔h8 12 f4 h6 13 fxe5 dxe5 14 ♗h4 g5 15 ♗g3 ♕e7 16 d4 and White is better, Janowski-Spielmann, Nürnberg 1906.

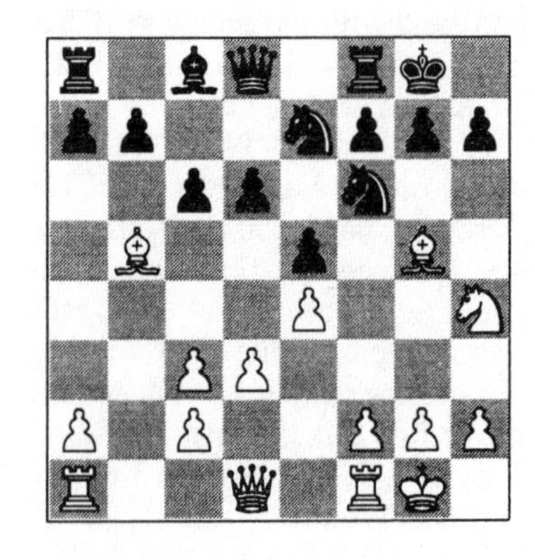

10 ♗a4

Or 10 ♗c4 d5 (10...♗e6? 11 ♗xf6 gxf6 12 ♗xe6 fxe6 13 ♕g4+ ♔f7 14 f4 ♖g8 15 ♕h5+ ♔g7 16 fxe5 dxe5 17 ♖xf6! ♔xf6 18 ♖f1+

♘f5 19 ♘xf5 exf5 20 ♖xf5+ ♔e7 21 ♕f7+ ♔d6 22 ♖f6+ ♔c5 23 ♕xb7 ♕b6 24 ♖xc6+ ♕xc6 25 ♕b4 mate is the famous game Capablanca-H.Steiner, exhibition game, Los Angeles 1933) 11 ♗b3 and now:

⇨ 11...dxe4 12 dxe4 ♕xd1 13 ♖axd1 ♘g6 14 ♘xg6 hxg6 15 ♗xf6 gxf6 16 ♖d6 ♔g7 17 f4 (this is good for White because Black has severe problems developing his bishop) 17...exf4 18 ♖xf4 ♗e6 19 ♗xe6 fxe6 20 ♖xe6 ♖ad8 21 e5 fxe5 22 ♖xf8 ♖xf8 23 ♖e7+ ♖f7 24 ♖xf7+ ♔xf7 with a winning pawn ending, consultation game Em.Lasker-Grigoriev, Nenarokov, Bobrov and Gentschorov, Moscow 1899.

⇨ The other idea is 11...♕d6 12 f4 dxe4 with the division:

1) 13 dxe4 ♕c5+ 14 ♔h1 ♘g4 15 f5, with a clear plus for White, is repeated uncritically in almost all opening books (for example Euwe, Keres and *ECO*). However, 14...♘xe4 is an obvious and massive improvement. Nigel Short informs me that this variation probably emanates from Golombek's book on the 1948 World Championship tournament. So far as I know, only Rellstab (in *Fernschach*) gave 14...♘xe4, continuing 15 ♗xe7 ♕xe7 16 ♕e1 ♘d2 with equality. This opinion is a bit pessimistic, for example after 16...♘c5! 17 fxe5 ♗e6 Black has an advantage.

2) 13 fxe5 ♕xe5 14 ♗xf6 gxf6 15 dxe4 a5? (the start of a bad plan; 15...♗e6 is more natural) 16 a4 c5 (the idea is to prevent 17 ♕f3 because of the reply 17...c4, but this wastes time and weakens the queenside) 17 ♕d3 ♗e6 18 ♗xe6 fxe6 19 ♕c4 ♖a6 20 ♖ad1 ♕c7 21 ♖d3 ♖c6 22 ♖df3 (Black is much worse) 22...♔g7 23 ♕e2 ♕e5 24 ♖g3+ ♔h8 25 ♘f3 ♕h5 26 ♖d1 ♕e8 27 e5 ♘g6 28 exf6 e5 29 ♘g5 ♖fxf6 30 ♖gd3 ♘f8 31 ♖d8 ♕e7 32 ♕h5 c4 33 ♘e4 ♖f7 34 ♖1d7 ♕xd7 35 ♖xd7 ♖xd7 36 ♕xe5+ ♖g7 37 ♘d6 (37...♖c7 38 ♕f6 ♔g8 39 ♘f5 wins) 1-0, Lundqvist-Borsony, 2nd World corr. Ch. 1956.

10...♘e8 11 ♗b3 ♗e6

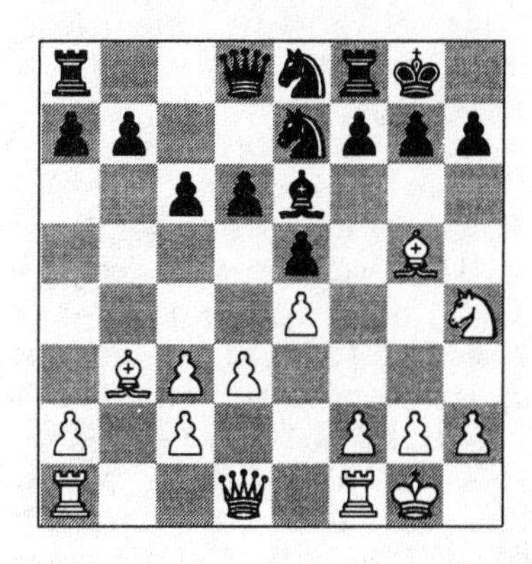

12 d4?!

⇨ 12 ♗xe6 (12 f4 ♗xb3 13 ♗xe7 ♗xc2! 14 ♗xd8 ♗xd1 15 ♗e7 ♗e2 16 ♖fe1 ♗xd3 17 ♗xf8 ♔xf8 is at least equal for Black) 12...fxe6 13 ♕g4 (this is identical to Chandler-Agdestein above, except that Black's pawn is on c6, not c7; here Black has the extra possibility of ...♘c7, although this doesn't seem to help) 13...♕d7 (13...♘c7 14 f4 exf4 15 ♖xf4 ♖xf4 16 ♕xf4 ♕d7 17 ♖f1 ♘g6 18 ♘xg6 hxg6 19 ♕g4 with a clear plus for White) 14 f4 exf4 15 ♖xf4 ♖xf4 16 ♕xf4 ♘f6 17 ♗xf6 ♖f8 18 ♕e3 ♖xf6 19 ♕xa7 (White has a favourable version of Chandler-Agdestein, but Marshall's technique was terrible) 19...g5 20 ♘f3 g4 21 ♕d4 ♖f7 22 ♘e5 c5 23 ♘xd7 cxd4 24 ♖f1 ♖xf1+ 25 ♔xf1 dxc3 26 ♘f6+ ♔f7 27 ♘xg4 ♘c6 28 ♘e3 b5 29 a3 b4 30 axb4 ♘xb4 31 ♔e2 d5 32 exd5 exd5 33 d4 ♔f6 34 g3 h5 35 h3 (White's winning chance have all but disappeared) ♔g5 36 h4+ ♔f6 37 ♔f3 ♔e6 38 g4 hxg4+ 39 ♔xg4 ♘c6 40 ♘f5 ♘b4 41 h5 ♔f7 42 ♘e3 ♘c6 43 h6 ♔g6 44 ♘xd5 ♘xd4 45 ♘e3 ♘xc2 ½-½, Marshall-Capablanca, match, New York 1909.

12...h6 13 ♗e3 b6? (after 13...exd4! 14 cxd4 d5 15 e5 ♘c7 White's b3 bishop is badly placed, so White would have to reply 14 ♕xd4, with an unclear position) **14 ♗xe6 fxe6 15 ♕g4** (very strong as both e6 and h6 are attacked) **15...♖f6 16 f4 exf4 17 ♖xf4 e5 18 ♖xf6 ♘xf6 19 ♕e6+ ♔h7 20 ♖f1** (the threat is ♖xf6, and this is also the reply to 20...♕d7) **20...♕f8 21 ♖f3!** (Black is paralyzed, so White has a better option than the obvious 21 dxe5) **21...♖e8**

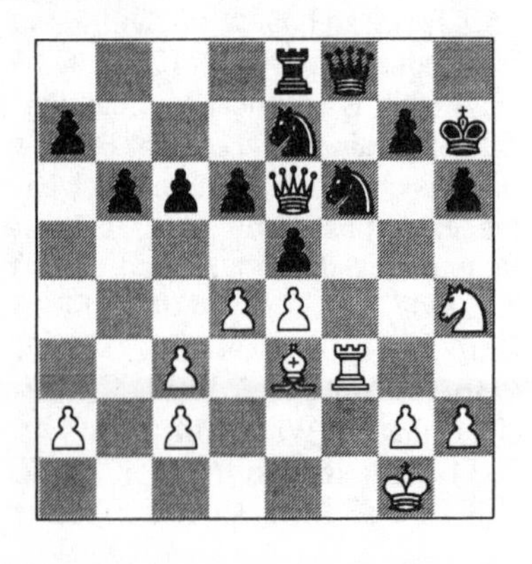

22 ♗xh6 ♔xh6 23 ♖h3 (White wins in all lines, for example 23...♘g6 24 ♘f3+ ♘h5 25 g4!, 23...g5 24 ♘f5+ ♔g6 25 ♖h6+ ♕xh6 26 ♘xh6 ♘eg8 27 ♕xd6, 23...♔h7 24 dxe5 dxe5 25 ♘f3+ ♔g6 26 ♘xe5+ ♔g5 27 g3! with the deadly threat of mate in three starting with 28 ♖h5+!, or 23...exd4 24 cxd4 retaining all the threats) **1-0**

Game 40

Nunn-Smejkal
Bundesliga 1991/2

1 e4 e5 2 ♘f3 ♘c6 3 ♘c3 ♘f6 4 ♗b5 ♗b4 5 0-0 0-0 6 d3 d6 7 ♗g5 ♗xc3 8 bxc3 ♗d7

The threat is 9...h6 10 ♗h4 ♘e7 and then neither 11 ♗xd7 ♘xd7 nor 11 ♗xf6 ♗xb5 promises White a real advantage, while otherwise the knight arrives on g6 with gain of tempo.

The alternative is 8...h6 9 ♗h4 and now:

⇨ 9...♔h8 (a curious idea; Black cannot play 9...g5 because of 10 ♘xg5, but now ...g5 is possible) 10 ♕d2 (10 ♖e1 ♖g8 11 d4 ♕e7 12 ♕d3 was probably better, as in Bolland-Euwe, Weston Super Mare 1924) 10...♖g8 11 ♗xf6 (White can only play for a draw after this move) 11...♕xf6 12 ♗xc6 bxc6 13 ♕e3 c5 14 d4 cxd4 15 cxd4 exd4 16 ♘xd4 ♗d7 17 ♖ad1 ♖ge8 18 ♖fe1 ♕e5 19 ♕a3 ♕f4 20 f3 a5 21 ♕c3 ♖ec8 22 ♘e2 ♕h4 23 ♘g3 with equality, T.Christensen-T.Wedberg, Gausdal Arnold Cup 1991.

➪ 9...♗d7 10 d4 (10 ♖b1 should transpose into the main line of this game) 10...♕e7 11 ♖e1 a6 12 ♗d3 ♔h8 13 d5? (a positional error, releasing the tension in the centre and conceding the c5 square; 13 ♖b1 was better) 13...♘b8 14 ♘d2 g5 15 ♗g3 b6 16 ♘c4 a5 17 ♘e3 ♘a6 18 ♕f3 ♘c5 19 ♘f5 ♗xf5 20 ♕xf5 ♖g8 and Black is better because White has no constructive plan, Campora-Anand, Thessaloniki Ol. 1988.

➪ 9...♗g4 10 h3 ♗xf3 (10...♗h5 11 g4 ♗g6 12 ♕d2 is good for White) 11 ♕xf3 g5 12 ♗g3 ♘h7 (12...♘d7 13 d4 f6 14 ♕g4 ♔h8 15 h4 ♖f7 16 hxg5 hxg5 17 f3 ♘f8 18 ♔f2 ♖h7 19 ♖h1 ♕e7 20 ♕f5 ♖d8 21 ♖xh7+ ♘xh7 22 ♖h1 was better for White in Capablanca-Em.Lasker, St.Petersburg 1914) 13 ♖ab1 ♕c8 (13...♕f6 is also possible, but 14 ♕g4 retains White's advantage) 14 ♖fd1 ♔g7 15 d4 f6 16 ♗e2 ♘e7 17 ♕d3 ♖b8 18 ♗g4 ♕e8 19 ♕c4 h5 20 ♗e6 ♕c6 21 ♕d3 h4 22 ♗h2 ♖fd8 23 d5 ♕a4 24 g3 ♘g6 25 ♖b4 ♕e8 26 ♖db1 b6 27 ♕a6 and White is clearly better, Janowski-Tarrasch, Vienna 1898.

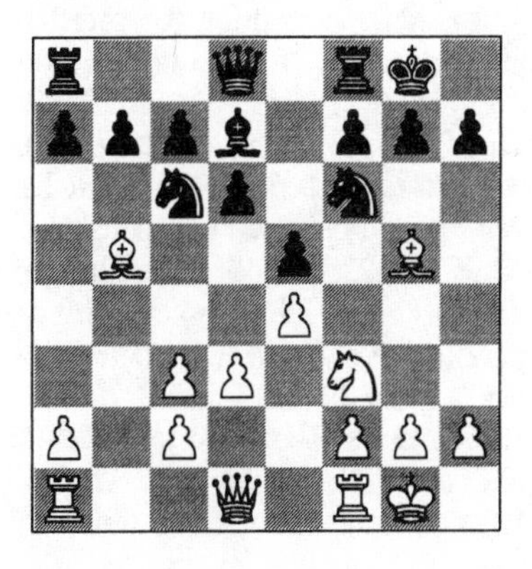

9 ♖b1 a6 10 ♗a4 (10 ♗c4 ♘a5 is equal) **10...♖b8** (renewing the threat of 11...h6 12 ♗h4 ♘e7) **11 ♗b3 h6** (11...♕e7 12 ♘h4!? prevents 12...h6 because of 13 ♘g6) **12 ♗h4 ♕e7 13 ♖e1**

➪ 13 ♕c1 ♔h7 14 ♖e1 ♗g4 15 ♕e3 b6 16 d4 ♖be8 17 ♗c4 ♘b8 18 h3 ♗d7 19 ♗d3 ♗c6 20 g4 gave White a distinct plus in Marciano-Lukacs, Montpellier 1991, but Black's play was unimpressive.

13...♘a5 14 d4 ♖bd8 (Black wants to play ...g5 without allowing ♘xg5, so he would like to play ...♔h7, but the immediate 14...♔h7? is bad after 15 dxe5 dxe5 16 ♘xe5! with advantage for White)

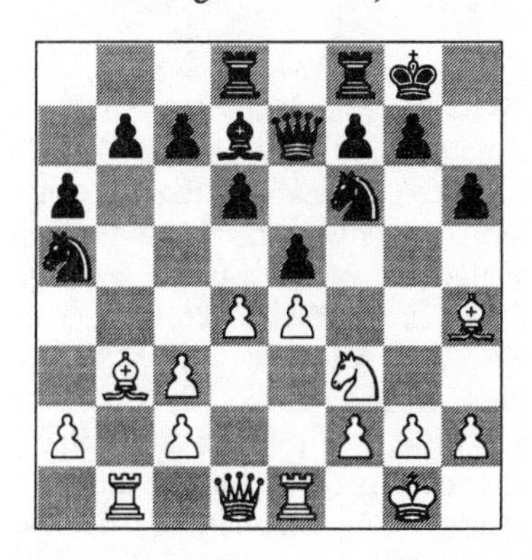

15 ♕c1

This move is an attempt to manage without wasting a tempo on h3. The alternative is 15 h3 ♔h7 (threat ...g5; after 15...c5 16 ♕c1! c4 17 ♕a3 cxb3 18 dxe5! bxc2 19 exf6 Black cannot play 19...cxb1♕? because of 20 fxe7! and White wins, but the alternatives 19...gxf6 20 ♖b4 b6 21 ♕c1! and 19...♕xe4 20 ♖bc1 are favourable for White) 16 ♕c1 (threat ♕a3) 16...♘xb3 (not 16...♗c8? 17 ♕a3 ♘xb3 18 dxe5! ♘c5 19 exf6 gxf6 20 e5! with advantage for White, nor 16...g5? 17 ♘xg5+ winning) 17 axb3 and now:

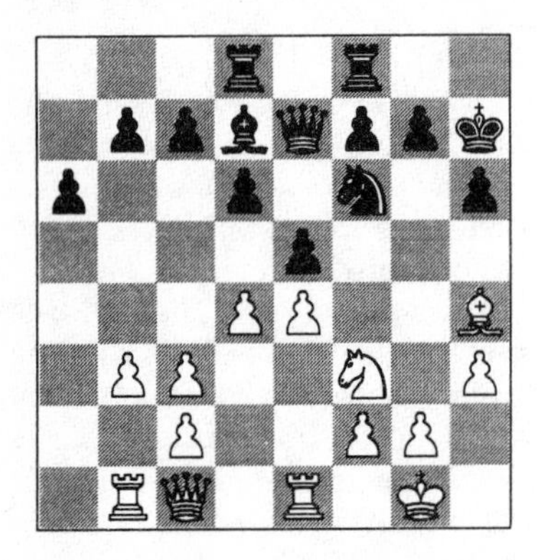

➪ 17...♗c6?! 18 ♖a1! ♖g8 (18...♖a8 19 c4 is a little better for White) 19 dxe5 dxe5 20 ♖a5 ♗b5 21 c4 b6 22 ♖a1 ♗c6 23 ♖xa6 g5 (Black's counterplay finally starts moving, albeit at the cost of the a-pawn) 24 ♗g3 ♘h5! 25 ♘xe5 ♗b7 26 ♖a7 ♘xg3 27 ♖xb7 ♕xe5 28 fxg3 ♕xg3 29 ♕e3 ♕e5 30 c5!? (30 ♕f3 looks good) 30...b5? (30...bxc5 31 ♖b5 is also bad, but 30...g4!? would have offered some counterplay) 31 ♖f1 (now White is winning) 31...♖d7 32 ♖xb5 c6 33 ♖b6 ♖g6 34 b4 ♔g7 35 ♕f3 h5 36 ♕xh5 ♕d4+ 37 ♔h1 g4 38 ♖b8 ♖d8 39 ♖b7 ♕f6!? 40 ♖xf7+ ♕xf7 41 ♖xf7+ ♔xf7 42 hxg4 ♖e8 43 ♕h7+ ♔f6 44 ♕d7 ♖e6 45 b5 ♔e5 46 b6 ♖g8 47 c3 1-0, Short-Speelman, London match 1991.

➪ 17...♗c8 18 ♕e3 b6 (not 18...♖g8 19 dxe5 dxe5 20 ♗xf6, when Black has to play 20...gxf6 because 20...♕xf6 21 ♕c5 forks e5 and c7) 19 c4 ♖de8 20 b4 (20 c5 is doubtful because of the line 20...bxc5 21 dxe5 dxe5 22 ♗xf6 ♕xf6! 23 ♕xc5 ♗xh3, but 20 ♖bd1 may be better) 20...♖g8 21 dxe5 (21 c5 bxc5 22 dxe5 dxe5 23 bxc5 g5 24 ♗g3 g4 is unclear) 21...dxe5 22 ♗g3 ♘d7 23 ♖ed1 f6 24 ♘h4 ♕f7! with equality, Chandler-Karpov, Reykjavik 1991.

15...♘xb3 16 axb3 ♗g4 (this is the only way to exploit the omission of h3; after 16...♗c8 17 ♕a3 White gains an important tempo and stands better) **17 ♘d2 g5 18 ♗g3 ♘h5 19 ♘c4 ♘f4 20 ♘e3**

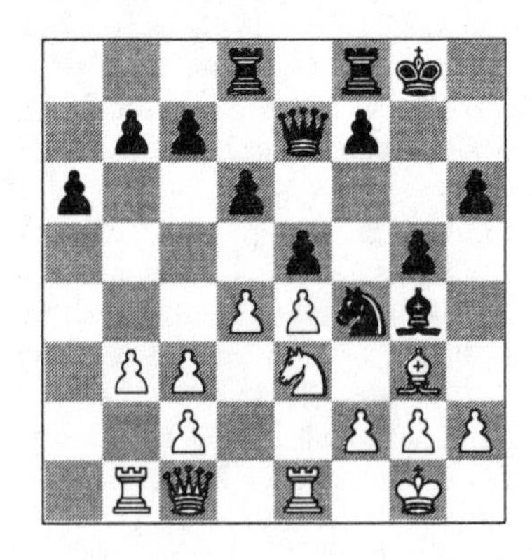

20...♗e6 (accepting the sacrifice is dangerous, for example after 20...♘e2+ 21 ♖xe2 ♗xe2 22 ♘d5 ♕e6 23 ♘xc7 ♕d7 24 ♘d5 f6 25 f3 ♗b5 26 ♕d2 ♗c6 27 ♘e3 White has very good positional compensation) **21 f3 ♕f6 22 ♕d2 ♔h7 23 ♖bd1 h5 24 ♔h1 ♖g8 25 c4 h4?!** (the preparatory 25...♖de8 was better) **26 ♗xf4 gxf4 27 ♘d5 ♗xd5 28 exd5 ♖g6?! 29 dxe5 dxe5 30 ♕c3 ♖e8 31 c5?** (31 h3! would have stopped Black's attack and threatened c5 followed by d6) **31...h3! 32 gxh3 ♕f5 33 ♕d3** (33 ♖g1 e4 is unclear) **33...♕xh3 34 ♖g1 ♖eg8 35 ♖xg6 ♖xg6 36 ♖g1 f5 37 ♖xg6 ♔xg6 38 ♔g1** (38 d6 e4! 39 ♕e2 exf3 40 ♕e8+ is a draw) **1-0** (Black lost on time, but he could have drawn by 38...e4 39 fxe4 f3 40 exf5+ ♔f7! 41 ♕d2 ♕g4+ 42 ♔f1 ♕h3+ 43 ♔e1 ♕h4+ 44 ♔d1 ♕g4!).

Game 41

Suttles-Gligoric
Sousse Iz. 1967

1 e4 e5 2 ♘c3 ♘c6 3 ♘f3 ♘f6 4 ♗b5 ♗b4 5 0-0 0-0 6 d3 d6 7 ♗g5 ♗xc3 8 bxc3 ♕e7 9 ♗xc6

9 ♗xc6 is an insipid continuation, normally used only if White is aiming for a draw. However, the examples below show that White very often fails to achieve his modest ambition, mainly because in the middlegame the opposite-coloured bishops tend to accentuate unbalanced situations.

9...bxc6

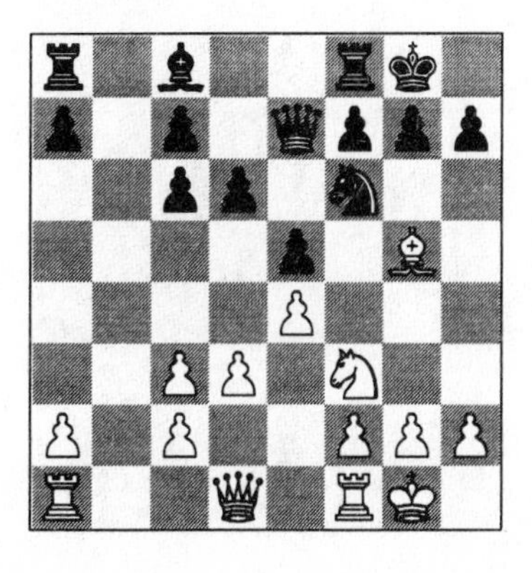

10 ♖e1

➩ 10 h3 h6 11 ♗d2 ♘h7 (playing for ...f5 is a good plan) 12 ♕e2 f5 13 exf5 ♗xf5 14 ♘d4 ♗g6 15 ♕g4?! (15 ♘xc6 ♕d7 16 ♘b4 ♘f6 gives sufficient compensation for the pawn) 15...♕e8 16 ♘e6?? (16 ♘xc6 ♗f5 is good for Black, but this is awful) 16...h5 0-1, A.Martin-Yusupov, Dubai Ol. 1986.

➩ 10 ♘d2 h6 11 ♗e3 ♘g4 12 ♕f3 ♗e6 13 h3 ♘xe3 14 ♕xe3 ♕g5 15 ♖fb1 ♕xe3 16 fxe3 ♖fb8 17 a4 a5 18 ♖xb8+ ♖xb8 19 ♖b1 ♖b6 20 ♔f2 ♔f8 21 ♔e2 ♔e7 22 ♔d1 ♔f6 23 ♔c1 ♔g5 24 ♘f3+ ♔h5 25 ♖a1 g5 26 ♔d2 ♖b2 27 ♔c1 ♖b8 28 ♔d2 c5 29 d4 cxd4 30 exd4 f6 31 ♘h2 ♗d7 32 d5 ♔h4 33 ♘f1 f5 34 exf5 ♗xf5 35 ♖e1 ♗g6 36 ♘e3 ♖f8 37 ♔e2 ♔g3 38 ♖b1 ♖f2+ 39 ♔e1 ♗h5 40 ♘g4 ♗xg4 41 hxg4 ♖xc2 42 ♖b5 ♖xc3 43 ♖xa5 ♖c4 0-1, Berg-Flear, London (Lloyds Bank) 1987.

10...h6 11 ♗d2 c5 12 ♘h4 (the start of a dubious plan; 12 h3 with the idea of ♘h2 and f4 is better) **12...♗g4 13 f3 ♗e6 14 ♘f5** (the knight cannot retreat to f3, so it has nowhere else to go) **14...♗xf5 15 exf5 c4! 16 dxc4** (*Informator* gives 16 d4 e4, but 17 fxe4 ♘xe4 18 ♕g4 is awkward; instead 16 d4 should be met by 16...♕d7 17 dxe5 dxe5 18 ♖xe5 ♖ad8 19 ♖e2 ♖fe8 20 ♖f2 ♕xf5 with advantage to Black) **16...♖fe8 17 g4 ♕d7 18 h4** (very risky) **18...e4?!** (this involves a piece sacrifice, but it was unnecessary because 18...♖ab8! would have improved Black's position without committing him to a sacrifice; note that 18...♖ab8 19 g5 hxg5 20 hxg5

♘h7 is good for Black) **19 g5** (Black is better after 19 fxe4 h5) **19...♕xf5 20 gxf6 exf3**

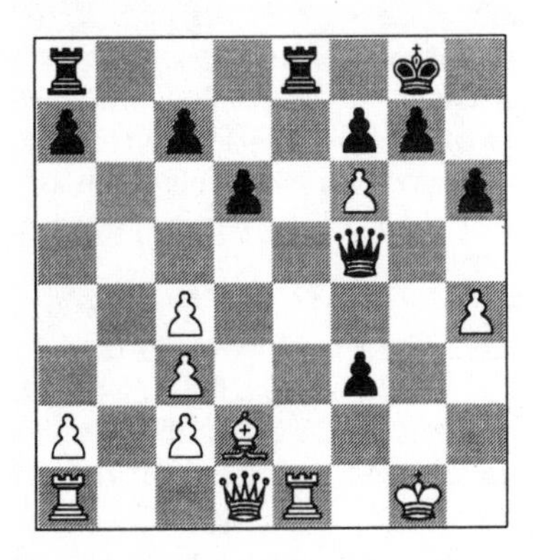

21 ♔f2 ♖e2+ 22 ♖xe2 fxe2+ 23 ♔xe2 ♕g4+ 24 ♔f1? (after 24 ♔f2 Black may have an edge but there is nothing clear) **24...♕h3+ 25 ♔g1 ♕g3+ 26 ♔f1 ♖e8** (now Black's attack is decisive) **27 ♗e1 ♕h3+ 28 ♔f2 ♖e6 29 ♕d3 ♕h2+ 30 ♔f3 ♖xf6+ 31 ♔e3 ♕g2 32 ♕d5 ♖e6+ 33 ♔f4 ♕f1+ 34 ♔g3 ♖e3+ 0-1**

Game 42

Speelman-Karpov
Linares 1992

1 e4 e5 2 ♘f3 ♘c6 3 ♘c3 ♘f6 4 ♗b5 ♗b4 5 0-0 0-0 6 d3 d6 7 ♗g5 ♗xc3 8 bxc3 h6

After 8...♕e7 we need to consider two unusual lines. The first is 9 ♘d2 h6 10 ♗h4 ♘d8 11 ♖e1 ♘e6 12 ♘f1 and now:

➩ 12...g5 13 ♗g3 ♘g7 14 f3 ♘fh5 15 ♗f2 ♘f4 16 d4 ♔h7 17 ♘e3 f6 18 ♗f1 ♗e6 19 g3 ♘g6 20 ♕b1 ♖fb8 21 ♕b5 ♕f7 22 ♗c4 ♗xc4 23 ♕xc4 ♕xc4 24 ♘xc4 with a roughly equal position, T.Taylor-Schüssler, New York Open 1987.

➩ 12...♘f4 13 ♘e3 c6 14 ♗c4 ♘g6 15 ♗g3 ♗e6 16 ♕f3 ♘h7 (16...♗xc4 17 dxc4 followed by ♘f5 is unpleasant) 17 ♗b3 ♖ad8 18 ♖ab1 b6 19 ♘f5 ♕f6 20 d4 c5 21 ♕h5 (threat ♘xd6) 21...♕g5 22 ♕xg5 ♘xg5 23 f3 c4 24 ♗a4 ♗xf5 25 exf5 with an edge for White, Smyslov-Bagirov, Lvov 1978.

➩ 12...♘f4 13 ♘e3 c6 14 ♗c4 g5 15 ♗g3 ♔h8 16 f3 ♖g8 17 d4 ♗e6 18 ♘f5 ♗xf5 19 exf5 ♖ae8 20 ♕d2 ♘6h5 21 ♖ad1 g4 22 ♗xf4 ♘xf4 23 g3 gxf3 24 ♔h1 ♕f6 25 dxe5 dxe5 26 ♕f2 ♘d5 (26...♘g2 leaves the knight with no retreat, but it seems to be good after 27 ♖e4 ♕xf5 or 27 ♖f1 e4) 27 ♕xf3 ½-½, Meier-P.Swidler, Dortmund Open 1991.

It seems that a timely ...g5 by Black solves most of his problems.

The second unusual line is 8...♕e7 9 d4 (trying to manage without ♖e1, but White must be prepared to sacrifice if he plays like this) 9...h6 10 ♗h4 and now:

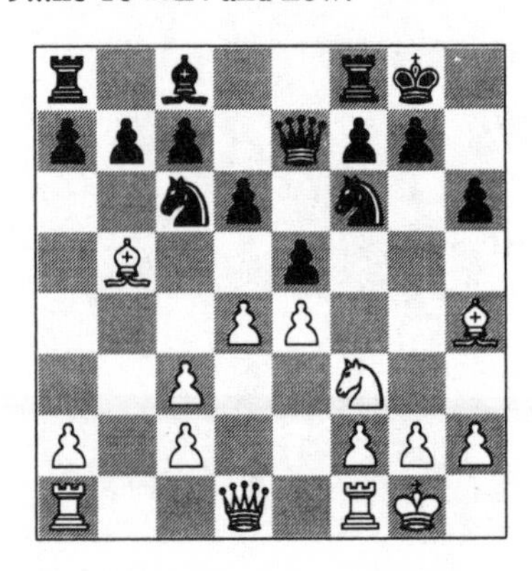

➩ 10...♗g4 11 h3 ♗xf3 12 ♕xf3 g5 13 ♗g3 exd4 14 ♗xc6 bxc6 15 ♖fe1 ♘d7 (the threat of e5 is very strong, so Black returns the pawn) 16 cxd4 ♕e6 (White has the advantage because he has bishop against knight and Black has weakened his kingside) 17 ♕c3 c5 18 d5 ♕g6 19 ♖ab1 ♘b6 20 ♖bd1 ♖fe8 21 e5 and White is clearly better, Imanaliev- Howell, Frunze 1989.

➩ 10...g5 (extremely risky) 11 ♘xg5 hxg5 12 ♗xg5 exd4 13 cxd4 ♔g7 14 ♖e1 ♕e6 15 f4 (15 d5 ♕e5 16 ♕d2! is just one of many very dangerous continuations) 15...♘xe4 16 d5 ♕f5 17 ♗d3 ♕xd5 18 ♗xe4 ♕d4+ 19 ♔h1 ♕xd1 20 ♖axd1 ♗g4 21 ♖b1 (White has a promising ending) 21...♖ae8 22 f5 ♖e5 23 ♗d2 d5 24 ♗d3 ♖fe8 25 ♖xe5 ♖xe5 26 ♖xb7 (a strange choice since 26 ♗f4 ♖e7 27 h3 ♗e2 28 ♖xb7 appears good for White) ½-½, Imanaliev-Yuneev, Frunze 1989.

9 ♗h4 ♕e7 10 ♖e1 ♘d8

➩ 10...♗d7 11 d4 ♖ad8 12 ♖b1 b6 13 ♕d2 ♘b8 14 ♗d3 ♗g4 15 ♕e3 ♘c6 16 ♗b5 ♘a5 17 h3 ♗d7 18 ♗d3 ♗c8 19 ♗g3 ♘d7 20 ♘h4 ♕g5 21 ♕e2 ♖fe8 22 ♘f5 ♘f6 23 ♗h4 ♕g6 24 d5 ♗xf5 25 exf5 ♕h7 26 ♗xf6 gxf6 27 ♖b4 ♔h8 28 ♕h5 ♖g8 29 ♖h4 c6 30 c4 ♖c8 31 ♕xh6 (White misses a win by 31 ♖ee4! cxd5 32 cxd5 ♖c5 33 ♖eg4 ♖xg4 34 ♖xg4 followed by ♕h4) 31...♕xh6 32 ♖xh6+ ♔g7 33 ♖h4 cxd5 34 cxd5 ♖c3 35 ♖ee4 ♖c5 36 c4 ♘b7 37 ♗c2 ♖a5 38 ♗b3 ♘c5 ½-½, Euwe-Ree, Netherlands 1973.

11 d4 ♘e6 (normally White meets ...♘e6 by ♗c1 in the Metger unpin, but here White's bishop is already committed to h4; White can still play slowly, but he can also try grabbing the pawn on e5) **12 dxe5 dxe5 13 ♘xe5 ♕c5 14 ♗xf6 ♕xb5** (14...gxf6 15 ♘g4 ♕xb5 16 e5 fxe5 17 ♖xe5 gives White a very strong attack in return for the piece)

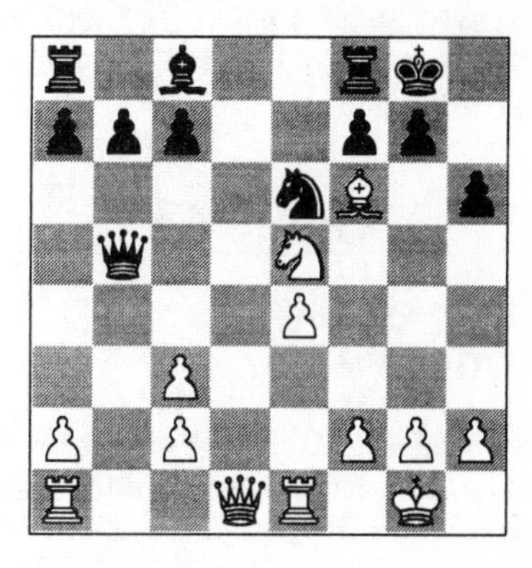

15 ♘g4 (it is hard to say whether a preliminary a4 or ♖b1 helps White or not) **15...h5**

➩ 15...♘f4!? (an interesting alternative) 16 ♕f3 (16 ♗d4 ♕g5 17 ♘e3 c5 is good for Black) 16...♘g6 17 ♗d4 c5 18 ♗e3 ♖e8 (18...h5!?) 19 h4 ♗xg4 20 ♕xg4 ♕c4 21 ♗xh6 gxh6 22 h5 ♕e6 23 ♕xe6 ♖xe6 24 hxg6 fxg6 25 ♖ab1 ♖b8 26 ♖b5 b6 27 f3 ♖d8 28 ♖bb1 ♖d2 29 ♖bc1 ♔f7 30 ♔f1 ♖ed6 31 a4 ½-½, Bus-Xu, World Student Ch., Antwerp 1992.

16 ♘e3 (Karpov gives 16 e5 hxg4 17 ♕xg4 ♖d8 18 ♖e3 ♔f8, and here I do prefer White's chances after 19 ♗xd8 ♘xd8 20 ♕h4) **16...gxf6 17 ♘d5 ♖d8** (17...♔g7 18 ♕f3 c6 19 ♕xf6+ ♔h7 20 ♕f5+ ♔h6 is a draw according to Karpov) **18 ♕xh5**

♖xd5 19 exd5 ♘g7 20 ♕h6 ♗f5 21 ♕xf6 ♕b6! (White is slightly better, but Karpov defends without apparent difficulty) **22 ♕h4 ♗xc2 23 ♖e7 ♕d6 24 c4 b5 25 cxb5 ♕xd5 26 a4 c6 27 bxc6 ♕xc6 28 h3 ♗g6 29 ♖e5 ♖c8 30 ♖ae1 a6 31 a5 ♘e6 32 ♕f6 ♘f8 33 ♕xc6 ♖xc6 34 ♖d1 ♘e6 35 h4 ♔g7 36 h5 ♗h7 37 ♖d7 ♔f6 38 ♖e3 ♗f5 39 ♖d5 ♘f4 40 ♖d4 ♘e6 41 ♖d5 ½-½**

Game 43

Spassky-Gligoric
Sarajevo 1986

1 e4 e5 2 ♘c3 ♘f6 3 ♘f3 ♘c6 4 ♗b5 ♗b4 5 0-0 0-0 6 d3 d6 7 ♗g5 ♗xc3 8 bxc3 ♕e7 9 ♖e1 ♘d8 10 d4 ♗g4

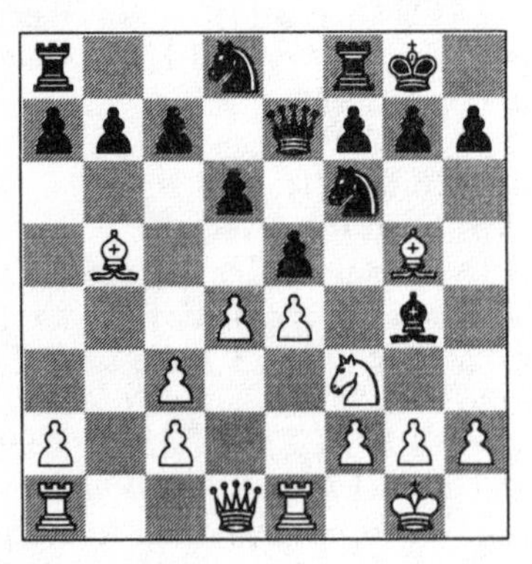

11 h3 ♗h5

➪ 11...♗xf3 (inconsistent) 12 ♕xf3 ♘e6 13 ♗e3 c6 14 ♗d3 ♘d7 15 ♕g3 ♕f6 16 ♖ad1 ♖fd8 17 ♗c4 ♘b6 18 ♗b3 h6 19 a4 ♘d7 20 ♖d2 ♘f4 21 ♕g4 ♘f8 22 g3 ♘4e6 23 f4 with a large advantage for White, Tischbierek-M.Hermann, Bad Wörishofen Open 1992.

12 g4 ♗g6 13 d5

➪ 13 ♗f1 ♘e6 14 ♗h4 ♘f4 15 ♖b1 b6 16 ♗g5 ½-½, Pedzich-Panczyk, Polish Ch. 1991.

➪ 13 ♘h4 (this may be best) 13...h6 14 ♘f5 (14 ♗c4 ♘e6 15 ♘xg6 fxg6 16 f4!? is very unclear) 14...♗xf5 15 ♗xf6 ♕xf6 16 exf5 a6 17 dxe5 dxe5 18 ♗d7 (a courageous move, but probably best) 18...♘c6 19 ♕f3 ♘b8 20 ♖ad1 c6 21 ♖d2 ♖d8 22 ♖ed1 ♖a7 23 ♖d6 e4 ½-½ (an incomprehensible decision since 24 ♕e3 ♖xd7 25 ♕xa7 wins outright) Lundqvist-Ragozin, 2nd World corr. Ch. 1956.

➪ 13 ♗h4 h5? 14 ♘h2 (after this it becomes clear that Black has weakened his kingside for no real gain) 14...c6 15 ♗c4 ♘e6 16 gxh5 ♗h7 17 ♘g4 ♘f4, Ivkov-Portisch, Santa Monica 1966, and now 18 ♔h2! ♘4xh5 19 ♘h6+! gxh6 20 ♕xh5 ♘xh5 21 ♗xe7 would have been very strong.

➪ 13 ♗h4 ♘e6 14 dxe5 dxe5 15 ♘xe5 ♕c5 16 ♘xg6 hxg6 17 ♖b1 g5 18 ♗g3 ♕xc3 19 ♕d3 (White has a slight advantage) 19...♕c5 20 ♕e3 ♕xe3 21 ♖xe3 ♖fd8 22 ♗c4 b6 23 ♗xe6 fxe6 24 ♗xc7 ♖dc8 25 ♗e5 ♖xc2 26 ♗xf6 gxf6 27 ♖a3 ♖e2 28 ♖a4 ♔f7 29 ♔g2 ♔g6 30 ♔g3 ♖c8 ½-½, Ivkov-Unzicker, Santa Monica 1966.

13...c6 14 ♗d3

Or 14 ♗f1 ♖c8 and now:

➪ 15 ♖e3 cxd5 16 exd5 ♖c5! 17 c4 b5 18 cxb5 ♗xc2 19 ♕d2 ♗g6 20 ♖c1 ♘b7 21 ♖xc5 ♘xc5 22 ♕e1 ♕b7 23 ♗xf6 gxf6 24 ♗c4 ♔h8 25

Nh4 Rg8 ½-½, Bagirov-I.Zaitsev, USSR 1969.

➪ 15 c4 b6 16 a4 Nb7 17 Ra3 Nc5 18 Nd2 h6 19 Bh4 Bh7 20 f3 a5 21 Nb1 g5 22 Bf2 cxd5 23 cxd5 Bg6 24 Nd2 with advantage to White, Batik-Ragozin, 2nd World corr. Ch. 1956.

➪ 15 c4 b6 16 Nd2 Nb7 17 Bd3 Nc5 18 Qf3 Ncd7 19 Nf1 cxd5 20 cxd5 Rc3 21 Ng3 h6 22 Bd2 Rc7 23 h4 Ne8 24 h5 Bh7 25 Kg2 Nc5 26 Rab1 Kh8 27 Be3 Nf6 28 g5 Ng8 with a distinctly unclear position, T.Petrosian-Furman, Semi-Final, USSR Ch. 1950.

14...cxd5?!

Gligoric criticised this move. The alternative is 14...Rc8 15 c4 b6 16 Nh4 (it isn't logical to put the knight on h4 if White doesn't intend going to f5 or g6; 16 Nd2 is better, as in Batik-Ragozin above) 16...h6 17 Bd2 Nb7 18 a4 Nc5 19 f3 Nfd7 20 Ng2 Nxd3 21 cxd3 Nc5 22 Ra3 cxd5 23 cxd5 Qd7 24 Qa1 f6 25 Ne3 Be8 26 Rc1 Rc7 27 Nf5 Bg6 28 d4 Nb7 29 Rxc7 Qxc7 30 Rc3 Qd7 31 Rc6 Bxf5 32 gxf5 Nd8 33 Rc4 Nf7 34 Be3 ½-½, Lundqvist-Endzelins, 2nd World corr. Ch. 1956.

15 exd5 e4?!

➪ 15...Rc8 (15...b6 16 Nd4 intending f4 is good for White) 16 c4 e4 17 Bf1 (17 Bxe4! Bxe4 18 Qd4 is still possible and appears good for White) 17... Ne6! 18 dxe6 exf3 19 exf7+ Qxf7 20 Qxd6 Ne4 21 Qe7 Rfe8 22 Qxf7+ Bxf7 and now Black is better, Belavenetz-Panov, Leningrad 1935.

16 Bxe4! Bxe4 17 Qd4

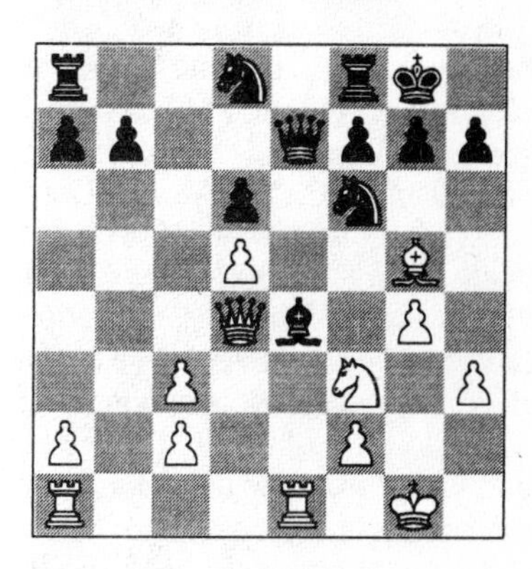

17...Ne6 (17...Re8 18 Nd2 and 17...Qd7 18 Bxf6 Bxf3 19 Bxg7 Re8 20 Bh6 are also very good for White) **18 Qxe4 Nxg5** (this is hopeless, but there was little else) **19 Qxe7 Nxf3+ 20 Kf1 Nxe1 21 Rxe1 Nxd5 22 Qxb7 Nf4 23 Re7 Rab8 24 Qxa7 g5 25 Qd4 Nxh3 26 Qxd6 Nf4 27 Qf6 Ng6 28 Rd7 h6 29 c4 Nf4 30 Ke1 Rb1+ 31 Kd2 Rf1 32 Qxh6 Rxf2+ 33 Kc3 Rf3+ 34 Kd2 Rf2+ 35 Ke1 Re2+ 36 Kd1 Re5 37 Qf6 Rc5 38 Kd2 Ne6 39 Rd3 Nf4 40 Rd8 Ne6 41 Rd3 Nf4 42 Rb3 Ng6 43 Rb4 Rfc8 44 Rb7 1-0**

We have finally arrived at one of the key variations in the Four Knights Opening, the so-called Metger Unpin. Johannes Metger (1850-1926) was a strong German player who won a number of local events in the period 1876-1896. According to *The Oxford Companion to Chess*, Metger's name became associated with this opening line as a result of a game he played in a tournament held at Kiel in 1893. The Metger Unpin runs 4 ♗b5 ♗b4 5 0-0 0-0 6 d3 d6 7 ♗g5 ♗xc3 8 bxc3 ♕e7 9 ♖e1 ♘d8 10 d4 ♘e6. Various continuations have been played over the years, but these days the most common line is 11 ♗c1 c5 12 ♗f1 ♖d8. In games 44 and 45 we examine deviations from this variation.

Game 44 covers 11 ♗h4 and the alternative Black 11th moves 11...c6 and 11...♖d8. The former is inferior, but the latter is perfectly playable and may transpose to game 46.

The rest of the chapter deals with 11...c5. After 11...c5 there are many possibilities for White and it is far from clear which is the best. 12 ♗c4 has been played, but there is a strong argument for 12 a4, reserving the option of retreating the bishop to c4 or f1 according to Black's reply (in game 45 we only deal with the retreat to c4, because ♗f1 transposes to game 46). These lines are covered in game 45, which also analyses 12 ♗f1 ♕c7.

Finally game 46 deals with the pivotal line 11 ♗c1 c5 12 ♗f1 ♖d8. Once again the best move is not clear, but 13 g3 has been the most popular in practice.

Game 44

Nunn-Prasad
Manila Ol. 1992

1 e4 e5 2 ♘f3 ♘c6 3 ♘c3 ♘f6 4 ♗b5 ♗b4 5 0-0 0-0 6 d3 d6 7 ♗g5 ♗xc3 8 bxc3 ♕e7 9 ♖e1 ♘d8 10 d4 ♘e6

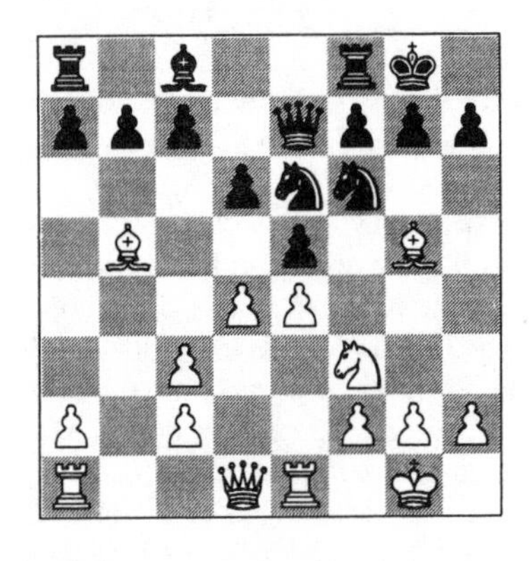

11 ♗c1

➪ 11 ♗h4 (a dubious move, because we reach the same position as in game 42, but with Black having saved a tempo by missing out ...h6) 11...♘f4 12 ♘d2 (the knight is ultimately heading for e3) 12...♔h8 13 ♗f1 h6 14 f3 g5 15 ♗g3 ♖g8 (with the obvious plan of a kingside attack based on doubling rooks on the g-file) 16 ♘c4 ♖g7 17 ♘e3 h5 18 c4 ♗d7 19 c3 (19 c5 dxc5 20 dxe5 ♕xe5 21 ♘c4 ♕e6 22 a4 is unclear according to Kamsky) 19...♖ag8 20 ♘f5 ♗xf5 21 exf5 h4 22 ♗f2 g4 23 ♗xh4 gxf3?! (Kamsky recommends 23...♘e4, when 24 ♗xe7? ♘h3+ is mate in five, so White's best is 24 fxe4 ♕xh4 25 g3 ♘h3+ 26 ♔h1 ♘f2+ 27 ♔g2 ♘xd1 28 gxh4 ♘xc3 29 dxe5 dxe5 30 a4 with a very double-edged position) 24 ♕xf3 ♖g4 25 ♗g3 ♘6h5 26 ♗xf4 ♘xf4 27 g3 (White quickly takes over the initiative) 27...♕h4 28 ♖e3 ♘h5 29 ♕f2 exd4 30 cxd4 ♖xd4 31 ♖ae1 (Black's king is too exposed) 31...♕f6 32 ♖e4 ♖xe4 33 ♖xe4 ♕g5 34 ♕d4+ ♔h7 35 ♖h4 ♖e8 36 ♕d1 ♔h6 37 ♗e2 ♖xe2 38 ♕xe2 a6 39 a4 b6 40 ♖h3 ♕c1+ 41 ♔g2 1-0, Kamsky-Timman, Tilburg 1991.

11...♖d8

Or 11...c6 12 ♗f1 and now:

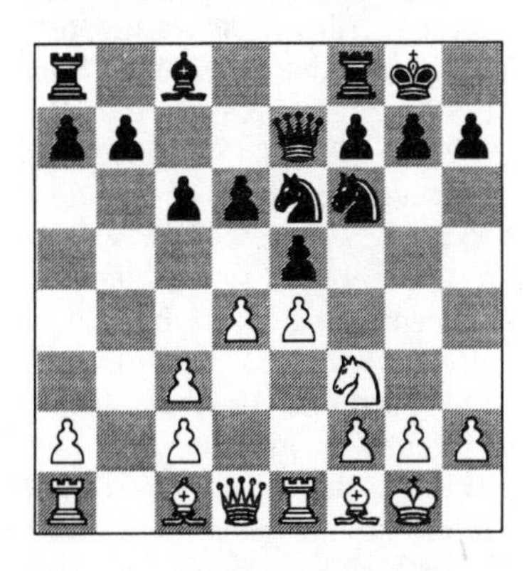

⇨ 12...♖d8 13 ♘h4 g6 14 g3 (14 a4 would transpose to Nunn-Prasad) 14...♘e8 15 ♗g2 ♘8g7 16 ♗e3 ♗d7 17 ♕d2 (a typical miserable position for Black in this variation; he cannot force through ...d5 and any opening of the position, for example by ...f5, would only activate White's bishops) 17...♗e8 18 f3 (White intends ♕f2 followed by f4, so Black has to react) 18...c5 19 d5 ♘f8 20 c4 (this may be too slow; 20 ♕f2 intending f4 is more aggressive) 20...♗d7 21 ♖ab1 b6 22 ♗f1 (the tempting 22 f4 exf4 23 ♗xf4 f6 24 e5 runs into 24...dxe5 25 d6 ♕f7 26 ♗xa8 ♖xa8, a promising exchange sacrifice) 22...♖e8 23 ♗d3 ♗h3 24 ♗f2 (White is ready for f4, but Black gets in first) 24...f5 25 ♕h6 fxe4 26 fxe4 ♕d7 27 ♘g2 ♘h5 28 ♖f1 (White still has an edge and Black goes wrong at the time control) 28...♕g7 29 ♕g5 ♕e7 30 ♕d2 ♘d7 31 ♗e3 ♘df6 32 ♗g5 ♖f8 33 ♖f2 ♕d7 34 ♗h6 ♘g7 35 ♖bf1 ♘g4 36 ♖xf8+ ♖xf8 37 ♖xf8+ ♔xf8 38 ♗e2 ♘xh6 39 ♕xh6 ♗g4 40 ♗d3 ♔g8 41 ♕g5 ♗f3? (41...♗h3) 42 ♘e3 (trapping the bishop) 42...♕f7 43 h3 ♔f8 44 ♘f1 ♘e8 45 ♘h2 ♗d1 46 ♕d2 ♗f3 47 ♕f2 ♗d1 48 ♕e1 ♗f3 49 ♕f1 ♗xe4 50 ♕xf7+ ♔xf7 51 ♗xe4 1-0, Nikolenko-Malaniuk, Budapest 1990.

⇨ 12...♕c7 13 ♘h4 ♖e8 14 ♕f3 ♔h8 15 ♘f5 ♘g8 (again Black has been driven back into an unpleasantly passive position) 16 h4 f6 17 ♖d1 ♖f8 18 d5? (this cannot be right when the knight has the active square c5 available; if White wanted to close the centre then 18 ♗a3 c5 19 d5 was best, but it was also good to retain the tension) 18...♘c5 19 ♘e3 ♘e7 20 c4 cxd5 21 ♘xd5 ♘xd5 22 cxd5 (now Black is slightly better, but White manages to hold the draw) 22...♗d7 (22...f5! looks strong) 23 ♗d3 ♖ae8 24 ♗e3 b6 25 ♖ab1 ♘a4 26 ♖b4 ♘c5 27 ♗xc5 bxc5 28 ♖b3 ♖b8 29 ♖db1 ♗a4 30 ♖xb8 ♖xb8 31 ♖xb8+ ♕xb8 32 g4 ♕d8 33 ♔h2 ♔g8 34 c3 ♗d7 35 ♔g3 ♕a5 36 ♗c4 ♕b6 37 ♕d1 a5 38 ♗b3 ♕b5

39 a4 ♕b6 40 h5 ♗c8 41 ♕c2 ♕a6 42 ♕d1 ♗d7 43 ♔f3 h6 44 ♔g3 ♔f7 45 f3 ♔e7 46 ♔g2 ♕c8 47 ♕b1 ♕b8 48 ♕a2 ♕e8 49 ♔f2 ½-½, Levenfish-Lisitsin, Moscow 1940.

⇨ 12...♘d7 13 g3 c5 14 dxe5 (an interesting decision, in some ways a forerunner for a similar plan adopted in Short-Anand, analysed in game 45 below; 14 d5 is also possible) 14...dxe5 15 ♘h4 g6?! 16 ♘g2 (the knight cannot move to f5, so it heads for d5 instead) 16...♘g7 17 ♘e3 ♘f6 18 ♗g2 ♗e6 19 c4 ♖ad8 20 ♕e2 (Black's knights are far away from d4) 20...♘d7 21 ♗b2 f6 22 f4 (the threat of ♘d5 is stronger than actually playing the move) 22...♖de8 23 ♖ad1 b6 24 ♖d2 exf4 25 gxf4 g5 26 fxg5 fxg5 27 e5 ♕f7 28 ♘d5 ♘h5 29 ♖f1 ♘f4 30 ♕e4 ♕f5 31 ♕xf5 ♗xf5 32 ♘xf4 gxf4 33 ♗d5+ ♔g7 34 e6+ ♘f6 35 ♖xf4 ♔g6 36 ♖g2+ ♘g4 37 ♖gxg4+ ♗xg4 38 ♖xg4+ ♔f5 39 ♖g3 ♖g8 40 ♗g7 ♖e7 41 ♗f8 1-0, Botvinnik-Panov, USSR Ch. 1939.

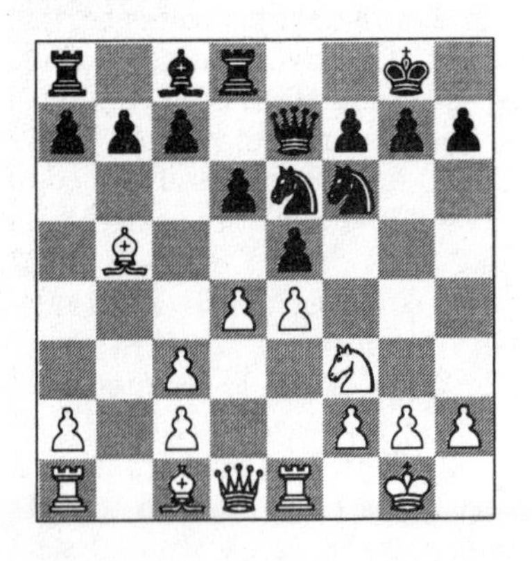

The move 11...♖d8 is not illogical, because if Black plays 11...c5 he usually follows it up with ...♖d8. By playing the rook move first he reserves the option of missing out ...c5.

12 ♘h4

⇨ 12 ♗f1 ♘f8?! (12...♘d7 13 g3 ♘df8 14 ♘h4 ♕f6 15 ♗e3 ♘g6 was just very slightly better for White in Alexander-Barcza, Munich Ol. 1958; 13 ♕e2!? is possible, in order to tie the d7 knight to the defence of e5) 13 ♘h4 (this move is characteristic of the whole system in that White would like to meet ...♘f8 by ♘h4, in order to answer ...♘g6 by ♘f5; if this is possible then it almost always gives White the advantage) 13...♘g4? (this just wastes time; White must always be careful when playing ♘h4, because the trick 13...♘xe4 14 ♖xe4 f5 is also typical, but here it loses to 15 ♗c4+ ♔h8 16 ♕h5 fxe4 17 ♗g5 ♕d7 18 ♗f7 and Black is helpless against the reinforcement of the attack by ♖e1-e3; notice also that 13...exd4 14 cxd4 ♘xe4 is bad after 15 g3 and there is no decent way out of the pin) 14 g3 ♕f6 15 f3 ♘h6 16 ♗e3 ♖e8 17 ♕d2 (White has a large advantage) 17...♘g6 18 ♘g2 ♗h3 (18...♕xf3 19 ♗e2 ♕f6 20 ♗c4 ♕e7 21 ♗xh6 is also very good for White) 19 ♗e2 ♗xg2 20 ♔xg2 d5 (desperation) 21 exd5 exd4 22 cxd4 (White is a pawn up with the better position; owing to time-trouble Botvinnik didn't win in the most efficient way, but the result is the same) 22...♘f5 23 ♗f2 ♖ed8 24 c4 h5 25 h4 b5 26 ♕g5 ♕xg5 27 hxg5 h4 28 ♗d3 hxg3 29 ♗xg3 ♘xd4 30 ♖ad1 c5 31 dxc6 ♘xc6 32 ♗e4 ♖ac8 33 ♖xd8+ ♘xd8 34 ♗f5

♖a8 35 ♖e8+ ♔h7 36 cxb5 f6 37 ♗c7 ♘e6 38 ♖xa8 ♘xc7 39 ♖xa7 ♘xb5 40 ♖d7 fxg5 41 a4 1-0, Botvinnik-Reshevsky, The Hague-Moscow World Ch. 1948.

12...g6

⇨ 12...♘f8 13 g3 (13 ♗f1! would have transposed to Botvinnik-Reshevsky) 13...♗h3! 14 a4 h6 15 ♗f1 ♗xf1 16 ♔xf1 d5! (Black takes his chance to break out; now the position is unclear) 17 exd5 ♖xd5 18 c4 ♖dd8 19 ♕e2 e4 20 f3 ♕d7 21 ♗b2 g5 (the rest of the game is a tactical mess) 22 d5 ♘8h7 23 ♘g2 ♕h3 24 fxe4 ♘g4 25 e5 ♖e8 26 ♕d3 ♕xh2 27 ♕f3 ♕h3 28 ♔g1 ♕h2+ 29 ♔f1 ♕h3 30 ♔g1 ♘hf6!? 31 ♗d4 c5 32 ♗b2 ♕h2+ 33 ♔f1 ♕h3 34 ♔g1 ♕h2+ 35 ♔f1 ♕h3 36 ♔g1 ½-½, Yurtaev-Yusupov, Frunze 1979.

13 a4 (White has forced a weakness with ...g6, but at the cost of decentralising his knight, so the next couple of moves revolve around the possibility of ...d5) **13...c6** (a necessary preliminary, because 13...d5 14 ♘f5! is even more unpleasant than in the game) **14 ♗f1 d5** (otherwise a constructive move is not so easy to find; 14...♘xe4 15 ♖xe4 f5 16 ♘xf5 gxf5 17 ♖e1 leaves Black's king exposed) **15 ♘f5!** (the point of White's play) **15...gxf5 16 exf5 e4** (more or less forced because 16...♘f8 17 ♖xe5 ♕c7 18 ♕d2! and 16...♘c7 17 ♖xe5 ♕d7 18 ♕f3 are extremely dangerous for Black) **17 fxe6 ♕xe6** (White has some positional advantage) **18 f3** (18 ♗f4!?) **18...♕f5 19 ♗e3 ♕g6 20 ♔h1 h5 21 ♕d2 ♗f5 22 ♗g5 ♖e8 23 ♕f4?** (23 ♗xf6 ♕xf6 24 fxe4 ♗xe4 25 ♗d3 would have been much better, liquidating to a position in which Black's weakened kingside gives White a long-term advantage) **23...♘h7 24 ♗h4 f6 25 ♖e3 ♘g5** (Black has supported e4 and the position is now equal; in the remaining moves White over-presses and falls into a bad position, but eventually there is a peaceful result) **26 ♖ae1 ♘e6 27 ♕d6 ♖ad8 28 ♕b4 ♖d7 29 ♕b2 ♔h7 30 ♕c1 ♖g8?! 31 ♕d2?!** (31 fxe4 dxe4 32 ♖xe4!? ♗xe4 33 ♖xe4 is promising for White) **31...♘g5 32 ♗xg5 ♕xg5 33 ♕f2 ♖dg7 34 g3 h4 35 fxe4 ♗xe4+ 36 ♗g2 ♗xg2+** (36...f5! is good for Black) **37 ♔xg2 ♖g6 38 ♖f3 hxg3 39 hxg3 ♖h6 40 ♖h1 ♖xh1 41 ♔xh1 ♔g6 42 ♖f4 ½-½**

Game 45

Nunn-Norri
Manila Ol. 1992

1 e4 e5 2 ♘f3 ♘c6 3 ♘c3 ♘f6 4 ♗b5 ♗b4 5 0-0 0-0 6 d3 d6 7 ♗g5 ♗xc3 8 bxc3 ♕e7 9 ♖e1 ♘d8 10 d4 ♘e6 11 ♗c1 c5

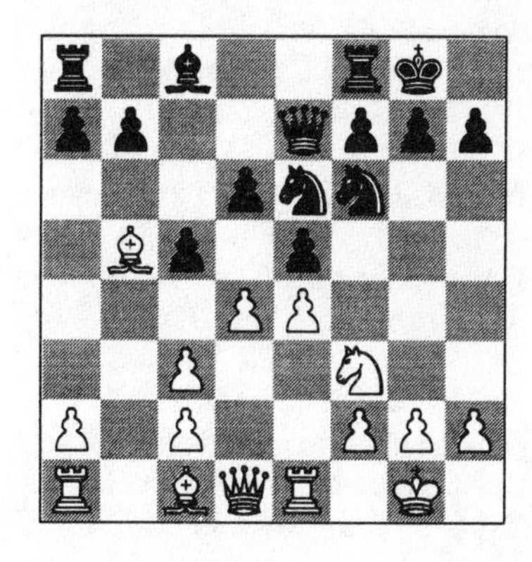

124 Main Line: Metger Unpin 124

12 a4

Note that 12 dxe5 dxe5 13 ♘xe5 is impossible because of 13...♘c7. The various possible White 12th moves all prevent this trick and so force Black to defend his e5 pawn, either directly or indirectly.

➪ 12 ♗c4 (in this game White adopts the plan of transferring his bishop to d5 and cementing it in place with c4; this idea is known from some lines of the Nimzo-Indian, but here it is not especially effective) 12...♖d8 13 ♗d5 ♘f8 14 dxe5 dxe5 15 c4 (White has achieved his objective, but Black can manoeuvre around the bishop) 15...♘g6 16 h3 ♖b8 17 a4 b6 18 ♘h2?! ♗e6 19 ♕f3 ♘e8! 20 ♘g4 ♘d6 21 ♘e3 ♕h4 22 ♘f5 ♗xf5 23 exf5 ♘e7 24 g4 ♘xd5 25 cxd5 f6 (the situation has stabilised; Black's pawns form an effective barrier to White's bishop and d5 is weak) 26 ♔g2 ♖d7 27 a5 b5 28 a6 ♖c8 29 ♖b1 ♔f7 30 ♗e3 ♖dc7 31 c3 g6 32 fxg6+ hxg6 33 ♗c1 ♖e8 34 c4 b4 35 ♗b2 ♔g7 36 ♕d3 g5 37 ♖bc1 ♕h7 38 ♕f3! ♕g6 39 ♖e3 ♖ce7 40 ♕e2 ♔g8 41 ♖a1 ♖h7 42 ♖a5 ♖c7 43 ♖a1 ♖ce7 44 ♖e1 ♖b8 45 ♖a1 ♖c7 46 ♖a5 ♖b6 47 ♖a1 ♖c8 48 ♖a5 ♖c7 49 ♖a1 ♖c8 50 ♖a4? (50 ♖a5) 50...b3! 51 ♖c3 (or 51 ♗a3 ♖cb8! 52 ♕b2 ♕e8! 53 ♕b1 ♔g7 and the rook is trapped) 51...♕e4+! 52 ♕xe4 ♘xe4 53 ♖e3 ♘d6 54 ♖c3 ♖b4! 55 ♖xb4 cxb4 56 ♖xb3 ♖xc4 57 ♔f3 ♔f7 58 ♔e3 ♔e7 59 ♔d3 ♔d7 60 f3 ♔c7 61 ♗a1 ♔b6 62 ♖b1 ♔c5 63 h4 gxh4 64 g5 ♔xd5 65 g6 ♘f5 66 ♖g1 ♖c7 67 ♗b2 ♖g7 68 ♗c1 h3 69 ♖h1 ♖xg6 70 ♖xh3 ♖g1 71 ♗d2 b3 72 ♔c3 ♖d1 73 ♖h2 ♖a1 74 ♔xb3 ♖xa6 75 ♖f2 ♘d4+ 76 ♔b2 ♖b6+ 77 ♔c3? (77 ♔c1 ♖b3 78 f4 e4 is also winning for Black) 77...♖b3 mate, Chandler-Salov, Reykjavik 1991.

A second alternative is 12 ♗f1 ♕c7?! (12...♖d8 is better, as in game 46) and now:

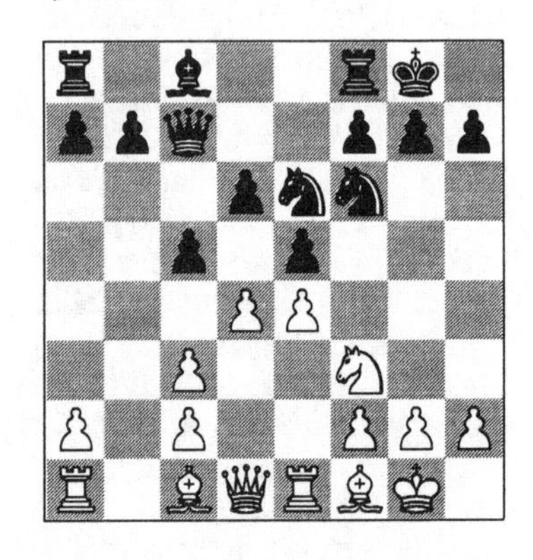

➪ 13 g3 (White should not give Black the chance to clear f8 for his knight) 13...♖e8 14 d5 ♘f8 15 c4 (the thematic line 15 ♘h4 ♘g6 16 ♘f5 fails to 16...♗xf5 17 exf5 ♘e7) 15...♘g6 16 ♗g2 (16 h4 with the idea of ♘h2 is possible, but I doubt if this gives White any advantage) 16...♗d7 17 a4 h6 18 ♕d3 ♖f8 19 ♘d2 ♘h7 20 ♖f1 f5 21 exf5 ♗xf5 22 ♗e4 ♕d7 23 ♗xf5 ♖xf5 (Black has sacrificed the e4 square in return for active piece play) 24 ♘e4 ♖af8 25 f3 ♘f6? (25...♘e7 is better, intending ...♖5f7 and ...♘f5) 26 ♘xd6! e4 27 ♘xe4 ♘e5 28 ♘xc5! (not 28 ♕e2? ♘xe4 29 ♕xe4 ♘xf3+ 30 ♔g2 ♘h4+ and Black wins) 28...♕c8 29 ♕e3? (29 ♕d4! ♘xf3+ 30 ♖xf3 ♖xf3 31 ♘e6 is good for

White) 29...♘fg4! 30 ♕d4 ♘xh2 0-1, Hodgson-Spassky, Brussels 1985.

➪ 13 d5 (a useful rule is that if White can play d5 at a moment when Black has to reply ...♘d8, then he should certainly do so because bringing the knight back into play from d8 is very time-consuming) 13...♘d8 (13...♘f4 14 ♗xf4 exf4 15 e5 dxe5 16 ♘xe5 ♖d8 17 c4 b5 18 ♕f3 is good for White after 18...♗b7 19 ♖ad1 bxc4 20 ♗xc4 ♖d6 21 ♗b3 or 18...bxc4 19 d6 ♕b7 20 ♕xf4) 14 ♘h4 ♘e8 15 g3 (Black's knights are far from e5, so White prepares f4) 15...♕e7 16 ♘f5 (White could still have played f4, for example 16 f4 exf4 17 ♗xf4 g5 18 ♘f5 ♗xf5 19 exf5 ♕f6 20 ♕g4, but perhaps he feared that after 17...f6 followed by ...♘f7 Black's badly placed knight would become active) 16...♗xf5 17 exf5 ♕f6?! (a waste of time, but White was better in any case) 18 ♕g4 ♕e7 (18...g6 19 ♗g5! wins the exchange) 19 ♗g5 (the rest of the game is a good demonstration of how to use the two bishops) 19...♕d7 20 a4 f6 21 ♗d2 g6 22 ♗h3 ♕xf5 23 ♕xf5 gxf5 24 ♗xf5 ♘g7 25 ♗d3 f5 26 f4 e4 27 ♗e2 ♖c8 28 c4 ♘e8 29 h3 ♘f6 30 g4 fxg4 31 hxg4 ♖c7 32 ♔f2 h6 33 ♖h1 e3+ 34 ♗xe3 ♘e4+ 35 ♔g2 ♘f7 36 ♗d3 ♖e7 37 ♖ae1 ♖fe8 38 ♗c1 ♘c3 39 ♖xe7 ♖xe7 40 a5 b6 41 axb6 axb6 42 ♗d2 ♘e2 43 c3 b5 44 ♔f3 1-0, T.Petrosian-Lilienthal, USSR Ch. 1949.

➪ 13 d5 ♘d8 14 c4 ♘e8 15 ♘h4 g6 16 g3 ♘g7 17 f4 f6 (in this game Black adopts a passive defence, which at least enables him to bring his knight into play) 18 ♗g2 b6 19 a4 a5 20 ♖a3 ♘f7 21 ♖f1 ♕e7 22 ♕e1 ♖b8 23 ♗b2 ♗d7 24 h3 ♘e8 25 ♔h2 (White's plan is ♗f3-g4, exchanging off his bad bishop for a useful defensive piece; Black can only wait) 25...♘h8 26 ♗f3 ♘c7 27 ♘g2 ♘f7 28 ♘e3 ♘e8 29 ♗g4 ♘g7 30 ♗xd7 ♕xd7 31 ♘g4 ♘h5 32 ♕e2 ♕e8 33 ♖f2 ♖b7 34 ♖af3 ♔g7 35 ♕e3 ♕e7 36 ♕d3 ♖bb8 37 ♗c1 ♖be8 38 fxe5 fxe5 (Black cannot recapture with the knight because of ♗h6+, and 38...dxe5 39 ♕f1 wins material) 39 ♕f1 1-0 (an early resignation, because Black could still play on by 39...♖b8 40 ♘h6 ♘h8, although his position is of course extremely bad), Campora-Giertz, Zürich Open 1990.

The idea behind 12 a4 is first of all to force Black to attend to his e5 pawn, and secondly to reserve the option of ♗c4 or ♗f1 according to Black's reply.

12...♖d8

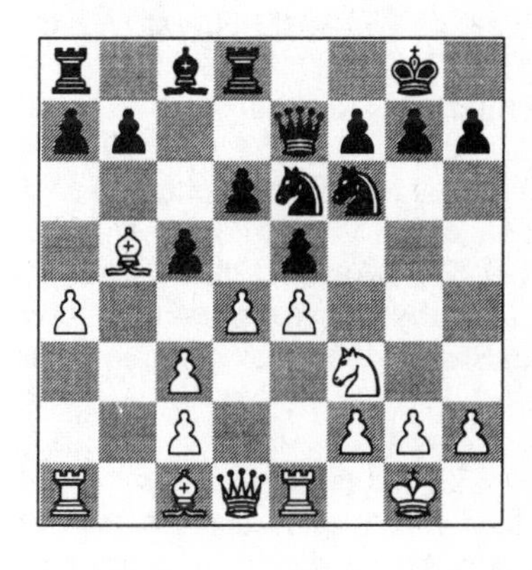

13 ♗c4

➪ 13 dxe5 dxe5 14 ♕e2 (Short's idea is reminiscent of that used in

Botvinnik-Panov given in game 44; I doubt if such a simple plan can really be good for White) 14...♕c7 (Anand suggests 14...♘f8 15 ♗c4 ♘g6 16 ♘g5 ♖f8 in *Informator*; indeed White cannot profit from his temporary activity, so this should be equal) 15 ♗c4 h6 (15...♖e8 16 ♘h4 ♘f4 would have saved time; of course White doesn't have to play ♘h4, but it is hard to see another useful move) 16 ♘h4 ♖e8 (Short gives 16...♘g5 17 ♗xg5 hxg5 18 ♘f3 ♗g4 19 h3 ♗xf3 20 ♕xf3 as good for White) 17 ♘f5 ♘f4 18 ♕f3 ♗xf5 (after this the two bishops start to present a real danger; Anand recommends 18...♗e6) 19 exf5 ♖ad8 20 a5 ♘4d5 21 ♕g3 ♔h7 22 h3 ♖e7 23 ♗f1 ♕c8 (23...c4!?) 24 ♖xe5 ♖xe5 25 ♕xe5 ♖e8 26 ♕g3 c4 (26...♕xf5 loses to the attractive continuation 27 ♗d3 ♖e1+ 28 ♔h1 ♘e4 29 ♗xh6! ♘xg3 30 ♖xe1 ♔xh6 31 ♗xf5 ♘xf5 32 ♖e5 ♘de7 33 g4 f6 34 ♖e1) 27 ♗b2 ♕xf5 28 ♗xc4 ♘e4 29 ♕f3 ♕xf3 30 gxf3 ♘exc3 31 ♔f1 ♖c8 32 ♗d3+ (32 ♗b3 is preferable, according to Short) 32...♔g8 33 ♖a3 b5?? (after 33...♖c7 White is just slightly better) 34 axb6 (34...axb6 35 ♗f5! wins at once) 1-0, Short-Anand, Linares 1992.

Finally note that 13 a4 transposes to Spassky-Yusupov given in game 46.

13...♘f8

⇨ 13...♖b8 (a mysterious move) 14 dxe5 (the idea is that the plan of Short-Anand should be better with an extra tempo; 14 d5 ♘f8 15 ♘h4 was bad after 15...♘xe4 16 ♖xe4 f5, but 14 ♕d3!? was superior) 14...dxe5 15 ♕e2 ♕c7 16 ♘h4 ♖e8! (not wasting time on ...h6) 17 g3?! (17 ♘f5 ♘f4 18 ♕f3 was better, even though 18...♗e6 is satisfactory for Black) 17...h6 (now this is good, because 18 ♘f5 ♘g5! exposes the weaknesses created by g3) 18 f4?! exf4 19 ♗xe6 fxe6 20 e5 (now Black has an edge) ½-½, Nunn-Zilberman, London (Lloyds Bank) 1992.

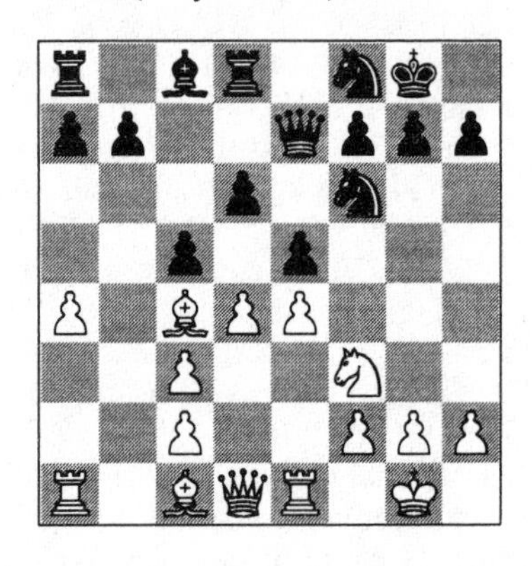

14 h3

⇨ 14 ♘g5 (an ineffective move) 14...♘e6 15 ♖b1 ♖b8 16 a5 h6 17 ♘xe6 (exchanging only relieves any pressure White has; 17 ♘f3 was better) 17...♗xe6 18 d5 ♗d7 19 h3 g5 20 ♗d2 ♘h7 21 ♖b3 ♔g7 22 ♕f3 ♖f8 23 ♗d3 f6 24 ♖eb1 ♗c8 (Black's only weak point is the b-pawn, but this is easily defended) 25 ♕g3 ♔h8 26 ♕f3 ♖f7 27 c4 ♘f8 28 ♕h5 ♔g7 29 h4 ♘g6 30 g3 ♕d7 31 ♗f1 ♕g4 32 ♕xg4 ½-½, Hort-Brunner, German Team Cup 1992.

14...♗e6 15 ♗f1 (after 15 d5 ♗d7 16 ♘h4 Black must not play 16...♘xd5? 17 ♕xd5 ♗e6 18 ♘f5 and White wins, but 16...♘xe4 17 ♖xe4 f5 and now White is worse)

15...♖ac8?! (15...d5 was probably best, although White has an edge after 16 dxe5 ♘xe4 17 ♕d3) **16 d5 ♗d7 17 ♘d2 ♖c7?** (this not only wastes time, it also creates a tactical weakness; 17...♘g6 was preferable, although 18 g3, with the idea of ♘c4 and f4, is better for White) **18 ♘c4 ♗c8** (18...♘g6 19 f4! is very good for White after 19...♘xf4 20 ♗xf4 exf4 21 e5 or 19...exf4 20 e5 ♘xe5 21 ♗xf4, exploiting the rook's position on c7) **19 f4 ♘g6** (there isn't much choice, but Black ends up in a hopelessly passive position) **20 f5 ♘f8 21 g4 ♘e8 22 g5 f6 23 h4 ♔h8 24 ♕f3 ♕f7 25 ♗g2 b6 26 ♘e3 g6 27 ♖f1 ♘g7 28 c4 ♘h5 29 ♘g4 gxf5 30 exf5 ♖e8? 31 ♘h6 1-0**

Game 46

Nunn-Howell
Sheffield 1991

1 e4 e5 2 ♘f3 ♘c6 3 ♗b5 ♘f6 4 ♘c3 ♗b4 5 0-0 0-0 6 d3 d6 7 ♗g5 ♗xc3 8 bxc3 ♕e7 9 ♖e1 ♘d8 10 d4 ♘e6 11 ♗c1 c5 12 ♗f1 ♖d8

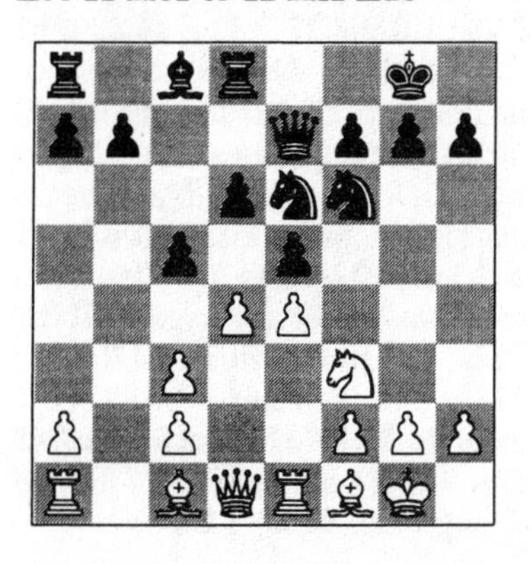

13 g3

This isn't the only possibility, although it has been the most popular.

➪ 13 d5 (premature) 13...♘f8 14 c4 (the usual rule applies; White cannot play 14 ♘h4 because of 14...♘xd5, so it was wrong to play 13 d5) 14...♘e8 (it is very bad to play ...f5 without any development; 14...♘g6 was correct, followed by ...♖f8 and ...♗d7, slowly building up the conditions for a successful ...f5) 15 g3 f5 16 exf5 ♗xf5 17 ♘h4 ♕d7 (17...♗d7 18 f4) 18 f4 exf4 19 ♗xf4 ♘g6 20 ♘xf5 ♕xf5 (White has the two bishops in an open position, plus a big lead in development) 21 ♗d3 ♕f6 22 ♗xg6 hxg6 23 ♖b1 g5 24 ♗e3 ♖d7 25 ♕g4 ♖f7 26 ♖f1 ♕g6 27 ♖xf7 ♕xf7 28 ♗xg5 ♘c7 29 ♗f4 ♕f6 30 ♕d1 b6 31 ♕d3 ♖e8 32 ♖f1 b5 33 cxb5 ♕d4+ 34 ♕xd4 cxd4 35 ♗xd6 ♘xb5 36 ♗b4 a5 37 ♗xa5 ♖a8 38 ♗b4 ♖xa2 39 d6 ♖a8 40 d7 ♘c7 41 ♖f8+ 1-0, Trifunovic-Van Scheltinga, Amsterdam 1950.

➪ 13 a4 ♘f8 14 d5 (an insipid plan which causes Black no problems) 14...♘g6 15 ♘d2 ♖f8 16 ♘c4 b6 17 g3 ♗d7 18 ♗g2 h6 19 ♘e3 ♕d8 20 ♕d3 ♕c7 21 ♗d2 ♖ae8 22 c4 a5 23 ♖f1 ♕d8 24 ♖fb1 ♘e7 25 ♕b3 ♘c8 26 ♖f1 ½-½, Spassky-Yusupov, Bugojno 1986.

➪ 13 a4 ♕c7 14 h3 b6 15 d5 ♘f8 16 ♘h4 ♘g6 (once again White cannot play 17 ♘f5 because of 17...♗xf5 18 exf5 ♘e7, so Black has equalised) 17 ♗g5 ♘xh4 18 ♗xh4 ♕e7 19 g3 h6 20 f4 ♔h8 21 f5 g5 22 fxg6 ½-½, Benjamin-Zarnicki, Buenos Aires 1992.

13...♘c7

This may not be the best. The critical line runs 13...♕c7 (13...d5 is playable, but has never been tested in practice) 14 d5 ♘f8 and now:

➪ 15 ♗g5 ♕e7 (Black appears to be wasting time, but he will regain it with ...h6, which is a useful move for him in any case) 16 ♘h4 h6 17 ♗c1 g5 18 ♘g2 ♘g6 19 f3 ♔h8 20 ♘e3 ♖g8 21 c4 ♗d7 22 ♖b1 b6 23 ♘f5 ♗xf5 24 exf5 ♘f8 25 ♗d3 ♘8d7 26 ♔f2 ♖ae8 27 ♗d2 ♕f8 28 ♗c3 ♕g7 29 ♔g2 h5 30 h3 h4 ½-½, Short-Tukmakov, European Club Cup 1991.

➪ 15 c4 (15 ♘h4 ♘g6 16 ♘f5 fails to 16...♗xf5 17 exf5 ♘e7, so 15 c4 is the critical move; the circumstances are favourable for c4 because White has gained a tempo with g3, while Black's queen has been misplaced at c7) 15...♘g6 16 h3 h6?! 17 ♘h2 ♖e8 18 ♕d3 (White is playing to force through f4 as quickly as possible; unless Black reacts quickly he will be crushed as in Nunn-Norri above) 18...♘h7 19 f4 exf4 20 gxf4 f5 21 ♕g3 ♘hf8 22 e5! dxe5 23 fxe5 f4 (23...♘xe5 24 ♗f4 ♘8d7 25 ♖e3 is crushing) 24 ♕c3 b5!? (24...♖xe5 25 ♗xf4 wins material, so Black tries to mix it up) 25 cxb5 ♗b7 26 ♗c4 ♕d8 27 ♘f3 (White has maintained control and made off with an important extra pawn) 27...♘h4 28 ♗b2? (28 ♗xf4 is winning for White) 28...♘e6! (but now the position is totally unclear) 29 dxe6 ½-½, W.Watson-R.Mainka, Prague 1992.

➪ 15 c4 ♘g6 16 h3 ♖e8 17 ♘h2 ♗d7! (so that if White plays the direct 18 ♕d3, intending f4, Black can inconvenience White by 18...♕c8) 18 ♗g5 ♕d8 19 ♖b1 b6 20 ♘g4 ♗xg4 21 hxg4 h6 22 ♗d2 ♘h7 23 ♖b3 f6 24 f4 (White has some kingside initiative) 24...♘h8 (the idea is ...g5 followed by ...♘g6 to block the kingside) 25 g5 (anticipating Black's plan, but it might have been better to allow ...g5 and respond by tripling White's major pieces on the f-file) 25...hxg5 26 fxg5 (26 ♗h3!?) 26...♘xg5 27 ♗xg5 fxg5 28 ♗h3 (White has a temporary initiative, but Black's position is solid) 34...♖h8 35 ♕b1 ♘f7 36 a5 ♖xh3 37 ♖xh3 ♘h6 38 axb6 axb6 39 ♖f3 ♖f8 40 ♕xb6 ♖xf3 41 ♔xf3 ♕f6+ 42 ♔e2 ♕f4 43 ♕c7+ ♘f7 44 ♔d3 ♕f3+ ½-½, Campora-Van der Sterren, San Bernadino 1991.

14 a4 ♗g4 (forcing White to close the centre, but this is promising for White when Black's knight is stuck on the queenside) **15 d5 ♖f8 16 h3 ♗d7 17 ♘h4 ♘fe8 18 c4 g6 19 f4 f6 20 f5 g5 21 ♘g2 ♘g7 22 h4 h6 23 ♘e3** (23 ♗e2! was more accurate as 23...♔f7 could be met by 24 ♗h5+, so Black would be unable to switch his rooks to the h-file) **23...♔f7 24 ♗e2 ♖h8 25 ♔g2 ♖h7 26 ♖h1 ♖ah8 27 ♗d2 ♘a6 28 ♕b1 ♗c8 29 ♖h2 ♘b8** (the knight is finally able to cross to the kingside) **30 ♕b5** (intending to meet 30...♘d7 by 31 ♕a5, forcing Black to weaken his queenside pawns) **30...♕d8 31 ♖ah1 ♔g8 32 ♘g4 ♘d7?** (leads to a forced loss) **33 hxg5 hxg5 34 ♖xh7 ♖xh7 35 ♘h6+ ♔f8 36 ♘f7! ♔xf7 37 ♖xh7 ♔g8 38 ♖h6 ♕b6 39 ♕xb6 axb6 40 ♖h1 ♘e8 41 ♗h5 ♘c7 42 ♖b1 ♔f8 43 ♗g6 ♔e7 44 ♔f3 ♘a8 45 ♔g4 ♘f8 46 ♔h5 1-0**